The Attorney General's Lawyer

THE ATTORNEY GENERAL'S LAWYER

Inside the Meese Justice Department

DOUGLAS W. KMIEC

FOREWORD BY EDWIN MEESE III

PRAEGER

New York
Westport, Connecticut
London

Library of Congress Cataloging-in-Publication Data

Kmiec, Douglas W.
The attorney general's lawyer : inside the Meese Justice Department / Douglas W. Kmiec : foreword by Edwin Meese III.
p. cm.
Includes bibliographical references and index.
ISBN 0-275-93983-9 (alk. paper)
1. Attorneys general—United States. 2. United States. Dept. of Justice. Office of Legal Counsel. 3. Meese, Edwin. I. Title.
KF5107.K57 1992
353.5′092—dc20 91-44006

British Library Cataloguing in Publication Data is available.

Library of Congress Catalog Card Number: 91-44006
ISBN: 0-275-93983-9

First published in 1992

Praeger Publishers, One Madison Avenue, New York, NY 10010
An imprint of Greenwood Publishing Group, Inc.

Printed in the United States of America

The paper used in this book complies with the Permanent Paper Standard issued by the National Information Standards Organization (Z39.48-1984).

P

In order to keep this title in print and available to the academic community, this edition was produced using digital reprint technology in a relatively short print run. This would not have been attainable using traditional methods. Although the cover has been changed from its original appearance, the text remains the same and all materials and methods used still conform to the highest book-making standards.

To the Kmiec and Keenan families

There's no question that . . . tough-mindedness, especially when combined with solid legal scholarship, can be a desirable quality for the head of the Office of Legal Counsel. OLC is an elite corps within the Justice Department, charged with making the difficult legal calls for the executive branch. It's supposed to be above politics—the arbiter of ethics, the conscience of Justice. With such alumni as Chief Justice William Rehnquist and Justice Antonin Scalia, OLC's history is illustrious, but its demands—making ostensibly apolitical decisions in a decidedly political atmosphere—are rigorous. Being the assistant attorney general in charge of OLC is not for the weak-willed.

The American Lawyer Magazine
December 1988

Contents

Foreword

Professor Kmiec provides an accurate and insightful look at the work of the Department of Justice and, in particular, the Office of Legal Counsel. As head of OLC and earlier as its principal deputy, Doug Kmiec was very much "the Attorney General's Lawyer," and I was glad for it. This book recounts many of the constitutional and statutory issues upon which Professor Kmiec provided principled and candid legal advice to the President, to me, and indeed, to the entire executive branch. More than anything else, his account reveals the thorough, searching intellectual examination the Department brought to controversial legal questions, such as affirmative action, abortion, property rights, and school choice. His chapters on federalism and the unitary executive illustrate his scholar's appreciation for the structural provisions and fundamental principles of our Constitution. They also show how his legal advice was critical to DOJ's work to preserve the constitutional authority of the presidency and a proper balance between state and federal power.

As the story unfolds, Professor Kmiec reveals how decisions were reached and describes the spirited and hard-hitting debate before—and sometimes after—positions were taken. More than anything else, the book completely debunks the myth that there ever was one monolithic, lock-step conservative agenda dictating legal outcomes before analysis. As his chapter on the search for original intent indicates, what all of us were after, then and now, was, quite simply, respect for the rule of law, including the Constitution as our nation's most important source of written law.

This book is a vital addition to the undistorted history of the Reagan presidency and American justice. It deserves serious attention by scholar and general reader alike. The student of law, politics, or government will benefit greatly from Professor Kmiec's counsel, as I have, and continue to do.

Edwin Meese III

The Attorney General's Lawyer

Introduction

This is a book about law. It is also a book about the people who are charged with the duty to faithfully execute it. Between 1985 and 1989, I served in the Office of Legal Counsel (OLC), an office described by those who know it as the attorney general's lawyer. The point of this book is not to reminisce about my experience as first deputy assistant, and then, assistant attorney general, overseeing this office, but to record the manner in which the law served as both an instrument of, and constraint on, the dramatic changes that occurred during the Reagan era.

The role of the attorney general since its inception in the Judiciary Act of 1789 has been to be "learned in the law" and to give opinions upon matters of law to the president and heads of departments. But the attorney general is also an administrator, overseeing a vast network of attorneys and nonlegal personnel in Washington, D.C., and throughout the United States. Frequently, attorneys general have been close friends (and even a brother in one notable case) of the President. These close relationships make attorneys general important policy advisors as well. With this many responsibilities, it is hardly surprising that the attorney general relies on lawyer-specialists for assistance with various parts of his great responsibilities. The heads of the criminal, civil, civil rights, antitrust, and land and natural resource divisions fit this bill.

But the attorney general has also come to rely upon one lawyer-generalist for objective advice with complex legal questions that implicate the Constitution or crosscut multiple legal fields. This constitutional lawyer and general legal advisor is the head of the Office of Legal Counsel. Their photographs hang in a small, oddly shaped conference room down the hall from the attorney general's office. Some of the faces are familiar: Chief Justice William Rehnquist and Justice Antonin Scalia both headed the office before appointment to the Supreme Court. Erwin Griswold, former dean of the Harvard Law School and Solicitor General is credited with helping nurture the office in its early years. Nicholas deB. Katzenbach served in OLC before becoming attorney general. Other names and faces may be less familiar, but their opinions continue to bind and shape legal thinking in the United States in significant, if unseen, ways.

The Office of Legal Counsel is small in the legions of the Department of Justice. OLC's 20 or so lawyers are but a fraction of the Department's thousands. Yet, OLC's influence is greatly disproportionate, and has been since its founding in 1933. It has been written that "[o]pinions originating in the Office of Legal Counsel have guided Presidents in many famous executive decisions. For example, in 1940, the 'Lend-Lease' opinion of Attorney General Robert H. Jackson gave President Roosevelt legal authority to transfer American destroyers to England in return for the right to establish naval and air bases in British possessions. In 1957, the Office of Legal Counsel justified the use of federal troops in Little Rock, Arkansas, to enforce a court order that the schools be desegregated. And in 1963, the Office devised the basis for the quarantine of Cuba during the missile crisis."[1]

Much of the work of OLC deals with the institution of the presidency. It is here that the legal contours of the presidential office are practically defined and guarded with great determination. I am certain that this function is important in any administration but it surely had special importance in January 1981 as newly elected President Ronald Reagan set about the task of reinvigorating a presidential office that had been adrift since Watergate and had begun to sink in Jimmy Carter's personally fashioned malaise.

Something related, but even more profound than assisting in the reestablishment of presidential leadership, occurred in OLC during President Reagan's second term. That something took the form of a comprehensive reexamination of what it means to serve under a written Constitution and the rule of law. This intense jurisprudential introspection over the deepest meaning of constitutional law was largely brought to the Department of Justice and OLC by President Reagan's longtime friend and counselor, Edwin Meese III. While for some, such constitutional theorizing would be arid and academic, for Ed Meese and his President, it was a matter of immediate application. And applied it was to reinvigorate the office of the presidency—by restoring Article II's unified executive oversight of executive agencies, by resisting a constant barrage of legislative encroachments on executive power, and by enriching the president's voice in the constitutional assessment of new legislation. The jurisprudence of Edwin Meese also gave new life to the

Constitution's original understanding as a color-blind document that respected the textual limits of national authority and understood the importance of federalism.

In making these claims, Ed Meese was challenging the established legal fraternity head-on. For this, he would be chastised by legal academics, vilified by the press, and ultimately hounded into a marginally early resignation. My service in OLC largely coincided with that of Attorney General Edwin Meese. These pages are about the legal thinking that he inspired. In the vernacular of the time, these pages are about a Department of Justice where "ideas had consequences." In recording them, it is hoped that they may again one day.

Before beginning, a brief word about sources. I have largely relied upon personal recollection, and where events preceded or followed my tenure, library and interview research. To verify facts and dates, I have consulted my unclassified chronological files and personal notes, being careful not to quote any material about events that have not yet become public or that might in any way disadvantage the current legal positions of my former client, the United States. Throughout, I have striven to make any criticism—of person or event—constructive and any praise objective.

I acknowledge the help and encouragement of many, especially my wife, Carolyn, and our five children who cheerfully kept tabs on their father's writing progress. The research assistance of the Notre Dame Law Library, particularly librarians Dwight King and Carmella Kinslow, and law students, Elena Baca and Martin Heli, was most welcome. The secretarial patience of Corinne Karlin and Darlene Carlson could not be exhausted. Finally, I here publicly acknowledge the legal achievements, integrity, and dedication of the lawyers and staff of OLC during my tenure.

NOTE

1. Huston, *The Department of Justice* 60 (Praeger 1967).

PART I

Beginnings

"I will not seek to have withdrawn my nomination for the office of Attorney General. I intend to pursue the vindication of my name, the honor of my family, and the confidence of the President of the United States in nominating me."

Attorney General-Designate Edwin Meese
March 24, 1984

Meeting the Press. One of the Attorney General's frequent press briefings at the Department of Justice. Standing on either side of Attorney General Meese are the author (left) and Patrick Korten (right), director of the Justice Department press office. (Photo courtesy of the U.S. Department of

1

Surmounting the Independent Counsel

Edwin Meese is an early riser. As he traveled south on the George Washington Parkway each morning, the morning light was barely visible over the bordering Potomac. I sometimes wondered if that was a painful ride for Ed. As he began his career as the 75th Attorney General of the United States in 1985, it had only been a few years since his son Scott—home for summer vacation from college in late July 1982—was killed in a single-car accident on that very same road. If the memory of that tragic loss haunted him, he never let on.

Knowing Ed Meese is to get an entirely different picture of him than the one flashed across newspapers or network television. In person, his stout stature and red complexion are counterbalanced by a pleasant laugh and subtle facial expressions that convey genuine interest in just about any subject brought to him. The public was never given a chance to pick up these nuances, however, since they were fed a daily diet of venal or inept or forgetful or reactionary Ed Meese. The first three characterizations were totally false, the last—the charge of being reactionary—was also a caricature, but at least it came closer to what really bothered the liberal press and the liberal academy: Ed Meese's unalloyed conservative values.

The Attorney General's conservatism opened him up to challenge, but so did his political innocence. Having served as Governor Reagan's chief of staff in California and as a tough Alameda County district attorney, the maintenance of that continuing innocence is somewhat baffling. Yet, it was there. Despite all the rubbish written about him, Ed Meese believed that if he simply articulated his understanding of legal issues, genuine debate would occur and truth would emerge. It didn't. Instead, independent counsels were appointed.

INDEPENDENT COUNSELS: CONGRESS' PROSECUTORIAL THREAT

The independent counsel law was not invented for Ed Meese, but it might as well have been. Ostensibly aimed at ensuring that no high official is above the law, its actual utility—if not its design—is as a malevolent political weapon. Like a number of other distortions of the executive-legislative balance, the independent counsel law originated out of the Watergate experience, and, in theory, it was benign and well intentioned. Nixon's desperate and intemperate firing of Archibald Cox, the special prosecutor appointed by the Department of Justice who subpoenaed the tapes, prompted congressional concern that the executive branch was incapable of investigating itself. In fact, however, executive federal prosecutors had a long history of ferreting out crime within or without the executive branch. Moreover, Watergate itself affirmed that executive competence. Leon Jaworski, Cox's replacement, was given a broad prosecutorial mandate by the Department, and he completed the investigation that ultimately led to Nixon's resignation. Had Jaworski failed, or had there been any credible evidence of executive laxness in the investigation of criminal behavior, an independent counsel law might have merited further consideration. That, however, was not the case.

The independent counsel statute needed no legal justification because it had a supremely political one: increasing congressional micromanagement of the executive, something the separation of powers theoretically denies. To be sure, members of Congress have a legitimate responsibility to inquire into the success or failure of their legislative handiwork. This responsibility may manifest itself as oversight or appropriations hearings or a simple phone call or letter on behalf of a constituent. Within the law, executive officials usually try to be accommodating to these legislative inquiries. Yet, however hazy, the line where lawmaking ends and executive administration begins must be observed or the notion of a government of law, rather than men, breaks down. If nothing else, the interventions of the so-called Keating Five into the executive regulation of the savings and loan industry reveals the mischief and economic cost that results when lawmakers seek to both make the law and not have it apply to their friends or political contributors.

A more subtle, but also more sweeping way for the legislative branch to manage executive decision making is to control the appointment of executive officials. After all, congressional staffs can organize only so many public hearings. And the old Washington saw, "policy is people," has much truth. There is only one problem—the Constitution by and large makes executive appointment an executive matter. Top officials—so-called principal officers—require confirmation by the Senate, but most officers are appointed by the heads of executive departments or the President alone. When the presidency is consistently in the hands of the other party, the absence of legislative control over executive appointments is an annoyance to Congress. When the White House falls into the hands of an ideologically principled and powerfully directed adversary like Ronald Reagan, acquiring "legislative" appointment power becomes a congressional cause.

There has been some debate over the proper scope of inquiry to be applied by the Senate to presidential appointments. In this, a distinction has been drawn between personal fitness and political philosophy and a further distinction between judicial and executive nominees. As the Bork hearings illustrated, with judicial nominees, the Senate has assumed that both philosophy and matters of fairness and propriety are fair game. Because judges have constitutional independence and are expected to apply the law dispassionately, philosophy at the time of appointment is said to matter. The Senate has not fully carried this policy inquiry over to executive nominations. With executive nominees, the prevailing operating principle is that the President is entitled to have the assistance of those who are best able and willing to carry out *his* policies—which, after all, are the ones that got him elected. Thus, with executive nominations, philosophy is said—theoretically—to matter less to the Senate. Theory is not always reality, and as it turned out for Ed Meese, his congressional opponents could make specious ethical concerns a stalking horse for opposition to his legal philosophy.

The independent counsel law is made to order for tarnishing a political opponent with spurious ethical charges. In this, the framework of the independent counsel law bears little resemblance to the rules and procedures that govern traditional criminal investigations. Generally speaking, such investigations proceed carefully and without publicity. It makes no sense to announce to a criminal suspect that you are about to investigate him. The confidential nature of criminal investigations preserves investigative methods, the identities of informants, and prevents the destruction of important evidence. Because of this confidentiality, however, the traditional criminal investigation is ill-suited to creating ethical doubt about a presidential nominee or a sufficient pretext for his Senate rejection. What is needed is not a mechanism that carefully analyzes serious allegations of criminal behavior in private, but a bullhorn that blares the fact that one is SUSPECTED OF WRONGDOING to all the world. This is the independent counsel law. Like Saddam Hussein's scud missile, it is not a weapon prized for its accuracy, but its terror.

That the independent counsel law is fraught with partisanship was apparent long before Ed Meese became one of its prime targets. Former

University of Chicago Law School Dean and U.S. Attorney General Edward Levi condemned the act when it was first proposed in 1976. Levi stated: "[i]t would create opportunities for actual or apparent partisan influence in law enforcement; [and] publicize and dignify unfounded, scurrilous allegations against public officials; . . ."[1] When the law came up for reauthorization in 1987, Meese's predecessor, the late William French Smith, confirmed that the law had lived up (or more accurately down) to Levi's expectations. The act, said Smith, has been used on a continuing basis "for essentially political purposes—in some cases blatantly—by members of Congress and others."[2] Griffin Bell, the Attorney General under Jimmy Carter, did not originally oppose the legislation because Carter was one of the law's supporters. However, seeing the gross politicization of law enforcement that resulted prompted even Bell to testify against the law's continuation. The law from beginning to end, observed Bell, "seems almost to be set up to create publicity."[3]

Despite this damning, bipartisan criticism from the nation's chief law enforcement officers, Congress not only extended the life of the independent counsel law in 1987, it enhanced the law's capability to be used as a political weapon. The law always had a hair trigger—requiring only that the allegations investigated not be wholly incredible or vague. However, under the law as reauthorized, even cases with no evidence of criminal intent are required to be pursued. This is contrary to common sense, let alone common prosecutorial practice.

To counteract normal prosecutorial fairness and judgment, the reauthorized independent counsel law mandates that the attorney general make his evaluation of the credibility of allegations against covered executive officials within 15 days. If he cannot make his determination during that extremely short time—tough. After 15 days, the attorney general must publicly notify the court that a preliminary investigation is underway of a named executive officer. The critical word in that sentence is *publicly*; that, after all, is the whole point. Moreover, since the 1987 reauthorization, the attorney general is explicitly forbidden from considering whether the subject of the allegation had the requisite state of mind to commit a criminal violation. No sense letting the law get in the way of a jerry-rigged investigative enterprise too early.

After a preliminary investigation is launched, the design of the statute is to press almost inevitably for the formal appointment of an independent counsel. During the preliminary investigation, the attorney general is denied all of the usual investigative tools; he may not convene grand juries, grant immunity, or issue subpoenas. Yet, the statute insists that the attorney general apply—*publicly* again—for the appointment of an independent counsel unless he determines within 90 days that there is nothing to merit further investigation. There will almost always be *some* ground for further investigation, especially since the attorney general was given few means by which to investigate. So, on it goes—the independent counsel is appointed, the executive official is nearly always placed on administrative leave, and as far as headlines might reveal, the executive branch equivalent of the Boston Strangler has just been nabbed.

With the appointment of an independent counsel, the reputation and career damage to an official is extensive. In fact, except for the millions of dollars in private legal defense fees that the publicly discredited official will now need to finance against the family home, and the equivalent and disproportionate expenditure of public prosecutorial resources, it seldom seems to matter very much what the independent counsel actually discovers. Public officials smeared in the press are often quickly distanced from the President and the White House—lest the reading public be too quick to generalize. And the work of government must go on. An acting official soon becomes identified with the job's responsibilities and the political victim of the independent counsel forgotten.

THE ATTEMPT TO BAR THE DOOR: THE INDEPENDENT COUNSEL INVESTIGATION TO KEEP MEESE OUT

One cannot help but speculate that it was Ed Meese's intended fate to be forgotten in the shadows of suspicion created by an independent counsel. It didn't work out that way. Perhaps, his political opposition underestimated his tenacity borne of innocence or the willingness of Ronald Reagan to defend a valued colleague under attack. Moreover, in passing the independent counsel law, Congress seemingly overlooked one thing: once that independent counsel is appointed, he or she might be just that—independent—not just from the executive, but from Congress as well. While Congress could legislatively stack the deck to get an investigation started and disclosed, it could not insure a desired outcome. Much to the chagrin of Meese's opposition, Jacob A. Stein, the independent counsel appointed during the pendency of his confirmation battle, concluded after a five-month investigation that there was "no basis with respect to any of the 11 allegations for the bringing of a prosecution against Mr. Meese for the violation of a Federal criminal statute."[4]

The events that led to Stein's vindication of Ed Meese started with the January 1984 announcement by William French Smith that he intended to resign his position as attorney general in order to return to law practice in California. Smith agreed to defer the effective date of his resignation until his successor was confirmed. Little did Smith realize, however, when the President nominated then-presidential counselor Ed Meese that some 13 months would elapse before that confirmation would occur.

The first confirmation hearings were held in March 1984. From the beginning, the tone of the hearings was decidedly negative. Critics claimed that Meese was insensitive to the needs of poor minorities and Senator Edward Kennedy used Meese's presence before the Senate Judiciary Committee to attack Reagan's civil rights policies generally. Simply stated, Mr. Meese thought the law ought to be color-blind, applying equally regardless of race or gender. The Kennedy view was strongly opposite, favoring the use of race and gender when such classifications could be argued to be "benign" or advantageous to women and minorities.

Staying with this theme, Kennedy lambasted Reagan through Meese for not appointing more black and Hispanic judges to the federal courts. President Carter had relied openly upon race, ethnicity, and gender in judicial selection. While President Reagan was not unmindful of the need to search for a representative sampling of the American population on the courts, his first priority was to find judges of ability who would not encroach upon legislative policy making. In this, Reagan and Meese were of like minds, and thus, Meese was a logical target for those who conceive of civil rights as an allocation of preferences rather than a commitment to equality. Meese's unwillingness to subscribe to racial and gender quotas was patently offensive to Kennedy, Metzenbaum, and the like. His belief in judicial restraint only made matters worse.

Despite these substantive or philosophical gripes and "round after round of partisan jabs,"[5] *U.S. News and World Report* reported on March 12, that Meese "appeared certain to win Senate confirmation."[6] While the press had reported on various Meese financial matters brought up at the hearings—and this had been Senator Metzenbaum's almost exclusive focus from the second day of the hearings—these so-called ethics matters had not yet gelled into a confirmation stumbling block. The opportunities for ethical aspersion multiplied, however, when Meese disclosed that he had inadvertently failed to report a $15,000 loan made by a personal friend to his wife, Ursula, on his annual financial disclosure form.

Blood had now been drawn. An admission of error—even innocent error—now could be easily coupled with broader, unsubstantiated allegations that he received favorable loan treatment on overdue mortgage payments on his unsold home in California or favored his friends for federal jobs. His Senate opponents had sufficiently clouded the atmosphere to cast doubt on the confirmation. What was impossible from the standpoint of legal philosophy—the Senate liberals' true concern—now seemingly came within reach by an orchestrated questioning of Meese's integrity. Whether there were honest explanations or answers to these questions didn't matter.

Given the hair trigger of the independent counsel statute, Meese knew that it was only a matter of time before someone raised the allegations made at the Senate hearings as a basis for launching a preliminary investigation under the independent counsel law. Over the weekend of March 17 and 18, 1984, Attorney General Smith agonized over whether to take the preliminary steps under the independent counsel structure. Perhaps underestimating the ease with which a preliminary inquiry would quickly lead to the appointment of an independent counsel, Meese relieved Smith of the problem by requesting that a preliminary inquiry be opened and his confirmation hearings be suspended.

In retrospect, Meese's call to bring an independent counsel upon himself may appear as a preemptive strike to regain the moral high ground. Less cynically, it may have simply been that prosecutor Meese believed that innocent citizens do not run from the police. It was only natural for him to stand resolute when his own integrity was challenged. If that was Meese's thinking, he was drawing a far too generous analogy between the usual motivations for police behavior and the more Machiavellian designs behind the independent counsel law. That said, by bringing on the independent counsel, Meese was also demonstrating his unswerving loyalty to Ronald Reagan. In an election year, it was abundantly evident that opponents of the President would have screamed "foul" and "cover-up" had the independent counsel mechanism not been placed into service.

On April 2, 1984, Jacob A. Stein, a distinguished Washington, D.C., lawyer and former Washington, D.C., Bar president, was given the broad mandate to investigate and prosecute "any allegation or evidence of violation of any federal criminal law by Mr. Meese." An occasional teacher at Harvard, Georgetown, and George Washington universities, Stein had also represented James Brady, the White House press secretary paralyzed in the Reagan assassination attempt. Despite the bias inherent in the structure of the independent counsel law, Stein was certain to conduct a thoroughly professional investigation. This was fine with Meese. Planting his flag, Meese proclaimed: "I will not seek to have withdrawn my nomination for the office of Attorney General. I intend to pursue the vindication of my name, the honor of my family, and the confidence of the President of the United States in nominating me."[7]

The matters investigated by Stein ranged from whether Meese improperly retained a gift of cuff links given to him by the government of South Korea to whether he was given preferential treatment in his change in status from retired to active Army Reserve and subsequent promotion from lieutenant colonel to colonel. The most serious allegations pertained to whether Meese helped friends obtain federal jobs. Those interested in the mundane details of these charges will have to turn to Mr. Stein's 385-page report. For every allegation, however, Stein's concluding refrain was the same: "no basis for any criminal charge" or "no evidence of special treatment." Stein did find that Meese—or at least the White House staff member responsible for assembling the material for his annual financial disclosure—neglected to disclose the $15,000 loan a former associate had made to Ursula Meese. Meese, of course, had already admitted as much. And even here, Stein found "no evidence of any motive" on Mr. Meese's part to conceal the underlying facts of this transaction and that responsible prosecutorial discretion "counsels strongly against a prosecution in such a case."[8]

An outside observer might have thought that the Stein investigation and its exoneration of Ed Meese would have been the end of the public sniping about Meese's fitness for the office of Attorney General. It was not. Archibald Cox, the Harvard law professor and martyred special prosecutor from the Nixon era, wailed to the media and the Senate Judiciary Committee that the Stein report meant nothing. After all, said Cox, then-chairman of the liberal lobbying group Common Cause, Stein had refused requests to evaluate Meese's personal suitability for the job. Of course, he had. As Stein reported: "[n]either the statute nor the [court] order affords a basis for me to submit an evaluation of fitness for public office.... There is always the danger that a finding based on such an inquiry would be the product of preconception rather than objective statement."[9] Watching the anguished look of Meese's detractors, one almost heard them respond: "Gee, Jake, we never thought you'd be objective!"

As the Meese confirmation hearings resumed, Senators Metzenbaum and Mitchell complained that mere innocence under the law was not enough. Picking up the theme of Archibald Cox, they insisted that Meese's actions demonstrated ethical insensitivity. When David Martin, the head of the Office of Government Ethics, concluded that Mr. Meese had not violated *any* code of ethics, the Senate Judiciary Committee probed whether staff members in Martin's ethics office had been pressured to reach that result. They said they had not. Surely, someone in authority would be sufficiently obliging to conclude that Ed Meese was morally reprehensible. No one did. No one who knew him could.

The Stein investigation revealed more than Ed Meese's honesty and resilience against scurrilous attack. The financial information unearthed portrayed a person of overriding public dedication who had spent little time, and showed virtually no interest, in amassing personal wealth. Unlike many high government officials—elected and appointed—whose personal fortunes were necessary to win election or secure appointment, Ed Meese rose through the ranks of Reagan followers largely because of his sincere belief in conservative, traditional values and long hours of hard work. His was the life of the modestly paid public servant and one-time law teacher who provided the best he could for his family within respectable, but nevertheless average, means. Ironically, Meese's bout with the independent counsel may thus reveal that those who strive to patch together meager private resources to undertake public service are more, not less, vulnerable to false accusation.

An example may illustrate the point. One of the most widely reported allegations against Ed Meese involved Thomas Barrack, a California real estate agent. Shortly after Meese's son was killed it is not unreasonable to assume that the family had terrible second thoughts about the move to Washington. To make matters worse, the Meeses were struggling with tremendous personal expenses—partly because of the extraordinary expensiveness of Washington, but mostly because the Meese family home in La Mesa, California, had yet to sell. At a family dinner in August, Ursula Meese related some of these difficulties to Pen James, a family friend who was serving with her husband in the White House. On his own initiative, James contacted Barrack who some months later arranged a private sale of the Meese home in the course of business.

Unbeknownst to Ed Meese, Barrack had applied for a job with James Watt, then Secretary of Interior. As Stein expressly found by "uncontradicted evidence," Barrack obtained the job independent of any connection with Ed Meese. Yet, fueling wholly unwarranted inferences, the *Washington Post* reported the very day the independent counsel was appointed to investigate Meese that "Thomas J. Barrack, Jr., a wealthy California real estate developer, was named to a job at the Interior Department and then nominated as an assistant secretary at the Commerce Department after arranging sale of Meese's California home.[10] In itself, the bare facts of the story were of course true. What bore no relation to the truth was the inference. Combine such disparaging inferences, the low pay of public service, and the cost of fending off Congress' independent counsel law, and most people would likely forego the "honor" of public service. Not Ed Meese.

That Meese survived his ordeal cannot erase the hidden, and troubling, message the raising of baseless charges to the level of independent counsel investigations has for public service generally: the average citizen need not apply. It is easily recognized that the excessive cost of congressional campaigns precludes the citizen of moderate means from pursuing election to public office. Were this income exclusion to spread to high-ranking, executive and administrative positions, notions of popular, representative government would be increasingly fatuous. Titles of nobility would clearly then be abolished in name only by our constitutional charter.

On a strictly partisan vote, Edwin Meese III was confirmed as Attorney General on February 23, 1985, 13 months after his nomination. With characteristic grace, Meese stated that he was "not bitter at all" about the lengthy investigation and mudslinging. His opposition did not reciprocate. Instead, his Senate detractors piously stated that they would be watching Mr. Meese very closely in the years ahead. As it turned out, they would be closely watching him restore the original meaning of the Constitution.

NOTES

1. *Committee on the Judiciary Subcommittee on Administrative Law*, 100th Cong., 1st Sess. 5 (1987) (statement of William French Smith before the House Judiciary Committee 5 [quoting Edward H. Levi]).

2. Smith statement, *supra*, at 6.

3. *Committee on the Judiciary Subcommittee on Administrative Law*, 100th Cong., 1st Sess. 2 (1987) (statement of Griffin B. Bell before the House Judiciary Committee).

4. N.Y. Times, Sept. 21, 1984, at B10, col. 1 (city ed.) (quoting the report of Independent Counsel Jacob A. Stein).

5. *Edwin Meese Takes His Turn in Hot Seat*, U.S. News and World Rep., March 12, 1984, at 12.

6. *Id.*

7. N.Y. Times, March 23, 1984, at D17, col. 1 (citing letter from Edwin Meese to Attorney General William French Smith).

8. N.Y. Times, *supra* note 4.

9. *Id.*

10. Thornton, *Special Prosecutor Named to Probe Meese Allegations*, Wash. Post, April 3, 1984, at Al.

2

In Search of Original Intent

There are, in my judgment, two personality types attracted to Washington: managers and movers. Managers would do well in any organization, public or private, keeping matters orderly and running smoothly. Movers, on the other hand, are excited by the pursuit of ideas and ideals, bothering little with organizational detail. To be fully successful, any political administration needs both types, and in fact, the perfect executive officer would have elements of each quality. The Reagan administration attracted more movers than managers. They were answering the President's rhetorical call "to curb the size and influence of the federal establishment and to demand recognition of the distinction between the powers granted to the Federal Government and those reserved to the states or the people."[1]

Now government could be reigned in by cutting revenue and removing administrative regulation. Reagan did both. But the nature and scope of government interference in daily life also depends on consistently observing that the federal government is constitutionally limited. The President deeply felt that the high level of federal intrusion in personal life and the decline of state responsibility could be traced to legal and judicial attitudes that either lost sight of, or wholeheartedly disregarded, the limits placed on the federal government by the Constitution.

Ronald Reagan was always the first to admit that he was a nonlawyer. Given the prevalence of lawyers in government, the President would make the disclaimer—as probably most Americans do—as a source of authority, not disability. Notwithstanding this common sense distrust of lawyering, the President recognized well that there was a pressing need to affirm the Constitution as the embodiment of the rule of law. For the Attorney General, this was the doctrine of original intent.

ORIGINAL INTENT

To explore original intent, or any other theory of constitutional interpretation, requires an excursion into what is meant by that terminology, the excuses given for ignoring it, and alternatives. What follows is that excursion, and for the nonlawyer, nonacademic, it will most certainly resemble a visit to Oz. I apologize for this, but I know of no shortcut. As a mover,[2] Ed Meese knew that restoring legitimacy to constitutional thinking required that the table be cleared of extraneous claims and assertions. There had to be a return to "first principles." That is what this chapter is all about.

"In the main," said Edwin Meese, "a jurisprudence that seeks to be faithful to our Constitution—a Jurisprudence of Original Intention . . . —is not difficult to describe. Where the language of the Constitution is specific, it must be obeyed. Where there is a demonstrable consensus among the framers and ratifiers as to a principle stated or implied by the Constitution, it should be followed. Where there is ambiguity as to the precise meaning or reach of constitutional provision, it should be interpreted and applied in a manner so as to at least not contradict the text of the Constitution itself."[3] To the nonlawyer, this might seem both unexceptional and somewhat abstract. Of course, the text of the law, including especially the Constitution as a higher, foundational form of law, should govern. Were this not the case, who would obey the law? Judicial opinions unfaithful to the Constitution and laws democratically enacted would be just that—personal opinions—nothing more.

To those who had become accustomed, however, to using the courts to obtain political results masked in constitutional language, Meese's seemingly unexceptional pronouncement constituted fighting words. Meese's words had particular sting for the practitioners of constitutional make-believe—the activist members of the federal bench. The intellectual leader of this group was Justice William Brennan. Scarcely a few months after the Attorney General articulated his Jurisprudence of Original Intention before the American Bar Association, where it received a standing ovation, Justice Brennan lashed out at the notion, calling it "arrogance cloaked as humility."[4]

What immediately followed Justice Brennan's visceral blast of words, and since, has largely been caricature. Many have deliberately or disingenuously distorted the Attorney General's meaning. For example, Floyd Abrams, a prominent first amendment lawyer, claimed that the effect of Meese's theory would be to allow "New York to ban newspapers, California to establish a state religion, and Kansas to deny citizens the right to assemble for the purpose of protesting governmental misconduct."[5] This kind of ridiculous hyperbole became commonplace, even in so-called elite law schools. Its obvious purpose was to discredit. If that was not possible, at least the constitutional noise would obscure, rather than enlighten.

The Substance of Original Intent

Fundamentally, the Attorney General argued: words matter. The words of the Constitution matter because they are written and they are law. The Constitution was written down, of course, in striking contrast to the unwritten British example that the founding generation no longer trusted. Any study of the constitutional convention of 1787, the drafting of the Bill of Rights by the first Congress, or the Civil War amendments of the 39th Congress illustrates the debate engendered and the care taken in choice of words.

That one word then, or now, could make all the difference is aptly illustrated by the recent controversy over the respective roles of the President and Congress in the war in the Persian Gulf. The framers changed the draft of Congress' war power from the power to "make" war to the power to "declare" war, recognizing—in part—that events external to either Congress or the President could place the United States in a state of war. The meaning of that change in phraseology was a central focus numerous times during the Reagan era in Grenada, Libya, and Lebanon, and was recently litigated as President Bush mobilized troops in the Persian Gulf. Certainly, this was not an abstract legal quibble to the thousands of lives affected by these military deployments.

Some may posit that, at least in the Persian Gulf situation, constitutional words mattered less than the fact that ultimately, despite his argument that no statutory authorization was needed, Congress narrowly gave Bush approval to move against the lunacy of Saddam. What that view would fail to perceive, however, is that in matters of foreign policy, the Constitution was carefully designed not to provide a uniform answer on the respective powers of the political branches. The juxtaposition of the commander-in-chief and war clauses is a form—if you will—of prescribed nonprescription, allowing a certain elasticity of action to meet unforeseen national security needs. Thus, the words of the Constitution are important for both the answers they do and do not provide. Some matters have been deliberately left open in the Constitution, so that future generations of participants in the political branches could supply them.

Ed Meese: John Marshall's Direct Descendant

In calling for a better acknowledgement of constitutional words, or original intent, Meese was echoing John Marshall, whom many historians observe as our nation's most preeminent Chief Justice. In the early decision of *Marbury v. Madison*,[6] Marshall is credited with establishing in Supreme Court case law, the concept of judicial review; that is, the authority of the Court to declare state or federal law void as against the written Constitution. Marshall stated: "it is apparent that the framers of the Constitution contemplated that instrument as a rule for the government of *courts*, as well as of the legislature."[7] Because the words "judicial review" are not explicitly stated in the Constitution, Meese's reference to Marshall is held forth as a prime example that even the Attorney General is selectively unfaithful to original intent. This again is an attempt to defeat by distortion. It is an attempt to conflate faithfulness to original intention with an unbending, wooden literalism and then declare both to be unworkable. Of course literalism is unworkable, but that fact hardly responds to the Attorney General's plea for fidelity to original intention.

Judicial Review and Original Intent

The role of the Court was debated at the constitutional convention, but judicial review was not explicitly provided. Judicial review of legislative action under a written constitution before 1787 was a novelty. When the English Parliament spoke, its pronouncements were thought to be inviolate. In a 1701 case, an English court noted that "an act of parliament can do no wrong, though it may do several things that look pretty odd."[8] But the Townshend and Stamp Acts and other examples of British economic oppression would so distress colonial America that some intellectual means to review legislative action was obviously required. For this, reference would be made to Lord Coke's dictum in *Dr. Bonham's Case* that "when an act of Parliament is against common right and reason, the common law will control it and adjudge such Act to be void."[9] In 1761, James Otis would argue before a Massachusetts court that certain overbroad writs of assistance or search warrants could be said to be void as against "natural equity."[10]

Notwithstanding this asserted authority for judges to pass upon the validity of legislation in some respects, the convention on four occasions rejected James Madison's idea for a council of revision that would involve both the judiciary and the executive in the review of the wisdom of legislative acts even before they became effective. Yet, the convention discussion rejecting the council proves, rather than disproves, the framers' belief in judicial review as articulated by Marshall in *Marbury*. Gerry of Massachusetts urged that judges not be policy makers. However, he stipulated that judges, by their office, already had the authority to set aside laws that were unconstitutional. Nevertheless, it was quite foreign to the office of the judge to make them judges of the *policy* of public measures. Said Gerry: "[i]t was making Statesmen of Judges, . . ."[11] The convention largely accepted Gerry's observation and thus drew a sharp distinction between invalidating a law because it is contrary to the written Constitution and doing so because it is unwise.

EXCUSES FOR NOT RELYING ON ORIGINAL INTENT

Too Difficult

Justice Brennan's claim that original intent is "arrogance cloaked as humility" is premised on the proposition that it is largely undiscoverable. There is some truth to this difficulty. However, the difficulty exists not because the language of the Constitution is unintelligible, but because most—if not all modern constitutional lawyers—are taught to pay almost exclusive attention to the decisions of the Court, itself, as the meaning of the Constitution. There are several long-winded explanations for this, but it primarily stems from the fact that it is the easier course of study. Court decisions are nicely indexed and accessible. The notes of the 1787 constitutional convention are far less so. Judicial decisions are the meat of law study. They form discrete packages of knowledge that are easily presentable in the classroom. Convention or congressional debates, by contrast, are unwieldy and discursive. Because of the idiosyncrasies of state practice, the records of ratification debates are not always even kept.

The difficulty encountered with the academic or practical use of non-judicial materials dovetails all too conveniently with those who are quite content leaving the country subject to the unelected policy edicts of the Court. But dwelling on inconsistencies or lapses in the historical record misunderstands original intent. Yes, the original understanding of constitutional words is informed by the historical and social context in which they were used, but the most important clue as to meaning are the words themselves. These words are not hard to find. The importance of relying upon the text—even over the subjective intentions of the principal founding actors—was made clear by Hamilton who noted that "whatever may have been the intention of the framers of a constitution . . . that intention is to be sought for in the instrument itself."[12]

Ambiguity

When the Attorney General would point out the availability of real, meaningful words in the Constitution, he often met with two objections: one somewhat understandable and one discernible only by academics who have been working in windowless rooms too long. The first claim is that significant portions of the Constitution contain deliberately opaque terminology like "due process" or "equal protection of the law." In this regard, Meese's chief Court antagonist, Justice Brennan, called the due process clause a "particularly empty vessel" that can accommodate "changing conceptions of social justice."[13] In fact, however, even this terminology can be understood in historical context traceable as far back as the Magna Carta (1215) as the basic notion of adequate or appropriate legal procedures in relation to the legal interest at issue.[14] Even the "majestic generalities"[15] of the Constitution, as the Court has called them, have some meaning and are not a complete blank into which the Justices can transcribe their will.

Words Without Meaning

The second objection to reliance upon the words of the Constitution is the more fantastic, it is, quite simply, that words have no meaning, such that "[i]nterpretation is not the art of construing but the art of constructing."[16] This view originated in the area of literary criticism, but legal academics have not been shy about applying these notions wholesale to the Constitution.[17] This uncritical transference of a theory where meaning is created rather than discovered is wholly unwarranted. It might have been thought that the dissimilarity between the Constitution as a source of law with life and death consequence, in contrast to the less obligatory subtleties of literature, might be enough to make this point. Beyond this, if words are "empty vessels," they present a profound dilemma for the settlement of disagreements—not only under the Constitution, but as to every written document from a person's will to everyday contracts. To overcome this illogic, the proponents of nonmeaning doctrines fall back on shifting communities of understanding to find meaning. The nature of these communities, however, is none too clear. At best, the communities embrace a wide array of ill-defined and value-laden approaches that yield little stability, and like the philosopher Nietzsche, posit that the notion of good or bad or "ultimate truth-seeking is based on philosophical error."[18]

Perhaps the best response to the intellectually lazy excuse that the Constitution's language is ambiguous, and the more bizarre position that language is meaningless, was penned by Professor Frederick Schauer. Schauer writes: "[t]he general intelligibility of language enables us to understand the mandate of numerous constitutional provisions without recourse to . . . standard interpretive supplements."[19] Schauer admits there are hard cases, but to make the hard cases the governing perspective unnecessarily tends toward nihilism. Even in hard cases, the proper response is not to throw up one's hands, or succumb to judicial assertion, but to utilize constitutional language in a way that at least excludes wrong answers where the language does not specifically point to the precisely correct one. Professor Richard Kay makes a similar point in saying that "[a]lmost every decision we make and action we take is based on a judgment of probabilities, often as to the probable intended meaning of what we read or hear. To insist on certainty would lead to paralysis. In asking judges to make decisions in this way, we demand nothing more or less than the same kinds of decisions everyone makes everyday."[20]

Undesired Outcomes

Law professors have suggested a number of other reasons for resisting the Attorney General's exhortation to return to original understanding. Many of these so-called reasons can be easily summarized as: original intent might not produce the favored result. Surely manufactured rights, such as the abortion right the Court made up in *Roe*, would fall within this category. However, there is a tendency of some critics to greatly overstate their case in other areas. Floyd Abrams' complaint mentioned earlier about Meese's interpretations leading to the likelihood of a state religion in California is an example, but it is not alone. For instance, Stanford law professor Thomas Grey argues that under original intent the Bill of Rights would not apply to the states and that even racial school segregation might return.[21]

Both of Grey's points cannot be seriously maintained. A half century ago, Justice Black admirably revealed that while the Court was straining to sandwich the entire Bill of Rights into the due process clause, these rights could be applied against the states on "the language of the entire first section of the Fourteenth Amendment, as illuminated by the legislative history surrounding its adoption."[22] As for the segregation of public schools, there is some evidence that some drafters of the fourteenth amendment did not contemplate the language of that amendment precluding the practice.[23] But, as already indicated, subjective intent is not the touchstone of original intent—it is the words used. The Constitution, said Justice Story, "must be judged by its words and sense, and not by any private intentions of members of the legislature."[24] The words of the equal protection guarantee mean unequivocally that "in respect of civil rights, all citizens are equal before the law."[25] Thus, the Court's landmark decision in *Brown v. Board of Education.*[26] is fully consistent with original understanding. As Attorney General Meese reflected:

> The *Brown* decision was correcting the damage done 50 years earlier, when in *Plessy v. Ferguson*, an earlier Supreme Court had disregarded the clear intent of the Framers of the civil war amendments to eliminate the legal degradation of blacks, and had contrived a theory of the Constitution to support the charade of "separate but equal" discrimination.[27]

The Legal Tender Bugaboo

Bernard Schwartz argues against original understanding by suggesting that this would preclude the issuance of paper money.[28] Under article I, Congress has the power "to coin Money, [and] regulate the Value thereof." That language did lead the Supreme Court to invalidate the use of paper money shortly after the Civil War,[29] however, the decision was reversed almost immediately in the *Legal Tender Cases*.[30] Schwartz attributes the reversal to the happenstance of two new Court appointments, and thus contends that were original intent our sole guide, modern America would be constrained to a currency of coins alone.

Hardly. The primary monetary concern of the constitutional convention of 1787 was addressed less to the issue of paper money versus coins than to the respective powers of the federal and state governments over the value of money. To be sure, under the Articles of Confederation, state issuance of paper had proven to be a problem—not so much because it was paper, but because it was paper not backed by value. Moreover, the Articles had failed to reserve to the central government the exclusive power to set the value of money in relation to foreign currency. Joseph Story reports that: "[t]he constitution has, with great propriety, cured this defect; . . ."[31] Yet, Story also makes it reasonably clear that Schwartz's federal paper money concern is a false one. As to whether either the states or the federal government had the power to issue paper money, Story denies it to the states and implies it for the federal government with a rhetorical question:

> The states cannot coin money. Can they, then, coin that, which becomes the actual and almost universal substitute for money? Is not the right of issuing paper, intended for circulation in the place, and as the representative of metallic currency, derived merely from the power of coining and regulating the metallic currency? Could congress, if it did not possess the power of coining money and regulating the value of foreign coins, create a bank with the power to circulate bills? It would be difficult to make out.[32]

Elsewhere in his book, Schwartz accuses those devoted to finding original intent, including the present Chief Justice of the United States, to a selective use of history, to what is called office history. Yet in making his argument against original intent depend upon an emphasis upon the use of the word "coin," rather than a complete understanding of the derivation of the congressional power at issue, Schwartz has done even less than what we would expect of office historians. In addition to Justice Story's commentary, a thorough-going effort to define the scope of Congress' power to issue paper money would draw on the interaction between this congressional power and the power "to borrow money on the credit of the United States,"[33] the power "to provide for the Punishment of counterfeiting the Securities and current Coin of the United States,"[34] as well as Congress' power "to make all Laws which shall be necessary and proper" to carry out those express grants.

SUGGESTED ALTERNATIVES TO ORIGINAL INTENT

The alternatives to original understanding are no more persuasive than the excuses for ignoring it. Most of the alternatives to original intent have one common and very noticeable feature: vagueness. They draw inspiration from an amalgam of philosophical traditions, most unidentified. Most often, they originate not in the constitutional text or history or even longstanding American tradition, but in the abstract will of a judge or legal academic with life tenure. In light of this, it is well to reflect at the outset how strenuously these nonconstitutional methods of constitutional interpretation—if that is not the ultimate oxymoron—were opposed by the Constitution's primary drafter, James Madison. Madison wrote:

> I entirely concur in the propriety of reasoning to the sense in which the Constitution was accepted and ratified by the nation. In that sense alone it is the legitimate Constitution. And if that be not the guide in expounding it, there can be no security for the consistent and stable, more than for a faithful, exercise of its powers. If the meaning of the text be sought in the changeable meaning of the words composing it, it is evident that the shape and attributes of the government must partake of the changes to which the words and phrases of all living languages are constantly subject. What a metamorphosis would be produced in the code of law if all its ancient phraseology were to be taken in its modern sense![35]

Despite the wisdom of Madison's warning, the alternatives for disregarding constitutional meaning continue to multiply.

Neutral Principles

The most moderate of the suggested alternatives can be found in Herbert Wechsler's call for the application of neutral principles in constitutional decisions.[36] Wechsler's suggestion predates Meese's call for reinvigorated original understanding, but it addresses the difficulty posed by hard cases. Wechsler instructs judges to follow the Constitution where its words are decisive, and where it is not, to at least fashion neutral principles that transcend the case before them. Rightly, Wechsler seeks to avoid the dilemma of the result-oriented judge, and his injunction to treat similar people similarly provides an important element of equality. What is lacking, however, is a persuasive justification for why anyone should accept the judge's neutral principle, rather than some other, if it is not founded on the Constitution. Judicial law making is still judicial law making even if it is evenhandedly applied.

Implied by Wechsler is the notion that a judge must make some decision. True enough, but it must be one guided by either the Constitution's terms or its structure. If the terms of the Constitution do not provide a specific answer, its structure does. This is because if Congress lacks the enumerated authority to legislate on a question, the structure of the Constitution as affirmed by the tenth amendment places the decision with the states. If a decision is reserved to the states, and no part of the Constitution precludes state action, federal judges—except in the extremely rare case where a true natural law principle underlying the Constitution is offended—have no basis to opine. Even a neutral intervention that is unauthorized is still without authority.[37]

Balancing

Balancing conjures up the statue of Justice, blindfolded with the scales carefully calibrated in her hand. Despite this figurative allure, however, the notion that constitutional cases can be resolved by identifying the interests involved and weighing them against each other is both nonconstitutional and fanciful. The Constitution does not assign values to particular rights; instead, individual liberties are secured by disabling particular governmental action or checking it with the division of governmental power. Nevertheless, the Supreme Court's cases are legion with multipronged or balancing formulas.[38] In dormant commerce clause cases, for example, the Court weighs the interest of the regulating state against the Court's conception of interstate commerce. In procedural due process cases, the Court weighs its conception of the importance of the individual right affected by a government decision against the Court's conception of what costs the government would suffer with better procedures.[39]

Without an external standard by which to balance, balancing as a method of constitutional decision making is delusive. Rather than identifying and addressing the source of decision, it hides it. The entity that is most often hiding is the Court itself. Even Justice Brennan voiced concern with the seductive capacity of balancing to distract judicial decision makers from the Constitution calling it "doctrinally destructive nihilism."[40] As one commentator put it, "[u]nder a balancing approach, the Court searches the landscape for interests implicated by a case, identifies a few, and reaches a reasonable accommodation among them. In so doing, the Court largely ignores the usual stuff of constitutional interpretation—the investigation and manipulation of texts . . ."[41]

Noninterpretivism

The more adventuresome alternative to original understanding is noninterpretivism. Scholars and judges of this school openly abandon traditional interpretive sources altogether. Thus, text in its historical and purposive context, the statements of drafters and ratifiers, and the meaning that can be drawn from the structure of the constitutional document as a whole is simply forsaken. But substituted with what?

Dean Paul Brest of the Stanford Law School suggests that the touchstone of constitutional decision making is "[h]ow well, compared to possible alternatives, does the practice contribute to the well-being of society."[42] Recognizing that this is a "designedly vague criterion," Brest proposes several factors that may reveal when "well-being" is advanced. Among other things, Brest proposes to have judges evaluate whether the practice "conduce[s] to a political order that is relatively stable but which responds to changing conditions, values and needs."[43] This may sound reasonable enough, but on reflection "stability with change" is more a bumper sticker than a constitutional standard. As a prescription it also seemingly argues for two contradictory things. Attempting to say everything is a stale academic trick, but it cannot possibly be of assistance to a federal judge. Saying everything is to effectively say nothing.[44]

Another noninterpretivist standard is whether a decision coincides with "values deeply embedded in the society."[45] These embedded values are apparently wholly outside the document, however. Lamely, they are defined as values behind which "the society and its legal system have unmistakably thrown their weight," but have not been "enshrined" in statute or constitutional amendment. The small matter of authoritative enactment is foregone and "gap-filling" is turned over to the Court. It seldom occurs to these noninterpretivists that the absence of statute or constitutional provision, however, strongly suggests that there is no gap to be filled.

Still a third noninterpretivist standard is constitutional right by "settled weight of responsible opinion."[46] Responsible opinion is said to consist of "the American Law Institute, the Commissioners for Uniform State Laws, and more specialized commissions of inquiry such as the Administrative Conference." These are respected and responsible voices, and their collective wisdom may be enormous. But as important sources in legal matters, they would likely be the first to refrain from presuming that their pronouncements somehow authoritatively amend the Constitution.

Any survey of noninterpretive standards could go on at length, but, except for capturing the rhetorical flare of various commentators, it would find most, if not all, to be nebulous and unhelpful. Even Professor Laurence Tribe who has contributed to legal literature a challenging and interesting constitutional volume is unable to articulate a substitute constitutional standard beyond "the living development of constitutional justice."[47] Nevertheless, Tribe, too, by his own admission, is a noninterpretivist. A judicial role demonstrating fidelity to constitutional text is misconceived, argues Tribe, because "the Constitution is an intentionally incomplete, often deliberately indeterminate structure for the participatory evolution of political ideals and governmental practices."[48] Thus, Tribe draws on the excuse that original intent is too difficult. But a closer look suggests that Tribe has another purpose for disregarding the Constitution: namely, keeping the Court's field of operation as wide as possible in order to achieve political victories not forthcoming from the democratic process. To accomplish this, Tribe must convince us that the restraints of the Constitution on judges are "rote unreality, profoundly misconceived in light of the inevitable social and cultural constraints on judicial intention and impact."[49] Judges must "take sides," claims Tribe, because judicial neutrality is a myth.

Tribe's words are alarming. If they were true, there would be no rule of law. There would only be rule by elite judges constrained only by their social and cultural positions in making decisions. The guarantees of life, liberty, and property would be ephemeral. Their sanctity or existence would depend on little else than the mores of the time. Does this mean that Tribe believes there is no need for restraint on governmental power? No, but the restraints he advocates are not necessarily, or even likely, founded on the consent of the governed. Indeed, instead of the ratified constitutional text, Tribe, who is often mentioned as a likely nominee to the Supreme Court in a Democratic administration, finds more insight in the scientific study of pigeon behavior.

Pigeon behavior? Yep, pigeon behavior. Professor Tribe writes: "the question . . . is why a nation that rests legality on the consent of the governed would choose to constitute its political life in terms of commitments to an original agreement . . . "[50] The outlines of an answer, advises Tribe, can be found in the report of a pigeon feeding experiment in the *Journal of the Experimental Analysis of Behavior*.[51] It seems that some pigeons had a choice between a small amount of immediate food or a large amount of delayed food. Overwhelmingly, the pigeons chose to get their food now. Tribe reports that the pigeons "regretted" this choice. It would be interesting to know how Tribe learned of this regret. No matter, the story continues, and when researchers gave the pigeons the option of waddling into a waiting room for the delayed food, about 30 percent of the pigeons could forego the temptation of the immediate food. Tribe finds in this "an apt model for constitutionalism."[52]

Pigeon sh__t! Pardon my expression, but this is the kind of stuff that makes it darn hard to explain to parents why they should work two jobs to pay the ever-increasing tuition at private, and even public, universities.

When a bright, able constitutional law teacher at one of America's elite law schools finds more insight into the Constitution in an isolated pigeon study than in the rich text and history of the document and the writing of the likes of Madison, Hamilton, and their contemporaries, is it little wonder that the judges and elected officials "trained"—or should I say "conditioned"—by such instruction bring little appreciation and respect for the Constitution as law?

Noninterpretivism and Morality

There is one more noninterpretivist school that deserves mention, not because it steers us toward proper constitutional decision making in itself, but because it identifies an original intent weakness that was never fully addressed by the Attorney General or other prominent originalists. This weakness is the failure of original intent to answer the possibility that the positive law may be immoral. Employing the language of morality, Michael Perry argues for departing from constitutional text as a type of "moral evolution."[53] Perry writes: "[i]n twentieth century America there have been several such issues: distributive justice and the role of government, freedom of political dissent, racism, sexism, the death penalty, and human sexuality. Our electorally accountable policy-making institutions are not well suited to deal with such issues in a way that is faithful to the notion of moral evolution and, therefore, to our religious understanding of ourselves."[54]

Perry is very quick to deny that his reference to religion is meant in any "sectarian, theistic, or otherwise metaphysical sense."[55] Of course, the moment Perry says that, he separates morality from the manner in which that term was understood by the framers, and I dare say, most of us today. If no objective truth stands behind Perry's moral claim, it is vacuous. It is the morals of the particular judge, nothing more. But morality need not be the empty, malleable term of a Michael Perry. Instead, it might have the immutable, objective content of natural law. Since the Constitution was drafted against the background of the natural law, any faithful return to original intent cannot disregard it.

WHAT IS NATURAL LAW?

If you haven't heard of the natural law, it is not surprising. While teaching natural law at the turn of this century was a prominent part of elementary, let alone, law school education, it is now seldom taught, or taught correctly. Natural law fell out of favor with the rise of pragmatism and moral relativism, and the modern denial of God. Natural law is not necessarily a religious doctrine, but it does assume that every person and every thing has been created with an inherent or intrinsic nature and that no human or positive law can supersede this nature. This was a fairly easy proposition for Thomas Jefferson who of course observed that "all men are endowed by their Creator with certain unalienable rights," but it has been scoffed at by Holmes who wrote: "[t]he jurists who believe in natural law seem to me to be in that naive state of mind that accepts what has been familiar and accepted by them and their neighbors as something that must be accepted by all men everywhere."[56]

Holmes notwithstanding, the limits and inclination of nature are difficult to ignore. To take an obvious example, if the Congress of the United States declared the human consumption of motor oil healthful, it could not make it so. Now to the lay reader this may seem as obvious as day following night and maybe about as relevant as Professor Tribe trying to discern the meaning of the Constitution in pigeon behavior. But its significance is indeed much greater and threefold: first, natural law has an objective content discernible through reason; [57] second, natural law offers judges little support for new judicially-created fundamental rights; and third, natural law does supply judges with some important, but necessarily infrequent, authorization to displace the actions of legislatures. In other words, properly understood, natural law is a meaningful, but by and large background, principle in constitutional decision making.

Natural Law's Objective Content

The notion that there are characteristics of a person's nature that are intrinsic is an ancient one. In this respect, Cicero described "Law" as "the highest reason, implanted in Nature, which commands what ought to be done and forbids the opposite."[58] That a legislature cannot change that which is ordained in nature is also made clear by Cicero:

> [T]he most foolish notion of all is the belief that everything is just which is found in the customs or laws of nations.... But if the principles of Justice were found on the decrees of peoples, the edicts of princes, or the decisions of judges, then Justice would sanction robbery and adultery and forgery of wills, in case these acts were approved by the votes or decrees of the populace.[59]

Even though natural law teaching has been in desuetude, it is not a principle foreign to American law even today. The ready distinction drawn in criminal law between offenses that are *malum in se* (something wrong in itself—like murder), as opposed to *mala prohibita* (something wrong because it is prohibited—like running a stop sign) is an example. Moreover, as will be discussed more fully later, legal historian Edward Corwin found natural law to be the essential purpose of the ninth amendment. The only difference, noted Corwin, is phraseology, since "the principles of transcendental justice have been [there] translated into terms of personal and private rights."[60] Corwin is clear that the founders' intent in the ninth amendment was not to confer legitimacy on these personal rights by their incorporation into the Constitution or to indulge the pretense that natural rights can be legislatively limited. Corwin thus writes that these transcendental rights "owe nothing to their recognition in the Constitution—such recognition was necessary if the Constitution was to be regarded as complete."[61]

A Check on the Judicial Creation of Rights

The rights derived from natural law have been stated differently over time, but chiefly they are

> [t]he "rights" revealed by nature, "animate and inanimate," includ[ing] a right to be, and therefore includ[ing] a right to continue to be (from which [is] derive[d] the right of self-defense and a duty of protecting from wanton destruction human, animal and vegetable life); [and] these imply "a right to the conditions of existence," from which [is] implie[d] the right to the exclusive ownership and possession of property.[62]

These same sentiments are captured by the shorthand employed by the framers of "Life, Liberty and the pursuit of Happiness"[63] known to every schoolchild. Fundamentally, natural law prescribes the right of self-preservation or life as well as the right to live and develop in community.[64]

As thus stated, natural law cannot be relied upon to create new rights because there is very little, if anything, new about the nature of the human person. In the words of Professor Charles Rice, "natural law . . . is not a hunting license empowering judges to impose their own morality to invalidate legislative decisions in genuinely debatable cases."[65] Economic regulation that does not threaten personal existence or disregard private property, subject of course to the explicit constraints of other provisions of the Constitution like the taking clause, would not be subject to challenge on natural law grounds. Thus, the state could take one's property for public use upon the payment of just compensation and the state could also regulate that property ownership without compensation so long as it performed its task in evenhanded and proportionate ways. What the state could not do, because the natural law against theft would preclude it, is redefine property ownership in ways that would render the taking clause and the due process clause meaningless. Property being in part a natural law concept could not be wholly subject to state redefinition.

Similarly, claims for new rights of privacy are seen as counterfeit under the natural law. Obviously, a judicial decision striking down state laws protection of human life can have no natural law foundation. Indeed, a decision like *Roe v. Wade* which manufactured the right to kill the unborn, is perhaps the best example of where the natural law context of the Constitution has been most seriously offended.[66] So, too, a claim that the Constitution guarantees individuals the right of homosexual practice would have no natural law foundation. Insofar as homosexual behavior is one of the primary ways in which the deadly HIV or AIDS virus is transmitted, a law limiting that behavior promotes natural law by safeguarding existence and promoting health. The Court's conclusion in *Bowers v. Hardwick* that "to claim that a right to engage in [homosexual] conduct is 'deeply rooted in this Nation's history and tradition' or 'implicit in the concept of ordered liberty' is, at best, facetious"[67] is an echo of natural law understanding.

Respect for Positive Law

Properly understood, natural law accords great respect for positive law. This bears emphasis because it highlights the chief difference between natural law and the open-ended, noninterpretivist constitutional theories discussed earlier. Natural law does not pretend to supply a detailed code of conduct to be copied verbatim into positive law. While natural law has been caricatured in this fashion, the natural law disavows such simplistic, judicially active notions.

This proper relationship between natural and positive law was outlined long ago by the respected American philosopher, Dr. Mortimer Adler. Adler observed that "[o]f political justice part is natural, part legal—natural, that which everywhere has the same force and does not exist by people's thinking this or that; legal, that which is originally indifferent, but when it has been laid down is not indifferent."[68] Thus, there are distinct, immutable principles of natural law, such as to seek the good, and precepts, such as not killing, stealing, or committing adultery, but "many things [are left] undetermined which must be determined by the conventions of political or civil law."[69]

To fully understand how natural law gives wide, but not unlimited, berth to the operations of positive law, it is necessary to comprehend the fundamental differences between natural and positive law.[70] If one wanted to learn the law of a particular state, Adler commented, one would not ask someone to teach us this law by demonstrating rational conclusions from sound premises. "The law of [a state] can only be taught by statement and it can only be learned by memory. This is due to its arbitrary character as positive law."[71] In contrast, natural law is discovered by the individual through rational inquiry and it can be taught by others through rational instruction. Adler highlighted other differences, too: positive law compels obedience through force and fear; there is no such temporal, external force with natural law; positive law involves a free choice among several options—indifferent possibilities as the philosophers would say; whereas, with natural law, as with an accurate mathematical answer, there is no choice; positive law is binding only within the limited sphere of temporal political authority; natural law is binding on everyone.

The differences Adler highlighted between natural law and its positive counterpart should not be taken to mean that they are irrelevant to each other. Quite the contrary, as Adler instructed: "[p]ositive law without a foundation in natural law is purely arbitrary. It needs the natural law to make it rational. But natural law without positive law is ineffective for the purposes of enforcing justice and keeping the peace."[72]

Over time, lawyers have sought to further elaborate the natural law/positive law difference by drawing a distinction between principles or precepts and rules. Principles and precepts—like the injunction to seek the good or the proscription against killing or theft—are not capable "by themselves of governing action, for different reasons, . . . : in the case of principles, because they specify only one end, and action depends on specification of means; in the case of precepts, because they specify the means only generally and without reference to the contingent circumstances which are always involved in action."[73]

It is the contingent circumstances that make rules, the usual stuff of positive law, far different from principles and precepts. Two consequences flow from the introduction of contingent circumstances, or facts: "[t]he first is that since facts are infinite in number, they cannot all be comprehended by human reason. Therefore any rule which is based upon them must be based upon the generality of experience and will be defective to the extent that it fails to provide for the unknown or the unusual case. The second is that facts change, and therefore laws must change, to preserve a reasonable relation to facts."[74] In short, natural law principles and precepts are immutable, whereas, rules are "relative, contingent and changeable."[75]

A third, very important consequence of the recognition of natural law is that it does not generally authorize judges to second-guess the legislative process. Only when the legislative process yields a true conflict between the explicit text of the Constitution or a natural law principle or precept would the Court be duty bound to act to set a statute aside. Thus, natural law, unlike any of the vacuous, noninterpretivist constitutional theories, is capable of harmonizing the judges' duty to follow the law as written with the judges' duty to do justice; to insure, that the positive law is not itself an injustice. But the use of natural law in *any* respect by judges has been assailed as a "serious problem"[76] by liberals *and* conservatives. Liberals see natural law as a return to principles of right and wrong that they thought were long ago forgotten. Some conservatives are unable to differentiate a genuine fundamental right founded in natural law from a counterfeit one resident only in the mind of its advocate. These liberal and conservative failings have a common origin: ignorance of the natural law elements contained within the written text of the Constitution. Properly understood, natural law is part of the original intent.

THE NATURAL LAW BACKGROUND OF THE CONSTITUTION

Natural law had a profound influence on the founders. Chester Antieau observed that "it would be amazing if any Revolutionary leader of the Commonwealth could be found who did not subscribe to the doctrines of natural law and right."[77] The higher law, or natural law, background of the Constitution was perhaps most eloquently taught by the late Dean Clarence E. "Pat" Manion of the University of Notre Dame. Manion began by tracing Jefferson's inspirational Declaration of Independence to the common law commentaries of Blackstone, in which Blackstone wrote:

> [W]hen the Supreme Being formed the universe and created matter out of nothing, he impressed certain principles upon that matter from which it can never depart and without which it would cease to be.... [S]ince man depends absolutely upon his maker for everything, it is necessary that he should in all points conform to his maker's will. *This will of his maker is called the law of nature.* ...[God] has not perplexed the law of nature with a multitude of abstracted rules and precepts...but has graciously reduced the rule of obedience to this one paternal precept *that man shall pursue his own true and substantial happiness.*[78]

From this passage, Manion carefully documented how the law of nature became interwoven with the English common law as well as with the "pursuit of happiness" formulation of the later Declaration. Natural law also led to the recognition of a "higher law" check upon legislative acts stated explicitly by Coke in *Dr. Bonham's Case.*[79] In this sense, natural law nurtured the seeds of revolution against a tyrannical king, the origin of judicial review, and the concept of fundamental right. As a young Alexander Hamilton would observe: "[t]he sacred rights of mankind are not to be rummaged for among old parchments or musty records. They are written as with a sunbeam, in the whole volume of human nature, by the hand of Divinity itself and can never be erased or obscured by mortal power."[80]

Contemporary students of constitutional law would be well advised to set aside their Perrys and Tribes long enough to read Manion's essay.

In but a fraction of the pages these noninterpretivist scholars exhaust, Dean Manion illustrates with clarity how our constitutional structure derives from a sublime understanding of "the laws of nature and of nature's God."[81] Moreover, Manion gives lie to the notion that this is somehow an ancient, irrelevant conception of constitutional decision making frozen in the 18th century. Mushy conceptions of dynamic, living constitutions pale in comparison to Manion's reference to James Wilson's delightfully clearheaded explanation of the growth of natural law knowledge. Wilson wrote:

> On these subjects one who has had the advantage of a common education in a Christian country, knows more and with more certainty than was known by the wisest of the ancient philosophers.... The *law of nature is universal.* For it is true, not only that all men are equally subject to the command of their Maker, but it is true also that the law of Nature having its foundation in the constitution and state of man, has an essential fitness for all mankind and binds them without distinction.... We may infer that the law of nature though immutable in its principles will be progressive in its *operations* and *effects.* In every period of his existence the law, which the divine wisdom has approved for man will not only be fitted to the contemporary degree but will be calculated to produce in future a still higher degree of perfection.[82]

Other contemporary scholars have followed Manion, relying upon the Declaration of Independence for interpreting the Constitution in the light of natural law. Professor Harry Jaffa, for example, has commented recently that it is the Declaration of Independence that provides the Constitution with its moral base.[83] In this, Jaffa references Jefferson and Madison's recommendation of the Declaration as the very best of the " 'best guides' to the principles of the Constitution of Virginia and of the United States.... "[84]

The Ninth Amendment

There is also explicit natural law reference in the Constitution. As briefly mentioned earlier, Columbia legal historian, Professor Edward Corwin argued that it could be found in the ninth amendment.[85] This amendment provides that: "The enumeration in the Constitution, of certain rights, shall not be construed to deny or disparage others retained by the people."[86]

There is much debate about the meaning of these words. Robert Bork argues that they are a meaningless "inkblot"; whereas, Professor Randy Barnett has premised the entire libertarian core of the Constitution upon them.[87] In constitutional litigation, the history of the ninth amendment is not encouraging. The amendment was glancingly relied upon by Justice Douglas to discover a constitutional right to contraceptive use, and the amendment had a nonspeaking role in Justice Blackmun's manufacture of the constitutional right to kill the unborn. It can be readily understood why the Attorney General and other originalists would fear the amendment as a "loose cannon."

Yet, Bork's inkblot assertion cannot stand. If the Constitution is law, then no part of it can go unenforced. Successful enforcement means that its history must be more carefully plumbed. That history began with many states ratifying the Constitution, but only on condition that a bill of rights be added. The reason for this insistence was made plain by Patrick Henry: to deny any implication of power to the federal government beyond that expressly enumerated. Henry insisted that "all nations have adopted this construction—that all rights not expressly and unequivocally reserved to the people are impliedly and incidentally relinquished to rulers, as necessarily inseparable from the delegated powers."[88]

To counter this construction, three states—Virginia, North Carolina and New York—drafted language that was the intellectual ancestor of the ninth amendment. The proposed amendments provided:

> That those clauses which declare that Congress shall not exercise certain powers, be not interpreted, in any manner, whatsoever to extend the powers of Congress; but that they be construed either as making exceptions to the specified powers where this shall be the case, or otherwise, as inserted merely for the greater caution.[89]

New York's language was even more blunt: "Powers, do not imply that Congress is entitled to any Powers not given by the said Constitution; but such Clauses are to be construed either as exceptions to certain specified Powers, or as inserted merely for greater caution."[90]

Madison took these state proposals designed to curtail the implication of federal power and subtly changed them to reference the "just importance of other rights retained by the people."[91] This change engendered considerable opposition and led to they initial rejection by the Virginia Assembly. Governor Randolph of Virginia thought that the rights retained formulation would be meaningless in much the same manner that Robert Bork has argued. In a letter to Madison from another Virginian, Randolph's concerns were stated as follows:

> there was no criterion by which it could be determined whether any other particular right was retained or not, it would be more safe, and more consistent with [the Virginia proposal] that this reservation against constructive power, should operate rather as a provision against extending the powers of Congress by their own authority, than as a protection to rights reducible to no definitive certainty.[92]

Madison didn't see the problem. In a letter to George Washington, he complained that Randolph was making something out of nothing. Madison wrote: "[i]f a line can be drawn between the powers granted and the rights retained, it would seem to be the same thing, whether the latter be secured, by declaring that they shall not be abridged, or that the former shall not be extended."[93] Stephen Markman, Ed Meese's legal policy advisor, argued that even though Madison failed to appreciate Randolph's concern, Madison's response to Washington confirms "his understanding that, notwithstanding the reference to rights instead of powers, the ninth amendment continued to operate as a restriction on the implied extension of federal powers."[94] The inference Markman draws may be the correct one, but it cannot fairly be said to be free from doubt.

That Madison also perceived the ninth amendment as incorporating natural law is suggested by his comments on the floor of the House introducing the Bill of Rights. As to the necessity of the amendments, Madison states: "[i]f they are incorporated into the constitution, independent tribunals of justice will consider themselves in a peculiar manner the guardians of those rights; they will be an impenetrable bulwark against every assumption of power in the legislative or executive; . . ."[95] Madison's assumption that the Bill of Rights, including the ninth amendment, would be judicially enforced directly rebuts Robert Bork who claims that the role of judges in this regard went "wholly unmentioned."[96] Madison's introduction also casts doubt on Markman's construction of the ninth amendment that it was meant only to refer to rights anchored in state constitutions, statutes and the common law.[97] It is illogical to conclude that the independent federal judiciary referenced by Madison would be the mainstay of enforcement for *state* provisions.

Bork is right, however, that words "retained by the people" indicate that the rights referenced must necessarily preexist, and are not to be discovered by the judiciary willy-nilly. The preexistence of the retained natural rights is also consistent with the remaining provision of the Bill of Rights—the tenth amendment which expressly provides that "[t]he powers not delegated to the United States by the Constitution, nor prohibited by it to the States, are reserved to the States respectively, or to the people."[98] Thus, the tenth amendment is the explicit limitation on federal power that Governor Randolph complained Madison's "rights retained" formulation of the ninth amendment slighted. But if the tenth amendment accomplishes that purpose, then the ninth amendment clearly must have some other.[99] That other purpose is not to specify *who* may exercise power (federal or state government), but over *what* (subjects) that power may be exercised by either the federal or state governments. But to know the *what*, Madison correctly observed that a line must be capable of being drawn "between the powers granted and the rights retained. . . ."[100] To draw that line, the rights must have a separate, ascertainable existence apart from executive, legislative, or judicial will. While the judiciary is charged with policing the line, the existence of the rights that form the line must be found elsewhere. The only credible source of right having any meaningful influence on the founders is natural law.

Meese's Omission of Natural Law—The Case of *Dred Scott* and Slavery

Professor Jaffa severely criticizes Attorney General Meese for neglecting the natural law foundation of the Constitution in his many lectures on original intent. Without that foundation, Jaffa believes Meese fails to appreciate that some rights are antecedent to society.[101] It was slavery and the Civil War, of course, that squarely posed the issue of antecedent civil rights. The Supreme Court's decision in *Dred Scott v. Sanford*[102] framed the dilemma. On the one hand, numerous provisions of the original Constitution seemingly provided that slaves were a form of property; in contrast, the natural law of the Declaration (arguably, incorporated by the ninth amendment) grandly declared that "all men are created equal, that they are endowed by their Creator with certain unalienable Rights, that among these are Life, Liberty and the pursuit of Happiness." In answering the specific question in *Dred Scott* whether Congress had the power to exclude slavery from United States territory, Chief Justice Taney chose the positivist course uniformed by natural law:

> [I]f the Constitution recognizes the right of property of the master in a slave, and makes no distinction between that description of property and other property owned by a citizen, no tribunal, acting under the authority of the United States . . . has a right to draw such a distinction. . . . [T]he right of property in a slave is distinctly and expressly affirmed in the Constitution. . . . The right to traffic in it, like an ordinary article of merchandise and property, was guarantied [sic] . . . in every State that might desire it, for twenty years. . . . And no word can be found in the Constitution which gives Congress a greater power over slave property, or which entitles property of that kind to less protection than the property of other description.[103]

Without a grounding in natural law, the Attorney General is left having to rationalize or explain away *Dred Scott*. In this respect, both Ed Meese and Robert Bork have mistakenly, in my opinion, tried to bolster original intent by denying that it was the original intent of the Constitution to treat slaves as property. Bork declares that "there is no . . . constitutional provision that can be read with any semblance of plausibility to confer a right to own slaves."[104] Echoing this view, Meese characterizes *Dred*

Scott as Roger B. Taney's effort to "read blacks out of the Constitution in order to invalidate Congress' attempt to limit the spread of slavery."[105] These sentiments are very hard to square with article IV, section 2, paragraph 3 of the original Constitution which provided: "No Person held to Service or Labour in one State, under the Laws thereof, escaping into another, shall, in Consequence of any Law or Regulation therein, be discharged from such Service or Labour, but shall be delivered up on Claim of the Party to whom such Service or Labour may be due."

In an attempt to respond to article IV, the Attorney General pointed to article I, section 9 of the original Constitution that provides that "[t]he migration or importation of [slaves]... shall not be prohibited by the Congress prior to the year one thousand eight hundred and eight...." Meese argued that the Constitution thus "made explicit provision for a time in the not-so-distant future when Congress could seek to restrict not only the slave trade but the institution itself."[106] But, with all due respect, this provision merely permitted Congress to prohibit the migration or importation of slaves after 1808; it did not require it.

What does seemingly require the abolition of slavery, and what makes Taney's opinion in *Dred Scott* a mockery of the Constitution and original intent, are the "Laws of Nature and of Nature's God" referenced in the Declaration of Independence and the natural law "rights retained" in the ninth amendment. As Jaffa has put it: "[t]he central question in *Dred Scott* was this: Which took precedence when a slaveowner entered a Territory with his slave, the Negro slave's human personality under 'the laws of nature and of nature's God,' or his chatteldom under the laws of the slave state whence he came?"[107] If the Declaration is recognized as the best guide to the meaning of the Constitution's terms, then the Court in *Dred Scott* was not called upon to simplemindedly cite the proslavery provisions of the Constitution, but to reconcile them with the conflicting due process rights of "persons" in the fifth amendment. The natural law easily resolves the conflict of constitutional provisions in *Dred Scott* because it unequivocally declares as wrong the treatment of a slave as subhuman; as something less than his nature requires. In this respect, Meese is right that Taney disregarded the Constitution's original intent by reading blacks out of the document. But unacknowledged by the Attorney General is that this original intent judgment is necessarily informed by natural law.

Why would the Attorney General make this omission? Perhaps, it was a simple matter of staffing. Having watched, and occasionally contributed to, the process by which drafts of the Attorney General's lectures on original intent were prepared, I largely believe these pronouncements were greatly influenced by the positivist views of his principal speech writers, Terry Eastland and Gary McDowell. Eastland and McDowell are able writers and strongly shared the Attorney General's commitment to original intent. More importantly, they shared his resistance to the importation into constitutional decision making of the type of amorphous, noninterpretivist theories alluded to earlier.

It is also quite likely that Meese encountered very little natural law in his own legal studies at the University of California. The natural law tradition is an analytically difficult course of study, and except at a few places like the University of Notre Dame, it is no longer part of the required law school curriculum. Both Eastland and McDowell were nonlawyers, trained as professional journalist and political scientist, respectively. While Meese would sometimes intuitively link the Constitution and the Declaration of Independence in brief remarks, that association very likely did not comprehend the full natural law tradition out of which the Constitution was born. In this regard, it was the tendency of Meese's speech writers to unthinkingly lump natural law with noninterpretive constitutional theory. In a speech Gary McDowell prepared and that I unsuccessfully urged the Attorney General not to deliver, there is a direct criticism of natural law as "mysterious and uncertain."[108] Insofar as this passage was aimed at precluding reliance upon nonconstitutional sources of interpretation, I understood Gary's reasoning for including it. What I believe Gary failed to perceive—and perhaps the Attorney General as well—is that natural law is not a nonconstitutional source.

Of course, there is another explanation, and that is that Ed Meese consciously rejected the proposition that there is an objective right and wrong to be found in the laws of nature. The denial of objective truth is certainly a prevalent view, and it is one that supports the widespread moral relativism found not only in courts, but even in such traditionally important sources of moral teaching as schools, churches, and families. Given his clear articulation of right and wrong in the criminal and family law contexts, and the upright example he sets and encourages in his own life, I find this explanation untenable.

Nevertheless, the failure to appreciate the natural law background of the Constitution may well be the undoing of original intent. To place entire reliance upon the will of the majority means an inability to distinguish the majoritarian policies of Churchill from that of Hitler or Saddam Hussein. True, the Bill of Rights by their terms should prevent serious curtailment of individual freedom. But without an objective moral anchor even the Bill of Rights can be turned inside out—not only failing to prohibit infringement of life and liberty, but also actively promoting its destruction, as in the case of abortion.

This is not to suggest that the Constitution be used to impose a theological orthodoxy.[109] The founders rightly guarded against an established religion. But as Jaffa so ably demonstrates, the "constitution was adopted because of the prior acceptance of a morality whose foundation was in the reason that recognized certain truths as self-evident. The will of the people was a rational and moral will, not a mere will."[110] All too cavalierly, even Chief Justice Rehnquist has confined the significance of these moral beliefs to private conscience. Rehnquist asserts that moral rightness flows only from the fact of majoritarian adoption, and not from "any intrinsic worth."[111] Yet, if majoritarian adoption has any true significance, it can only be derived from the deeper proposition that the original social compact and any law derived therefrom respects the natural, unalienable rights of all persons. If some persons have rights, and not others, there is an inequality of bargaining that vitiates any meaningful social compact.

NOTES

1. Wash. Post, Jan. 21, 1981, at Al (quoting President Reagan's inaugural address).

2. In actual fact, despite some half-truths about Meese's briefcase being the "black hole of Calcutta," the Attorney General was justly proud of his departmental management initiatives.

3. Speech by Edwin Meese to the D.C. Chapter of the Federalist Society Lawyers Division, November 15, 1985.

4. Speech of Justice William J. Brennan before the Text and Teaching Symposium, Georgetown University, October 12, 1985.

5. Abrams, *Mr. Meese Caricatures the Constitution*, N.Y. Times, July 25, 1986, at A31, col. 2.

6. 5 U.S. (1 Cranch) at 137 (1803).

7. 5 U.S. at 179–80 (emphasis in the original).

8. *City of London v. Wood*, 12 Mod. Rep. 669, 687–88 (1701).

9. 77 Eng. Rep. 646, 652 (K.B. 1610).

10. 2 *The Works of John Adams* (C. Adams ed. 1851).

11. 2 M. Farrand, *The Records of the Federal Convention of 1787*, at 75 (1966).

12. A. Hamilton, *Opinion on the Constitutionality of an Act to Establish a Bank, reprinted in* 8 *Papers of Alexander Hamilton* 97, 111 (H. Syrett ed. 1965).

13. Address by J. Brennan, "The Fourteenth Amendment" before the Section on Individual Rights and Responsibilities of the American Bar Association 8 (August 8, 1985).

14. II W. Crosskey, *Politics and the Constitution in the History of the United States* 1102–10 (1953).

15. *West Virginia Bd. of Education v. Barnette*, 319 U.S. 624, 639 (1943).

16. S. Fish, *Is There a Text in This Class?* 327 (1980).

17. Levinson, *Law as Literature*, 60 Tex. L. Rev. 373, 376–89 (1982).

18. *Id.* at 376–89.

19. Schauer, *Easy Cases*, 58 S. Cal. L. Rev. 399, 414–23 (1985).

20. Kay, *Adherence to the Original Intentions in Constitutional Adjudication: Three Objections and Responses*, 82 Nw. U.L. Rev. 226, 245 (1988).

21. Grey, *Do We Have an Unwritten Constitution?*, 27 Stan. L. Rev. 703 (1975).

22. *In re Winship*, 397 U.S. 358, 382–83 (1970) (Black, J., dissenting).

23. Bickel, *The Original Understanding and the Segregation Decision*, 69 Harv. L. Rev. 1, 58 (1955).

24. J. Story, 3 *Commentaries on the Constitution* § 1263 (1833).

25. *Pleasy v. Ferguson*, 163 U.S. 537 (1896) (Harlan, J., dissenting). Even the Plessy majority recognized that the words of the fourteenth amendment were "to enforce absolute equality before the law," but the majority failed to carry out the import of these words in fashioning the nonconstitutional edifice of "separate but equal."

26. 347 U.S. 483 (1954).

27. Address by Edwin Meese before D.C. Chapter of Federalist Society Lawyers Division, (November 15, 1985), *reprinted in The Great Debate: Interpreting Our Written Constitution* 37–38 (Federalist Society ed. 1986).

There is said to be greater difficulty reconciling original understanding with the desegregation of public schools in the District of Columbia. Public schools within the jurisdiction of a state are subject to the limitations of the fourteenth amendment; as a unique federal enclave, the schools in the District of Columbia are not. The federal government is bound by the due process clause of the fifth amendment, but it has been asserted by some originalists, most notably Robert Bork, that the Court's conclusion in *Bolling v. Sharpe*, 347 U.S. 497 (1954), that the due process clause includes an equal protection component "rested on no precedent or history. In fact, [states Bork,] history compels the opposite conclusion." R. Bork, *The Tempting of America* 83 (1990). Here Bork is in error. True, the originalist conception of due process is focused upon the provision of appropriate procedure, but it is analytically silly not to recognize that, at some point, procedure is substance and that appropriate procedures must include a check against arbitrary governmental actions. To posit that the framers were willing to allow life, liberty, and property to not be safeguarded against arbitrary decision making is almost to refute the argument by its mere statement.

Bork argues that allowing the Court to guard against arbitrary decision making is the revival of substantive due process—that is, the illegitimate policy review of legislative enactments by judges. Keeping judges out of the policy business is warranted as the rejection of Madison's council of revision discussed in the text illustrates. But Bork is overstating his case. A judge can inquire into the means chosen by government to further a desired end, including the classifications affected or created by the law, without second-guessing the end or objective of the political branches. Justice Scalia who has strongly argued for original understanding has adopted this view for the Court in the recent case of *Nollan v. California Coastal Commission*, 483 U.S. 825 (1987). There the Court concluded that a state legislative enactment was arbitrary because it could not accomplish the announced legislative goal. The *Nollan* Court also suggested that the law might be challenged if it misclassified—in that particular case, required a landowner who did not contribute to a public land use problem to solve it. Importantly, however, the Court never questioned the policy objective of the state.

28. B. Schwartz, *The New Right and the Constitution* 10 (1990).

29. *Hepburn v. Griswold*, 75 U.S. (8 Wall.) 603 (1870).

30. 79 U.S. (79 Wall.) 457, 575–78 (1872).

31. J. Story, *supra* note 24, at § 1112.

32. *Id.* at § 1115.

33. U.S. Const. art I, § 8, cl. 2.

34. U.S. Const. art I, § 8, cl. 6. John Jay's correspondence to George Washington reveals his assumption, and that of the early Congress, that a penal act applied to the counterfeiting of paper money.

35. Letter from James Madison to H. Lee, *reprinted in* 3 *Letters and Other Writings of James Madison* 441–42 (1865).

36. Wechsler, *Toward Neutral Principles of Constitutional Law*, 73 Harv. L. Rev. 1, 9 (1959).

37. Recognizing that a neutral principle without a substantive base means very little, Professor Mark Tushnet explored whether Wechsler's theory might be justified as an exhortation to judicial craftsmanship. Tushnet, *Following the Rules Laid Down: A Critique of Interpretivism and Neutral Principles*, 96 Harv. L. Rev. 781 (1983). Tushnet gives *Roe v. Wade*, the abortion decision, as an example of where "as a simple matter of craft, Justice Blackmun's opinion for the Court was dreadful." In this regard, Tushnet reveals that Blackmun provided almost no argument for how abortion might be located in the Constitution. This, says Tushnet, could have been done by a more skilled justice, and thus, Tushnet concludes that even as a definition of craft, Wechsler's neutral principle theory is a standard insufficient to constrain judicial tyranny.

38. *See, generally*, Nagel, *The Formulaic Constitution*, 84 Mich. L. Rev. 165 (1985).

39. *See, e.g.*, *Lassiter v. Department of Social Services*, 452 U.S. 18 (1981) and *Matthews v. Eldridge* 424 U.S. 319 (1976).

40. *New Jersey v. T.L.O.*, 469 U.S. 325, 369 (1985).

41. Aleinikoff, *Constitutional Law in the Age of Balancing*, 96 Yale L. J. 943, 988 (1987).

42. Brest, *The Misconceived Quest for the Original Understanding*, 60 B.U.L. Rev. 204, 226 (1980).

43. *Id.*, at 226.

44. The other factors of well-being that Brest proffers are no more helpful, and they are somewhat troubling. Thus, Brest thinks constitutional decisions should be acceptable to the populace. However, judicial decisions favoring individual liberty are often unpopular. Brest recognizes this and suggests that another factor might be how well a constitutional practice protects an individual. Again, Brest seems to be trying to have it both ways. Moreover, telling judges to protect the individual from governmental action when it advances "well-being" merely begs the question. Thus, while the text, history, and purpose of, say, the free speech clause may inform a judge that a dissenting view should be immune from governmental interference, Brest's well-being standard, even with its accompanying on-the-one-hand/on-the-other-hand factors, merely restates the problem.

45. Lupu, *Untangling the Strands of the Fourteenth Amendment*, 77 Mich. L. Rev. 981 (1979).

46. Tushnet, *The Newer Property: Suggestions for the Revival of Substantive Due Process*, 1975 Sup. Ct. Rev. 261, 279–80.

47. L. Tribe, *Preface to the First Edition, reprinted in American Constitutional Law* vii–viii (2d ed. 1988).

48. *Id.* at vii.

49. *Id.* at viii.

50. *Id.* at 10.

51. *Id.*, (citing Ainslie, *Impulse Control in Pigeons*, 21 J. Exper. Anal. Behavior 485 [1974]).

52. *Id.* at 11, n.4. Tribe reports in his second edition that he still likes the pigeon theory, but recognizes that it may overlook the role of the Constitution and its language. This is the beginning of insight, but it's a shame that for Tribe the pigeons get discussed in the text and the Constitution, however obliquely, in the footnote.

53. Perry, *Noninterpretive Review in Human Rights Cases: A Functional Justification*, 56 N.Y.U. L. Rev. 278 (1981).

54. *Id.* at 288–96.

55. *Id.* at 289.

56. Holmes, *Natural Law*, 32 Harv. L. Rev. 40, 41 (1918).

57. In the words of Aquinas, every man "has a share of the Eternal Reason, whereby [he] has a natural inclination to [his] proper act and end: and this participation of the eternal law in the rational creature is called the natural law." T. Aquinas, *Summa Theologica*, I, II Q. 91, art. 1.

58. M. Cicero, *Laws* in *The Great Legal Philosophers* 44 (C. Morris ed. 1959).

59. *Id.* at 48.

60. Corwin, *The "Higher Law" Background of American Constitutional Law*, 42 Harv. L Rev. 149, 152–53 (1928).

61. *Id.* at 153.

62. E. Patterson, *Jurisprudence* 368 (1953) (citing Lorimer, *The Institutes of Law* [2d ed. 1880]).

63. Antieau reports that from this the framers derived the following natural rights: "(1) freedom of conscience, (2) freedom of communication, (3) the right to be free from arbitrary laws, (4) the rights of assembly and petition, (5) the property right, [and] (6) the right of self government, . . . " Antieau, *Natural Rights and the Founding Fathers—the Virginians*, 17 Wash. and Lee L. Rev. 43, 45 (1960).

64. Rice, *Some Reasons for a Restoration of Natural Law Jurisprudence*, 24 Wake Forest L. Rev. 539, 562 (1989). In summarizing the work of Thomas Aquinas, another commentator describes the basic inclinations of man as follows:

1. To seek the good, which is ultimately his highest good which is eternal happiness.
2. To preserve himself in existence.
3. To preserve the species, that is, to unite sexually.
4. To live in community with other men.
5. To use his intellect and will, that is, to know the truth and to make his own decisions.

T. Davitt, *St. Thomas Aquinas and the Natural Law*, in *Origins of the Natural Law Tradition* 26, 30–31 (Harding ed. 1954).

65. Rice, *supra* note 64, at 568.

66. Professor Rice comments: "Only rarely would a judge be entitled or obliged to rely on supra-constitutional principles to refuse to uphold or enforce an enacted law. As the German courts indicated after World War II, judges should take this step only when the conflict between the law or precedent and justice is 'intolerable' or 'unendurable.' Such a conflict could occur in the context

of *Roe v. Wade*, since that ruling authorizes the execution of a certainly innocent human being." Rice, *supra* note 64, at 569.

67. 478 U.S. 186, 194 (1986).

68. Adler, *The Doctrine of Natural Law Philosophy*, 2 Natural Law Institute Proceedings 69 (A. Scanlan ed. 1947) [hereinafter 1947 Proceedings].

69. *Id.* at 70.

70. Adler relies for this distinction on the definition of law supplied by St. Thomas Aquinas: law is an "ordinance of reason, for the common good, promulgated by him who has charge of the community." *Id.* at 76.

71. *Id.* at 79.

72. *Id.* at 83.

73. McKinnon, 1947 Proceedings at 97.

74. *Id.* at 98.

75. *Id.*

76. Kinsley, *Democracy And Natural Law*, Time, 68 (August 12, 1991).

77. Antieau, *supra* note 63, at 43.

78. Manion, 1947 Proceedings at 9–11, (citing Blackstone's Commentaries [Lewis' Edition] Vol. I, pp. 27–31 [emphasis in the original]).

79. "[W]hen an act of Parliament is against common right and reason, or repugnant, or impossible to be performed, the common law will control it and adjudge such an action to be void." 8 Coke's Rep. 118(a).

80. Manion, 1947 Proceedings at 23–24 (quoting Hamilton's defense of the legality of the Continental Congress).

81. The Declaration of Independence, para. one (U.S. 1776).

82. Manion, 1947 Proceedings at 27–28 (citing 5 J. Wilson, *Works* 95 *et. seq.*).

83. Jaffa, *What Were the "Original Intentions" of the Framers of the Constitution of the United States*, 10 U. Puget Sound L. Rev. 351 (1987).

84. *Id.* at 363 (citing 19 *The Writings of Thomas Jefferson* 460–61 [1903] and 9 *The Writings of James Madison* 219–22 [G. Hunt ed. 1910]).

85. Corwin, *supra* note 60, at 152.

86. U.S. Const. amend. IX.

87. R. Barnett, *The Rights Retained by the People* (1989).

88. 3 *Elliot's Debates on the Federal Constitution* 445–46 (1836) [hereinafter *Elliot's Debates*]..

89. 3 *Elliot's Debates* 661 (Virginia); 4 *Elliot's Debates* 246 (North Carolina) (some variation in punctuation and style).

90. *Reprinted in* E. Dumbauld, *The Bill of Rights and What It Means Today* 189 (1957).

91. 12 *Papers of James Madison* 201–2 (W. Hutchinson, ed. 1977).

92. *Id.* at 456 (Letter from Hardin Burnley to James Madison [Nov. 28, 1789]).

93. *Id.* at 459 (Letter from James Madison to George Washington [Dec. 5, 1789]).

94. Office of Legal Counsel's Report to the Attorney General, *Wrong Turns on the Road to Judicial Activism: The Ninth Amendment and the Privileges or Immunities Clause* 22 (September 25, 1987).

95. 12 *Papers of James Madison* 206–7 (W. Hutchinson, ed. 1977).

96. R. Bork, *supra* note 27, at 184.

97. Caplan, *The History and Meaning of the Ninth Amendment*, 69 Va. L. Rev. 223, 254–55 (1983).

98. U.S. Const. amend. X.

99. *Cf.* J. Ely, *Democracy and Distrust* 36 (1980).

100. Letter from James Madison to George Washington, *supra* note 93.

101. Professor Jaffa States:

> The ground of all positive legal rights in civil society—above all, the right to property—is the antecedent natural right grounded in natural equality that every person possesses in himself. This right is a fortiori a right of each person to possess the fruit of his labor. The natural rights—to life, liberty, and property—are the ground of all authority, all sovereignty, in civil society. Jaffa, supra note 83, at 401.

102. 60 U.S. (19 How.) 393 (1857).

103. *Id.* at 451–52.

104. R. Bork, *The Tempting of America* 30 (1990).

105. Meese, *The Battle for the Constitution*, Policy Review 32 (Winter 1986).

106. Speech given by E. Meese at Dickinson College (Sept. 17, 1985).

107. Jaffa, *supra* note 83, at 411.

108. Speech by E. Meese at St. Louis University School of Law (Sept. 12, 1986).

109. Professor Charles Rice has ably demonstrated that the natural law is not necessarily a sectarian dogma. *See* Rice, *supra* note 64, at 555.

110. Jaffa, *supra* note 83, at 438.

111. Rehnquist, *The Notion of a Living Constitution*, 54 Tex. L. Rev. 693 (1976).

3

The Unitary Executive

The constitutional language directly bearing on presidential authority is fairly straightforward: the executive power is vested in the president of the United States.[1] That power, however, unlike the enumerated powers of Congress is largely undefined by constitutional text. Moreover, many statutes conferring power on an executive agency do so in broadly stated terms, authorizing actions in the "public interest." Because of this, presidential power is often best defined by the strength of presidential will.

The exercise of presidential will is not as easy as it might seem, however. While statutory ambiguity might appear to invite significant presidential supervision and direction, in fact, the sheer number of executive departments and agencies often thwarts meaningful oversight. In its place, agencies respond to the special desires of other constituencies. Unions corner the Labor Department, the construction trades dominate HUD, and universities inhabit Education. Members of Congress owing their election to these various constituencies sit on agency oversight committees for the express purpose of seeing to it that their particular needs are provided for in law, and most importantly, in the budget. This may all seem innocent enough, except that it results in one-issue departments responding to special interests, often pulling in opposite directions and frequently exacerbating public costs. No one person, or entity, thus supervises the executive functions to see, first, that their policies are consistent with overall national objectives, and second, that costs stay within a manageable range.

ASSERTING CONTROL OVER THE EXECUTIVE BRANCH

President Reagan had the will to exercise executive control, but needed a legal means to do it. One of those means was the executive order. Over twelve thousand such orders have been issued by presidents, and they have the force of law until modified or revoked by subsequent presidential action. Many of these orders cover arcane and technical subjects, establishing commissions, adjusting tariffs and the like. Two Reagan orders, one issued near the start of his administration and one at the beginning of the second term afforded the President the first meaningful control over the modern executive branch.

OMB Oversight

Executive Order 12291 issued in February 1981,[2] required that every executive agency submit proposed policies or rules to the Office of Management and Budget (OMB) in the White House. In essence, OMB was to be the President's eyes and ears in the regulatory field. The President bolstered his supervision of the regulatory process in January 1985 by requiring executive agencies to annually submit in advance their proposed regulatory programs and to demonstrate how these programs advanced the President's objectives.[3] OMB's job was to ensure that individual actions taken by federal agencies were well reasoned, economically sound and coordinated with the policies of other agencies. To accomplish this, the President required agencies to prepare an impact analysis assessing the costs and benefits of each major new rule and a determination of whether the objective could be accomplished at a lower cost. The agencies' analyses were submitted to OMB, which could raise objections.

Now OMB objections were interesting things. They were not technically dispositive, but then most cabinet members didn't need to be hit over the head. True, the rule-making authority undertaken by the agencies was provided by Congress, not the President. That's part of the constitutional design. Congress legislates. Yet, when an agency of government implements a statute, it is about the business of "executing the law," and that, says the Constitution, is wholly given to the President. And if this bit of constitutional theory were to somehow escape the mind of the agency head, the fact that he or she owed his or her job to the President could prove influential.

Despite general compliance with OMB direction by cabinet officers personally, cabinet agencies occasionally resisted. Generally, the closer the relationship of an agency with either its congressional oversight committee or its regulatory constituency, the greater the likelihood that OMB supervision might be thwarted. In the Reagan years, the Environmental Protection Agency (EPA) seemed to exhibit this "we know better than the boss" attitude more than most. In part, EPA's abstinence was traceable to its constant scrutiny by Congressman John Dingell, the powerful chairman of the House Energy and Commerce Committee.

From the beginning, Dingell sought to intercede between OMB and the EPA and other executive agencies as well. After the President's first executive order, Dingell demanded all sorts of internal documents concerning the manner in which OMB was carrying out its supervisory responsibilities. When OMB resisted, Dingell would issue a subpoena, and some, but not all, documents would be released. When the President tightened his supervision of the regulatory enterprise in the second term, Dingell was back at it again, but this time he sent his letters to the Secretaries of Transportation, Energy, and Health and Human Services, as well as the Director of the EPA. These letters demanded copies of all materials submitted by the agencies to OMB.

The demanded materials included the draft regulatory programs for the agencies. This suggested that Dingell wanted to rewrite the drafts, so that *his* personal influence, not the *President's* would "execute" the law. That this was his interest, rather than the legitimate congressional evaluation of legislative success or failure, was made plain by the fact that Dingell was seldom satisfied to receive the regulatory program information in its final form, which OMB would willingly provide. At OLC, we cautioned agencies against unthinking compliance with "President" Dingell's demands. Predictably, however, the EPA and others folded under the pressure of these demands.

After a while, Dingell and members of a similar mind in Congress directed an all-out assault on OMB itself. The law was changed to make the directorship of OMB subject to Senate confirmation.[4] In 1986, legislation was introduced that would have forced agencies to make public their communications with OMB on draft regulations, what OMB said in response, and how regulatory proposals were changed.[5] Citing the President's constitutional responsibility to "take care that the Laws be faithfully executed,"[6] we advised the President to veto such legislation if it passed. It didn't. Apparently, this time Congress understood we were serious. However, responding to threats to "defund" the subpart of OMB that did most of the supervising, Jim Miller, the President's second-term Director of OMB, informed Congress that he would make draft materials available on a more liberal basis. Specifically, drafts could be obtained after statutorily required notices of proposed rule making were published in the Federal Register. In addition, lists of draft rules could be obtained at the end of a calendar month in which OMB completed review. And, at the option of an agency, OMB would even place in a public reading room all written material received from persons outside the government concerning agency rules.

These were fairly generous concessions, especially since an appellate decision from the District of Columbia circuit had strongly affirmed the President's need for confidential communications in the regulatory process. In *Sierra Club v. Costle*,[7] the court rejected an argument that the Administrative Procedure Act required the President to note his comments in the public rule-making record. The court wrote that it recognized:

> the basic need of the President and his White House staff to monitor the consistency of executive agency regulations with Administration policy. He and his White House advisors must be briefed fully and frequently about rules in the making, and their contributions to policymaking considered. The executive power under our Constitution, after all, is not shared—it rests exclusively with the President. The idea of a "plural executive," or a President with a council of state, was considered and rejected by the Constitutional Convention.[8]

Legislative Vetoes

The D.C. Circuit's recognition of the President's constitutional responsibility to oversee the executive branch free from legislative interference was seemingly echoed by the Supreme Court in its decision in *INS v. Chadha*[9] invalidating over two hundred statutes that contained a so-called legislative veto. Mirroring its attempts to throttle presidential management through OMB, Congress had gotten into the habit over a substantial number of years of passing a law while putatively assigning to a subpart of itself—usually either one house or a committee—the right to effectively veto the President's administration of the law. In the *Chadha* case, for example, the Attorney General had been given the legal authority to stay the deportation of Mr. Chadha whose student visa had expired. When the Attorney General exercised that authority, the House of Representatives vetoed the action. This, said the Supreme Court, was a constitutional impossibility. While acknowledging that a legislative veto might be a clever "political invention," the Court stated that the Constitution provides the Congress with a "single, finely wrought and exhaustively considered, procedure"[10] for acting: bicameral passage of legislation presented to the President. In essence, Congress' attempt to affect the rights, duties, and relations of persons outside itself, including its interference with the duty of the President to execute the law, was *ultra vires*—without legitimate authority.

Notwithstanding this judicial recognition of the proper and separate responsibilities of the President and Congress, the now-retired Justice

Brennan managed to write a farewell opinion for the Supreme Court, which contracted OMB's supervisory authority for the President.[11] Part of OMB's authority for reviewing the draft work of agencies is derived from statute, the Paperwork Reduction Act.[12] Under this Act, OMB is charged with reducing the burden on the private sector of federal record keeping and the collection of information. The Department of Labor had submitted regulations pertaining to information that must be disclosed to employees handling hazardous materials. OMB approved them all, save three, which it felt duplicated or were inconsistent with other labeling requirements under federal law or which provided little additional safety benefit in light of the paperwork burden. The Labor Department grudgingly complied with OMB by withdrawing the unneeded regulations, but disputed OMB's thinking in public.

Not surprisingly, Labor's airing of OMB's confidential direction and supervision prompted one of Labor's biggest regulatory clients—the United Steelworkers—to file suit challenging OMB's decision. Thus, Labor could pretend that it was obeying the President's direction, and still effectively challenge OMB's disapproval of the proposed regulation in the courts with the aid of the union. The Court construed the Act very narrowly. According to Brennan, it authorized OMB only to supervise paperwork burdens associated with information requested by the government, not that required by the government to be given to third parties. This was another bit of judicial activism so typical of the Brennan approach, for as the dissenters pointed out, it was hardly unreasonable for OMB to characterize as a "reporting requirement," to which the Act clearly applied, an employer's obligation to disclose information even if it was disclosure to an employee, rather than a federal agency.

Some have claimed that Justice Brennan's decision removed one-third to one-half of all agency information requests from OMB's oversight. If true, that would indeed be a serious, gaping hole in the President's ability to supervise his subordinates. Not addressed by Justice Brennan, however, was the President's constitutional, as opposed to statutory, authority to review costly agency regulation. As OLC advised the White House when the President first issued his executive orders, the primary basis for directing executive officers is the President's constitutional "take Care" duty.[13] The Supreme Court's recent construction of OMB's statutory authority cannot undermine this. In *Myers v. United States*,[14] the Court, itself, emphasized that as head of the executive branch, the President must supervise and guide executive officers in "their construction of the statutes under which they act in order to secure that unitary and uniform execution of the laws which Article II of the Constitution evidently contemplated in vesting general executive power in the President alone."[15]

Signing Statements

Another means employed by President Reagan to give greater presidential supervision to the executive branch was the signing statement. While Congress is the principal lawmaking body, no bill becomes law without it first being presented to the president. If the president signs the bill, then the law must be implemented by an executive agency. But laws do not implement themselves, and much law that passes Congress is decidedly vague, either because of imprecise language or political compromise. Vague language obviously creates room for interpretation and discretion, and thus, the question becomes who will exercise that discretion.

Attorney General Meese felt strongly that the initial effort to interpret a law must be the President's. The President is the one held electorally accountable for the law's implementation. Were the President not to give direction, the task would fall to a less accountable and visible federal bureaucrat. To facilitate presidential direction, the Attorney General asked OLC to take special care in its review of enrolled bills presented to the President for approval or disapproval. Moreover, so long as it did not defy the legislative language or clear intent, OLC was asked to include draft signing statements for the President that would be consistent with administration policy. This we did, and the Attorney General arranged for these signing statements to be published in the "U.S. Code Congressional and Administrative News" along with administrative rules and other interpretations of law.

Almost immediately, the heightened use of signing statements to provide greater presidential direction caused a stir. Two law clerks, who were obviously not being overworked by their clerking duties, moaned that signing statements "allow[ ] the president to substitute his judgment for that of both Congress and the judiciary."[16] This was gross overstatement, as it was never the President's purpose to disregard legislative language and intent. And quite obviously, if the President did, the Supreme Court would always have the final word. The complainers also had no sense of history, as the use of presidential signing statements could be traced back at least to 1830 when President Andrew Jackson employed the device to give his interpretation of a road appropriation.[17] Nevertheless, the chorus of those suspicious of any effort on the part of the President to supervise his troops expanded to include the counsel to the House of Representatives who inflexibly opined that the president's role "is limited to thumbs up or thumbs down, with no shades of gray [in between]."[18] One law professor even gratuitously commented that "[w]hat the president thinks a law says is no more relevant than what I think it says."[19] Well, we can agree on the last part of that comment.

The importance of the signing statement initiative grew as Congress continued the practice of lumping together numerous unrelated provisions in omnibus bills, often inserting the most controversial provisions in emergency appropriations measures passed at, or after, fiscal deadlines. This practice effectively denied the President his constitutionally provided veto authority. It also denied the people what Alexander Hamilton referred to as "the chances in favor of the community against the passing of bad laws, through haste, inadvertence, or design."[20] Toward the end of his term, President Reagan graphically illustrated the "Hobson's choice" these massive bills presented to him during a state of the union address in which he held up before the watching American public an unwieldy stack of papers which he identified as the latest appropriations bill. He told Congress: "Congress shouldn't send another one of these. No. And, if you do, I will not sign it."[21]

Regrettably, this type of congressional chicanery does not always leave the president with discretion not to sign legislation. The greatest dilemma faced by a president is when needed legislation is presented with serious constitutional defect. The most notable historical example, perhaps, was Franklin Roosevelt's approval of the Lend-Lease Act, which provided vital support to our allies in World War II. As presented to the President, the Act contained a provision for the termination of the President's authority upon the passage of a "concurrent resolution of the two Houses. . . ."[22] Roosevelt correctly thought this an unconstitutional infringement of the presidential office because it provided for repeal without following the required procedure for new or repeal legislation set out in the Constitution, which included presentment to the president. Interestingly, then Attorney General Robert Jackson, later a Justice of the Supreme Court, was more equivocal speculating that the statutory limitation on the president's authority might be viewed not as a repeal but "a reservation or limitation by which the granted power would expire or terminate."[23] Roosevelt would have none of it, and in a rare twist, issued a legal opinion to his Attorney General stating that he "felt constrained to sign the measure [to meet a momentous emergency of great magnitude in world affairs], in spite of the fact that it contained a provision which, in [his] opinion, is clearly unconstitutional."[24] Roosevelt directed the Attorney General to put his legal opinion in the "official files of the Department of Justice" in order to preclude his approval of the Act from being used "as a precedent for any future legislation comprising provisions of a similar nature."[25] Roosevelt was right about the unconstitutionality of this type of provision, as was confirmed later by the Supreme Court in *Chadha* in 1983.[26] He also correctly anticipated that Congress would continue its efforts to circumvent the presidential judgment and veto in similar ways.

As dramatic as the Lend-Lease case is, it did not pose as great a problem as it might have because there was little chance that the Congress was going to implement its illicit authority in the midst of a world war. But what if there is an unconstitutional provision in needed legislation that ostensibly requires immediate implementation, is the President obligated to enforce it? This problem confronted President Reagan with the passage of the Competition in Contracting Act of 1984 (CICA).[27] CICA gave executive authority to stay a procurement to a legislative officer, the Comptroller General.[28] Seeing this, the Department objected while CICA was pending. Congress ignored the objection and presented CICA to the President as part of a much larger Deficit Reduction Act. Once again seemingly caught in an impossible position, Reagan signed the measure, but in his signing statement directed the Department to inform executive branch agencies how they might comply with CICA in a manner consistent with the Constitution.[29]

OLC examined the law. Like the Court, itself, OLC has long taken the position that legislation should be construed whenever possible to avoid constitutional difficulty. For example, unconstitutional legislative veto provisions before and after *Chadha*, have been treated as "report and wait" requirements, whereby executive action would be drafted, but not immediately implemented, giving Congress a reasonable time to object by constitutional means.[30] However, any statutory construction must be a possible one; it cannot be entirely fatuous.[31] In the CICA case, OLC determined that no constitutional construction was possible. Quite simply, under the Court's decision in *Chadha*,[32] the vesting of a legislative officer with the power to affect the legal rights, duties, and relations of individuals outside of Congress without following the prescribed legislative process is impermissible.[33] There was no getting around it; this is what CICA did.

Having made the determination that CICA could not be enforced consistently with the Constitution, then-Attorney General Bill Smith notified Congress that CICA would not be defended in court by the Department and would not be implemented by the administration.[34] Subsequently, a few district and appellate courts in dubiously reasoned opinions found CICA constitutional and a nomination-battered Meese replaced Smith. Notwithstanding the lower court determinations, Meese still felt that CICA was unconstitutional under Supreme Court precedent, and he maintained the nonenforcement posture, until Congressman Peter Rodino, then chairman of the House Judiciary Committee, threatened to deny funding for the entire Department unless Meese would implement the disputed provision. The Attorney General relented, even though the CICA issue remains judicially disputed and not finally resolved by the Court.[35]

Should the President and the Attorney General enforce statutes that they believe are unconstitutional? It may be remembered that Andrew

Johnson didn't think so, and this thinking nearly got him impeached. Congress had passed the Tenure-of-Office Act over Johnson's veto. The Act precluded Johnson from freely removing members of his cabinet. Notwithstanding the law's passage, Johnson removed Secretary of War Stanton and this became one of the articles of impeachment. In Johnson's defense, his counsel stated:

> If the law be upon its very face in flat contradiction of the plain expressed provisions of the Constitution, as if a law should forbid the President to grant a pardon in any case, or if the law should declare that he should not be Commander-in-Chief, or if the law should declare that he should take no part in making of a treaty, I say the President, without going to the Supreme Court of the United States, maintaining the integrity of his department, which for the time being is entrusted to him, is bound to execute no such legislation; and he is cowardly and untrue to the responsibility of his position if he should execute it.[36]

Johnson's counsel had a winning argument. Chief Justice Salmon P. Chase, casting the deciding vote against Johnson's impeachment, declared that the president has no duty to execute a statute that "directly attacks and impairs the executive power confided to him by [the Constitution]."[37]

Was CICA such an occasion? Bill Smith and Ed Meese thought so. Smith, for example, pointed out to Congressman Rodino that "historical examples of refusals by the Executive to enforce or defend an Act of Congress have been precipitated for the most part by Congress's attempt to alter the distribution of constitutional power by arrogating to itself a power which the Executive believes the Constitution does not confer on Congress but, instead, reposes in him."[38] Encroachments on the executive were especially apt for nonenforcement since it is unlikely that anyone would have the legal standing to challenge the disputed statute.[39] Predictably, the *New Republic* and a host of liberal law professors opined that nonenforcement might be appropriate, but only if a statute would "significantly infringe individual liberties."[40] But constitutional principle cannot depend on whose ox is being gored.

If John Marshall was correct that "an act of the legislature, repugnant to the Constitution, is void,"[41] and insofar as the president has the express responsibility to "take care that the Laws [including the Constitution as the supreme law] be faithfully executed," enforcing an invalid law would be contrary to a president's constitutional duty and oath.[42] This is a proposition as old as the founding. For example, James Wilson, a principal drafter and advocate of the Constitution, wrote that "the President of the United States could shield himself and refuse to carry into effect an act that violates the Constitution."[43] Even my predecessor as head of OLC in the Carter administration opined that "the President's duty to uphold the Constitution carries with it a prerogative to disregard unconstitutional statutes."[44]

To be sure, the President must carefully and most reluctantly come to a decision of nonenforcement recognizing, as the Department testified at the time of the CICA controversy, that "a statute of questionable constitutionality raises sensitive problems under the separation of powers."[45] If a constitutional method of enforcement is not available, the primary recourse must be the veto. President Reagan followed this course when the freestanding Fairness in Broadcasting Act of 1987 was presented to him in June 1987. This Act would have codified the so-called fairness doctrine authorizing federal officials to supervise the editorial practices of broadcasters. Even though the Supreme Court sanctioned such content-censorship because of the supposed, but now outdated, understanding that the broadcast medium is technologically limited,[46] the President exercised his independent constitutional judgment in vetoing the legislation. He noted straightforwardly: "[t]his type of content-based regulation by the Federal Government is, in my judgment, antagonistic to the freedom of expression guaranteed by the First Amendment."[47]

Even when legislation is not presented in a freestanding form and the president is forced to sign a multisubject bill with a provision he believes is unconstitutional, in order to give proper deference to the role of the Court in matters of constitutionality, the president should seek a judicial determination. Only where the provision is not likely to give rise to a case or controversy or where the provision is manifestly repugnant to the Constitution should nonenforcement be considered. In all events, occasions for nonenforcement must be strictly limited to serious constitutional flaws, not policy disagreements. Thus, for example, Richard Nixon's impoundment of funds because he disagreed with certain educational assistance had no constitutional warrant.[48]

Putting the difficult issue of omnibus bills and the nonenforcement of unconstitutional provisions to one side, the use of signing statements by President Reagan allowed him to properly direct the executive branch in matters of statutory interpretation. As might be expected, there were occasions when officials advising the President, in my judgment, either underused the device or abused it. For example, in the case of the South African sanctions bill passed over the President's veto in 1986,[49] the White House Counsel's office chose to delete most of OLC's explicit constitutional objections to provisions that contravened the President's foreign affairs power. These deletions effectively left executive agencies without direct presidential guidance once the bill became law over President Reagan's veto. I raised this and other similar examples with the Attorney General, and through his efforts, OMB issued a directive to all cabinet agencies reminding them of the importance of OLC's review of any signing statement raising legal or constitutional issues.

At the other extreme, toward the end of the administration, there was a tendency for a few lawyers in the Department to strain legislative language or be insufficiently respectful of congressional intent. The most notable case of this occurred with the 1986 Immigration Reform Act where the sheer length of the statement suggested that too much was being read into, or out of, the statutory language. At a hearing, Senator Kennedy once questioned me about the propriety of signing statements generally, and I responded by referencing something I had previously written:

> [The Constitution] commands [of the President] a faithful and reasonable effort to make sure subordinates understand the law and enforce it. By the same token, any attempt by a President to supply additional terms or adopt an interpretation that would do violence to the terms provided by the Legislature would be unwarranted and antagonistic to legislative powers.[50]

I think that still pretty well sums things up. So did the Senator, and that kind of executive-legislative agreement over a separation of powers question is rare.

THE SO-CALLED INDEPENDENT AGENCIES

No matter what a president puts in a signing statement, there are executive officials who may refuse to be guided. In particular, some executive officials—those in the so-called independent agencies—owe their jobs to the President, but cannot be freely removed by him. This absence of unfettered removal authority is the hallmark of an independent agency, although the extent to which an agency can independently submit a budget to Congress, provide Congress with information, or bring litigation and enforcement proceedings also must be considered to get the complete picture. Naming even a few of the almost twenty independent agencies[51] reveals the importance of the subjects they control: from the stock market (Securities and Exchange Commission) to communications (Federal Communications Commission) to the grocery store and other consumer transactions (Federal Trade Commission) and the money supply (Federal Reserve).

The idea of independent agencies emerged in a more naive time, when it was supposed that regulation was more the product of dispassionate scientific inquiry than interest group lobbying and the press and pull of ordinary politics. In fact, the first independent agency, the Interstate Commerce Commission, emerged in 1887 "[w]ithout too much political theory"[52] at all. Its origins are said to be traceable to a Democratic Congress' suspicion of Republican Benjamin Harrison, a former railroad lawyer who was to be inaugurated two days after the ICC's formation.[53] Even at the time of their great expansion during the New Deal, however, independent agencies were thought of as something of a "headless fourth branch" of government. In a report to President Roosevelt, the Brownlow Committee stated that independent agencies were "in reality miniature independent governments set up to deal with the railroad problem, the banking problem, or the radio problem. [They constitute] a haphazard deposit of irresponsible agencies and uncoordinated powers."[54]

Independent agencies can claim no support from original understanding. In the so-called Decision of 1789, the First Congress, which included many of the framers, determined that the president alone could remove the heads of the executive departments. After considerable debate,[55] it was thought both unnecessary and unwise (because of a desire to avoid the erroneous implication that Congress had the power to statutorily limit the removal of executive officers) for Congress to expressly acknowledge the president's constitutional removal authority.

When President Reagan asserted meaningful supervisory control over the purely executive departments through OMB and with presidential signing statements, some consideration was given to imposing the same control on independent agencies. OLC advised that this would be constitutional. However, perhaps because OLC cautioned that various older Supreme Court comments clouded the extent of presidential control over the independent agencies, the President decided not to bring these agencies under OMB's supervision for rule-making purposes. The President apparently concurred with OLC's prediction that any attempt to rein in independent agencies would very likely "produce a confrontation with Congress."

As a soothsayer, OLC was probably right about the congressional reaction, but as a legal advisor, its timidity was unjustified. Again, the primary characteristic that makes an agency independent is that the president is statutorily or functionally limited from removing its officials, usually except for "inefficiency, neglect of duty, or malfeasance in office."[56] When Franklin Roosevelt sought to remove an FTC commissioner without reliance upon cause, the Court in *Humphrey's Executor v. United States*[57] responded by upholding Congress' ability to require a cause for removal. This is all the Court held. Despite some broad nonbinding language, the Court did *not* hold that a president is precluded from supervising the work product of independent agencies. Unfortunately, my predecessors in OLC speculated that the language might be taken as limiting the extent of the president's constitutional power over independent agencies to the power of appointment. This made independent agency compliance with presidential direction a voluntary matter.

Four years later when Solicitor General Charles Fried argued the case of *Bowsher v. Synar,* this undue caution was repeated.[58]

Bowsher did not deal with an independent agency, but an independent agent—the Comptroller General, an officer removable only by Congress. Under the so-called Gramm-Rudman Act, the Comptroller General had been charged with making certain executive determinations binding on the President about the budget. The Court squarely rejected this spurious delegation saying: "[t]he structure of the Constitution does not permit Congress to execute the laws; it follows that Congress cannot grant to an officer under its control what it does not possess."[59] Fried properly pointed out this defect to the Court, but when asked by Justice O'Connor at oral argument whether he meant to argue the further point that an officer assigned such executive functions must not only be free of congressional interference but also fully answerable to the president, Fried—like OLC earlier—declined to make this challenge to the status of independent agencies.[60] Strategically, Fried related to me that he felt compelled to make this limiting concession to win the case.[61] In hindsight, he may well have been correct, given *Bowsher's* 5–4 outcome. However, whether motivated by lawyer's caution or litigation strategy, it left independent agencies outside meaningful presidential control.

In my judgment, the Court did advance presidential supervision of independent agencies in another recent case, *Morrison v. Olson.*[62] This is not the usual assessment of *Morrison,* in part because the Court there upheld the constitutionality of the independent counsel statute. Given the dangers of independent prosecutors described earlier in reference to the first independent counsel investigation of Ed Meese, *Morrison's* result upholding their authorization is abhorrent. Nevertheless, Chief Justice Rehnquist's opinion may reasonably be read as going a fair distance in limiting the more expansive readings of *Humphrey's Executor* that have been immunizing independent agencies from presidential supervision.

The Court admitted that in its prior cases it had relied on terms like *quasi-legislative* and *quasi-judicial* to explain why Congress could impose a "good cause" limitation on an official exercising such hybrid power. However, in *Morrison,* the Court stated that this missed the essential point, which is: "not to define rigid categories of those officials who may or may not be removed at will by the President, but to ensure that Congress does not interfere with the President's exercise of 'executive power' and his constitutionally appointed duty to 'take care that the laws be faithfully executed' under Article II."[63] In essence, the Court seemed to be saying, worry less about whether an executive officer is removable at will and focus more on whether an officer performing executive duties (in or outside an independent agency) is carrying out the President's instructions. Even in *Morrison,* the Court stressed that its willingness to uphold the removal limitation was contingent on its finding that it would not "impermissibly burden the President's power to control or supervise the independent counsel. . . ."[64] *Morrison* correctly refocused the discussion on the control of the substance of independent agency work. In this, *Morrison* was reflecting the modern view that the regulatory work product of all executive agencies, including the independents, should directly reflect presidential policy choices.[65]

Not reining in the independents was a policy shortcoming, and Ed Meese, one of the prime architects of the President's management initiatives, would later reflect as Attorney General that, as a matter of pure constitutional structure, the independents just don't fit. Meese stated: "federal agencies performing executive functions are themselves properly agents of the executive. They are not 'quasi' this, or 'independent' that. In the tripartite scheme of government a body with enforcement powers is part of the executive branch of government."[66]

Meese put his finger directly on one of the most serious problems with independent agencies: their unsupervised enforcement of the law. It is one thing to authorize a loose cannon to prospectively make policy; it is another to allow it to apply coercive sanctions. The problem is both a practical and a legal one. Practically, enforcement decisions always contain an element of prosecutorial discretion. The setting of enforcement priorities and the allocation of scarce enforcement resources is properly for the president. Legally, enforcement by an independent agency poses a special anomaly when that enforcement activity is aimed at the executive branch itself. In essence, it amounts to suing oneself.

Whistle-blowing

Congress continued its efforts to fractionate the executive right up to the end of the Reagan administration. Usually these efforts would be embedded within popular or sensitive legislation to which Congress calculated the President could ill-afford to object. Take, for example a bill designed to protect government employees who report fraud, waste and abuse within government, so-called whistle-blowers.

Ensuring that those who report mismanagement in government do not suffer reprisals for their courageous efforts is an important policy objective. For some time, the special counsel of the Merit Systems Protection Board has had that function. As important as that function is, it is also critical that genuine claims of reprisal be capable of separation from counterfeit assertions masking employee misbehavior or failure. In this, a president's interests are little different from those of every other employer or personnel manager.

In mid-October 1988, I advised Tom Boyd, the head of the Department of Justice's Office of Legislative Affairs that the Whistle-blower

Protection Act of 1988 introduced by Senator Carl Levin would both unbalance the federal employer-employee relationship and contained serious constitutional problems. A law graduate of the University of Virginia, Tom had worked for many years at Justice and before that as an aide on Capitol Hill. Tom knew that the visceral reaction would be to support any legislation with "whistle-blower protection" in the title. Nevertheless, he quickly grasped the reasons for our opposition.

First, the bill authorized the special counsel, an executive branch employee, to bring lawsuits against executive agencies in personnel matters. This could not be done. As I explained, giving the special counsel authority to litigate against executive branch agencies "places the President in the untenable position of speaking with two conflicting voices in the federal courts." Under a system of separated powers, the courts should not be involved at all in such disputes. Certainly, the President must have the ability to resolve conflicts between two of his own employees without going to court. Arguably, article III of the Constitution, the judicial article, even precludes such a lawsuit from being brought since it is not a *bona fide* "case or controversy." These constitutional difficulties were further aggravated by the fact that the Congress had previously hampered direct presidential supervision of the special counsel by limiting the president's power to remove him, except for cause.

In addition to these constitutional concerns, the bill radically shifted the burden of proof to the employer. This was directly contrary to settled litigation practice where a party bringing the lawsuit must prove his claim. Moreover, the employer's burden was so greatly increased that it made it difficult to show that inadequate job performance, not retaliation, was ever the motivation for discipline or dismissal. As the President later observed, the bill "essentially rigs the Board's process against agency personnel managers in favor of employees. The interest of both employees and managers should be fully protected."[67]

In retrospect, Tom and I correctly assessed that when the bill came to his attention the President would share our constitutional concerns and pocket veto the legislation. What we didn't know was that the Office of Management and Budget (OMB), the President's watchdog, was on this occasion being less faithful to the President's prerogatives. Tom ably relayed OLC's concerns, in which he joined, to OMB for transmittal on behalf of the administration to Congress. What happened then is not entirely clear. Justice's objections were not plainly made by OMB to the congressional leadership of either party and the whistle-blower bill passed unanimously.

Asking the President to veto any bill, an expression of democratic preference, is a weighty matter; asking him to veto one passed unanimously is a massive one. Nevertheless, Ronald Reagan understood well that he was a guardian of the office of the presidency, and that if objections are not made to constitutional encroachment today, the encroachment becomes standard practice tomorrow. In his memorandum of disapproval, President Reagan stated: "[t]hese provisions could not have been implemented to the extent that they are inconsistent with the President's constitutional authority and duty to faithfully execute the laws, [and] supervise his subordinates in the Executive branch, . . ."[68]

But it was surely ironic that OMB, the internal coordinator of executive policy, the agency designed to keep the executive unitary in its operations, would fail to fully protect the President's interests, against legislation aimed at diluting, if not thwarting, the President's supervision. How could this happen? It frankly baffled me then, and now. Some speculated that OMB in failing to strenuously convey the Justice's objections was reflecting the will of the President—the *next* President. Quite a few Reagan appointees hoped to continue in public service in a Bush presidency, and the perception was that the "kinder, gentler" George Bush would take a more conciliatory stance toward Congress, and that the best way to impress the new boss was to demonstrate a similar trait. Conciliation and compromise might have seemed especially appropriate when the subject matter was the plight of whistle-blowers.

If this was the thinking, it was misguided and it surely underestimated Ronald Reagan's intention to uphold his constitutional oath until the final day of his term. Strongly applauding President Reagan's decision to veto the whistle-blower bill, the *Wall Street Journal* reminded Reagan's successor of the wise words of former Attorney General Caleb Cushing in 1855:

> I hold that no Head of Department can lawfully perform an official act against the will of the President; and that will is by the Constitution to govern the performance of all such acts. If it were not thus, Congress might by statute so divide and transfer the executive power as utterly to subvert the government, and to change it into a parliamentary despotism, like that of Venice . . . with a nominal executive Chief utterly powerless."[69]

In withholding his approval, President Reagan directed the Attorney General to work with Congress to enact constitutional whistle-blower protection. We set about the task almost immediately, and Congress passed a new bill, which became the first piece of legislation approved by President Bush.[70] In signing the new legislation, President Bush noted that this bill "addresses the chief constitutional concerns raised by earlier versions of this legislation. The most substantial improvement in the bill is the deletion of provisions that would have enabled the Special Counsel, an executive branch official, to oppose other executive branch agencies in court."[71] Quite rightly, being "kinder and gentler" did not include pursuing good ends by unconstitutional means.

One other constitutional deficiency of the original whistle-blower bill deserves mention. The original bill purported to authorize the special counsel to submit executive branch information to Congress "without review, clearance, or approval by any other administrative authority."[72] This provision represented another of the ways in which Congress sought to balkanize the executive branch: preclude review of information by the President prior to its submission to Congress. Obviously, such statutory restrictions impede the President's supervision of his subordinate officers, and it totally denies the President the opportunity to withhold information that the President believes merits confidentiality. The constitutional doctrine most frequently associated with confidential materials is executive privilege.

EXECUTIVE PRIVILEGE

Ronald Reagan's bold assertion of managerial control over executive agencies was enough to trigger a maelstrom of controversy. When the president supervises what his worker bees are doing, that lessens the grip outside special interests can have on agency decisions, and it edges Congress out of the administrative picture as well. Throughout the Reagan administration, congressional efforts would be made, via subpoena or other less formal means, to pry into internal executive discussions. By and large these incursions were resisted by the executive agencies. Almost invariably, agency officers would rely in these circumstances upon OLC advice as to the nature and scope of the executive privilege protecting deliberative material.

The concept of executive privilege retains a bad name from the Watergate era. Most people remember that Nixon had to give up his tapes, and that after he did, he caught the next presidential helicopter out of town. Few people remember that while the Supreme Court decided against Nixon's interests, it gave a constitutional blessing to the concept of executive privilege. The Court specifically acknowledged the "valid need for protection of communications of high Government officials and those who advise and assist them in the performance of their manifold duties; the importance of this confidentiality is too plain to require further discussion."[73] Despite the Supreme Court's pronouncement about matters being "too plain" for explanation, those out of government must surely be baffled by why the President must keep secrets from the Congress. After all, aren't they on the same side?

Actually, no. Oh yes, the President and Congress both want the best for the country, but the very nature of a presidential election is both an embrace of one policy view and a rejection of another. Thus, one undeniable justification for allowing the president to keep his confidences is to allow the full implementation of this electoral choice. If the loyal opposition up the street learns of regulatory initiatives before they are launched, you can bet that efforts will be made to scuttle them. Hearings will be held, budgets will be threatened, unrelated nominations will be delayed, and cabinet members will be called to explain their advice. Not surprisingly, therefore, the candor the President can expect is inversely proportional to the privacy he can guarantee. This is as true for the oval office, as it is for the confessional. Finally, the constitutional design has separated or divided the powers of government to prevent any one portion of it from growing overly powerful. When Congress both writes and administers the law, it has melded functions that the framers thought necessary to keep separate to avoid tyrannies that we know continue to exist where these powers are held in one hand. Even the putatively "democratized" former Soviet Union still evidences as much.

Congress does have a legitimate role to play, of course, in evaluating how well a given law is accomplishing its public purpose. A law may require repeal or amendment. Congressional funding decisions may need revision to meet unforeseen circumstances. For these reasons, OMB and other agencies did endeavor to release as much information directly relevant to congressional interests without throwing open the filing cabinets of the entire executive branch. More often than not, however, what Congress would obtain in the individual case was the subject of sensitive negotiations, where the level of bluff and bluster knew few parallels. One of the most protracted of these battles ensnared Theodore Olson, who served as head of OLC under Ronald Reagan's first attorney general, William French Smith.

The Saga of Theodore Olson

Theodore Olson is a careful, demanding lawyer, zealous in defense of presidential prerogatives. His former staff members would later recall Olson's penchant for encyclopedic treatments of even the most obscure legal points. They would also recall his strong will. That will ran head on into the equally immovable Elliott H. Levitas, Democratic congressman and chairman of a subcommittee of the Committee on Public Works and Transportation. Both Levitas, and Congressman John Dingell, sought enforcement documents from the President's administrator of the Environmental Protection Agency, Anne Gorsuch Burford. Relying on Olson's advice, the President directed Mrs. Burford not to release "open investigative files, [which] are internal deliberative materials containing enforcement strategy and statements of the Government's position on various legal issues which may be raised in enforcement actions . . ."[74] The President did allow the congressmen access to over 700,000 pages of less sensitive documents, which he thought adequate to meet the congressional inquiry. That inquiry focused on the administration of the so-called Superfund Act pertaining to the cleanup of hazardous waste sites.

Failing to get every document they wanted, the Levitas subcommittee, and ultimately the full House in late December 1982 voted Mrs. Gorsuch in contempt of Congress. Tip O'Neill, the Speaker of the House, referred the contempt citation to the local U.S. Attorney for criminal prosecution. Immediately thereafter, the Department of Justice filed a civil suit styled—somewhat like kissing (or in this case hitting) your sister—"United States v. United States House of Representatives." The suit sought to obtain a ruling that an executive official need not comply with a subpoena for documents that are the subject of a valid claim of executive privilege. Seeing that it was about to be thrust into the middle of a brawl, the trial court ran for cover, urging the legislative and executive branches to settle the matter without judicial involvement. They did, with Congress receiving edited copies of enforcement documents and oral briefings.

Unfortunately for Theodore Olson this wasn't the end of the episode. In a snit over his highly principled defense of the President's control of the executive branch and his law enforcement duties, the House Judiciary Committee demanded that Olson testify as to the nature of his legal advice. Olson did, but not to the Committee's satisfaction, and in a several-thousand-page report, the Democratic members of the Committee asserted that Olson misled them and demanded the appointment of an independent counsel to investigate. Independent counsels have already been introduced, so little is needed to explain how the grand inquisition that followed ran up close to two million dollars in legal fees for Olson and would occupy several years of his life. The result: no basis to prosecute. Case dropped.

You might say Olson won the battle. He certainly paid for it. But did Congress or the President win the war? After Olson left the Department of Justice in 1984, you couldn't say there was less desire to protect the President's interests in overseeing the executive branch, but there was a greater realization that constitutional fights could get very, very personal. If disclosure of internal advice chills executive decision making, more than a few of us thought of the effect taking out a second or third mortgage to finance an independent counsel defense would have on our families.

NOTES

1. U.S. Const. art. II, § 1.
2. Exec. Order No. 12, 291, 3 C.F.R. 127 (1982).
3. 50 Fed. Reg. 1036 (1985).
4. 31 U.S.C. § 502(c) (Supp. 1970).

5. S.2023, 99th Cong., 2d Sess., 132 Cong. Rec. 340 (1986) (Rule Making Information Act of 1986).

6. U.S. Const. art. II, § 3.

7. 657 F.2d 298 (D.C. Cir. 1981).

8. 657 F.2d at 405.

9. 462 U.S. 919 (1983).

10. 462 U.S. at 951.

11. *Dole v. United Steelworkers of America*, 110 S. Ct. 929 (1990).

12. 44 U.S.C. 3501 *et. seq.* (1982 ed. and Supp. V).

13. U.S. Const. art. II, § 3.

14. 272 U.S. 52 (1926).

15. *Id.* at 135. Moreover, while *Myers* permits the assignment of certain functions to subordinate officers for reasons of expertise, it reaffirmed that even such officers may be dismissed if they fail to base their decisions on policies the President lawfully seeks to implement. *Id.* at 135. *Cf. Kendall v. United States ex. rel. Stokes*, 37 U.S. (12 Pet.) 524 (1838), holding that the President cannot order an officer to take an action plainly contrary to the statutory responsibilities of that officer.

16. Garber and Wimmer, *President's Statements at Signings No Help to U.S. Judges*, Nat'l L. J., Sept. 8, 1986, at 42, col. 1.

17. Kmiec, *Judges Should Pay Attention to Statements By President*, Nat'l L. J., November 10, 1986, at 13.

18. Greenhouse, *Washington Talk: The White House; Signing Bills, Reagan Tries to Write History*, N.Y. Times, Dec. 9, 1986, at B14, col. 3 (quoting Steven R. Ross, Counsel to the House of Representatives).

19. Finlay, *You know what I mean?*, California Lawyer, March 1987, at 11 (quoting Professor John E. Ryan of the McGeorge School of Law).

20. *The Federalist No.* 73, at 443 (C. Rossiter ed. 1961).

21. *Text of President Reagan's State of the Union Address*, Wash. Post, January 26, 1988, at A10.

22. Pub. L. No. 11, 55 Stat. 32 (1941).

23. Jackson, *A Presidential Legal Opinion*, 66 Harv. L. Rev. 1353, 1355 (1953).

24. *Id.* at 1357.

25. *Id.* at 1358.

26. *INS v. Chadha*, 462 U.S. 919 (1983).

27. Pub. L. No. 98–369, 98 Stat. 1199, codified at 31 U.S.C. §§3551–56.

28. 31 U.S.C. § 3553(c) and (d) (1988).

29. 20 *Weekly Comp. Pres. Doc.* 1037 (July 18, 1984).

30. President Kennedy also treated legislative vetoes as requests for information. *Public Papers of the Presidents: John F. Kennedy* 6 (1963).

31. *See, e.g., United States v. Nichols*, 841 F.2d 1485, 1492 (10th Cir. 1988).

32. 462 U.S. 919 (1983).

33. *Chadha* makes this point clear, but the exact application of *Chadha* to CICA remains curiously mired in the lower courts. *See infra* note 35.

34. Letter from William French Smith to Thomas P. O'Neill, Speaker of the House (Nov. 21, 1948) (copy on file with the author). Since 1979, conditions in Department appropriations have required the Department to notify Congress

when it will either not enforce or defend statutes it believes to be unconstitutional. *See, e.g.*, Pub. L. No. 98–411, sec. 203(a), 98 Stat. 1558.

35. *See Ameron v. United States Army Corps of Engineers*, 809 F.2d 979 (3d. Cir. 1986) (held that the Comptroller General's stay of contract award was a legitimate use of legislative power but CICA did not authorize the Comptroller General to execute procurement laws or interfere with the executive's performance of procurement duties); *Lear Siegler, Inc., Energy Products Div. v. Lehman*, 842 F.2d 1102 (9th Cir. 1988) (held the CICA stay provisions did not violate the separation of powers, and the government's refusal to comply with the provisions was in bad faith).

36. 2 *Trial of Andrew Johnson* 200 (1868).

37. R. Warden, *An Account of the Private Life and Public Services of Salmon Portland Chase* 685 (1874).

38. Letter to Peter Rodino from William French Smith 5 (Feb. 22, 1985) (copy on file with the author).

39. *See* R. Berger, *Executive Privilege: A Constitutional Myth* 208 (1974) (arguing that nonenforcement is only appropriate where the President's power is infringed).

40. Waas and Toobin, *Meese's Power Grab*, New Republic, May 19, 1986, at 15.

41. *Marbury v. Madison*, 5 U.S. (1 Cranch) 137, 177 (1803).

42. The President promises to "preserve, protect and defend the Constitution of the United States." U.S. Const. art. II, § 1. Chief Justice Chase concluded that sincere presidential belief that an act was unconstitutional meant that "it was a proper and peaceful, if not the only proper and peaceful mode of protecting and defending the Constitution," to not enforce the disputed act. J. Schuckers, *The Life and Public Services of Salmon Portland Chase* 578 (1874).

43. 2 *The Documentary History of the Ratification of the Constitution* (M. Jensen ed. 1976) (statement of James Wilson on December 1, 1787).

44. Memorandum to Counsel to the President Robert J. Lipshutz from Assistant Attorney General John M. Harmon, Office of Legal Counsel (Sept. 27, 1977).

45. *Constitutionality of GAO's Bid Protest Function: Hearings Before the Legislation and National Security Subcomm. of the House Comm. on Government Operations*, 99th Cong., 1st Sess. 318–19 (1985) (statement of Acting Deputy Attorney General D. Lowell Jensen).

46. *See Red Lion Broadcasting Co. v. FCC*, 395 U.S. 367 (1969).

47. 23 *Weekly Comp. Pres. Doc.* 715 (June 19, 1987).

48. This was also the view of William Rehnquist when he was head of OLC. *See* Memorandum Re Presidential Authority to Impound Funds Appropriated for Assistance to Federally Impacted Schools (Dec. 1, 1969), *reprinted in Executive Impoundment of Appropriated Funds: Hearings Before Subcomm. on Separation of Powers of the Senate Comm. on the Judiciary*, 92d Cong., 1st Sess. 283–84 (1971). *See also, Kendall v. United States*, 37 U.S. 524 (1838).

49. Comprehensive Anti-Apartheid Act of 1986, Pub. L. No. 99–440, 100 Stat. 1086 (1986) (appearing generally in 22 U.S.C. §§ 5001 *et seq.* [1988]).

50. Kmiec, *Of Balkanized Empires and Cooperative Allies: A Bicentennial Essay on the Separation of Powers*, 37 Cath. U.L. Rev. 73, 82 (1987).

51. The Paperwork Reduction Act lists 17 independent agencies. 44 U.S.C. § 3502(1) (1982).

52. J. Landis, *The Administrative Process* 2 (1938).

53. *See* 5 Senate Committee on Governmental Affairs, *Study on Federal Regulation Prepared Pursuant to S. Rev. 71*, 95th Cong., 1st Sess. 28 (1977).

54. *Report of the President's Committee on Administrative Management* 39–40 (1937).

55. The debate is nicely summarized in L. Fisher, *Constitutional Conflicts Between Congress and the President* 60–70 (1985).

56. *See, e.g.*, 15 U.S.C. 41 (the FTC statute).

57. 295 U.S. 602 (1935).

58. 478 U.S. 714 (1986).

59. *Id.* at 726.

60. *See* 54 *U.S.L.W.* 3709–10 (April 29, 1986).

61. Fried has since described his thinking in C. Fried, *Order and Law* 160 (1991).

62. 487 U.S. 654 (1988).

63. *Id.* at 689.

64. *Id.* at 692.

65. *Chevron U.S.A., Inc. v. Natural Resources Defense Council, Inc.*, 467 U.S. 837 (1984).

66. Address of Edwin Meese before the Federal Bar Association (Sept. 13, 1985).

67. Memorandum of Disapproval for the Whistle-blower Protection Act of 1988, 24 *Weekly Comp. Pres. Doc.* 1377 (October 26, 1988).

68. *Id.*

69. *Finally Awake at the Wheel*, Wall St. Journal, October 31, 1988, at A18 (quoting Attorney General Caleb Cushing).

70. Statement on Signing the Whistle-blower Protection Act of 1989, 25 *Weekly Comp. Pres. Doc.* 516 (April 10, 1989).

71. *Id.*

72. S. 508, 100th Cong., 2d Sess. 134 Cong. Rec. 10632 (1988) (Proposed sec. 1217, S. 508 of the Whistle-blower Protection Act of 1988). The legislation signed by President Bush partially corrected this problem by requiring "concurrent" submission to the President and Congress. This is not a completely satisfactory answer, and President Bush stated as much: "I do not interpret these provisions to interfere with my ability to provide for appropriate prior review of transmittals by the Special Counsel to Congress." Statement on the signing of the Whistle-blower Protection Act of 1989, 25 *Weekly Comp. Pres. Doc.* 516 (April 10, 1989).

73. *United States v. Nixon*, 418 U.S. 683, 705 (1974).

74. P. Shane and H. Bruff, *The Law of Presidential Power* 188–89 (1989).

PART II

The Essence

" 'Family. Work. Neighborhood. Peace. Freedom.' Those five words from the 1980 campaign state the five great themes of this Administration."

Attorney General Meese
February 21, 1986

With the President. "Before I knew it, I was in the oval office" (p. 91). Discussing a proposed executive order restricting pornography are (left to right) the author, the Attorney General (obscured), the President, Senator William Armstrong (R-Colo.), White House Counsel A. B. Culvahouse, and Alan Kranowitz, Assistant to the President for Legis-

4

Family: Abortion, AIDS, Pornography, and School Choice

For too long, the traditional family has been ignored, or worse, equated with alternative lifestyles. The social revolution of the 1960s and 1970s heralded a type of "do your own thing," individualism, and unusual alliances. Business interests exploited heightened individuality to market the material things of the "good life." BMWs, condos, European vacations, second homes—none of these things are wrong in themselves, unless, that is, they become the organizing principles of life.

Counterpoised was the individualism of the social reformer—those who hugged trees more than their children—that is, if there were any children. The solemnity of marriage and children somehow got in the way of living together, professional career development, or the latest environmental cause. The sexual revolution, too, lessened the likelihood of children or parental commitment. The contraceptive society came to mean the abortion society.

When family concerns were raised by policy makers in the 1970s, it was not to extol the virtues of the traditional family, but to make the traditional family feel guilty for the increasing social dysfunction of others who shunned family responsibility. Candidate Reagan said simply: enough already. While the initial years of the Reagan presidency sometimes appeared naggingly preoccupied with military defense and other nonsocial issues, Edwin Meese in the White House, and later at Justice, kept a careful eye on social issues. Soon after Meese came to the Department of Justice, Meese reminded us that "[c]hanges in laws, policy, and values have, often inadvertently, tended to undermine the family."[1] The President reaffirmed those words in his 1986 State of the Union address, and subsequently directed the Domestic Policy Group, chaired by the Attorney General, to outline the ways in which the law might be revised to "strengthen the role and bond of families in American life."[2]

With the Attorney General's guidance, the President issued an executive order that directed all executive departments to assess their policies and regulations to determine, among other things, whether any proposed action would increase or decrease family earnings, and fundamentally, whether the federal action would impede the primary authority of parents or the local community in family matters. In addition, Attorney General Meese helped supervise the preparation of a Report on the Family[3] that addressed a considerable range of issues from child care to pornography to tax reform.

Part of the Family Report dealt with the contraceptive society already mentioned. It is probably not well known to many parents that the contraceptive mentality is delivered, if not promoted, by federal monies in public schools. Under a variety of federal programs, including Title X family planning, funding for Maternal and Child Health, Medicaid, and social service block grants, school-based clinics provide contraceptive services. In some cases, federal law has been construed to mandate that these services be delivered to students without parental permission. The message sent by such federal subsidy is that teenage sexual activity is commonplace, even expected. The Family Report urged the reversal of this policy. Specifically, the Report called for parental consent to be a prerequisite for the distribution of contraceptives or prescriptions for them.

ABORTION: THE LICIT MURDER OF FAMILY MEMBERS

The most profound tragedy of the contraceptive society is abortion. Until 1973, when the Court decided *Roe v. Wade*,[4] a majority of states severely regulated or prohibited abortion. Usually, state law permitted abortion only where the life of the mother was threatened or in cases of rape, including incest. *Roe* changed all that. Discovering (inventing would be more accurate) a fundamental right to elective abortion, the Court declared that an unborn child was not a person within the terms of the fourteenth amendment, and subjected any state regulation of this newly fashioned abortion right to a trimester analysis. In the first trimester, the state could not regulate; in the second, the state could regulate, but only for maternal health; in the third trimester—after the supposed point of viability—the state could act to protect what the Court termed "potential life." Even in the third trimester, however, the state could not prohibit abortion where the mother's health (including as a major loophole, mental health, construed to mean emotional depression) was affected.

At its core, abortion reveals the extent to which even basic human life can be disregarded for reasons of personal convenience. Yet, this is a convenience that comes at terrible cost. Writing for the *Human Life Review*, President Reagan observed: "Abortion concerns not just the unborn child, it concerns every one of us. We cannot diminish the category of one human life—the unborn—without diminishing the value of all human life. The real question today is not when human life begins, but, *What is the value of human life?*"[5]

The President's probing question deserved an answer. His legal team, unfortunately, was not fully responsive. And make no mistake, the law is a loomingly large accomplice in the rationalization that permits murder as abortion. This is because "personhood" has been effectively transformed from a condition that exists in nature to a legal construct. One is only a person if one is recognized as such in law.[6] In the words of John Noonan, abortion is a "legal mask" used to dehumanize. With slavery, Noonan writes, "law was the medium and lawyers were the agents responsible for turning one class of human beings into property."[7] With abortion, lawyers' hands are on the blunt instruments crushing out the lives of unborn children.

The legal mask perpetuating slavery was shattered by the Civil War. It was the hope of many of us who signed on with President Reagan that constitutional argument would succeed in unmasking the humanity of the unborn. We knew this challenge would be great, even greater perhaps than slavery, since in the case of abortion the legal mask is aided by the hidden nature of the child in the womb. While some progress was made, the cataclysmic losses were not avoided. As the President himself pointed out, the millions of lives ended by abortion is "over ten times the number of Americans lost in all our nation's wars."[8] The losses continue to mount.

Rex Lee

The initial responsibility for arguing the cause of the unborn was in the hands of Rex Lee, President Reagan's first Solicitor General. Lee is a genuinely kind man, a true gentleman. From a strict Mormon upbringing, he graduated from the University of Chicago Law School and was the founding dean of the Brigham Young Law School. He is presently BYU's president. The dedicated father of seven children, one supposes that Lee's antipathy toward abortion was shaped as much by his own life's experience as by legal analysis.

Yet, Lee is also a consummate lawyer, and as much as Reagan conservatives can ever be, an establishment lawyer. Seldom does one become a law dean or university president as a result of strongly held opinions. Administrators are diplomats; masters of bureaucratic maneuver and the carefully phrased statement. Lee brought this methodology to the abortion issue to moderate, not stop, the killing.

I have little doubt that Lee arrived at this strategy out of goodwill. In *Akron v. Akron Center for Reproductive Health*,[9] Lee made two arguments: first, state regulation of abortion should be upheld unless it "unduly burdens" the abortion choice, and second, federal courts should generally defer to state legislative judgment on the issue of whether a regulation is unduly burdensome. At issue in *Akron* were city regulations requiring all second trimester abortions to be performed in a hospital, parental consent for unmarried minors under the age of 15 seeking abortion, a 24-hour waiting period, and the humane and sanitary burial of any aborted child. Lee did not argue that these specific regulations should be upheld, but merely that the Court should send the issue back to the lower courts with an instruction to follow the deferential standard he outlined.

As far as it went, Lee's brief was well crafted and scholarly. Nevertheless, Lee was immediately assailed by the abortion lobby and their friends at the *New York Times*. Calling Lee's work a "political tract... better suited to the partisan purposes of an Administration eager to appease its disgruntled right wing,"[10] the *Times* grossly mischaracterized the legal quality of the argument Lee presented. But Lee was also battered from conservative quarters. Writing in *Benchmark*, James McClellan faulted Lee's position for being "at best ambivalent, and at worst supportive of the Court's rewriting of the Constitution."[11]

As moderate as it was, the Court did not take Lee's invitation to extricate itself from the nettle of abortion. Writing for a six-justice majority, Justice Powell stiff-armed Lee, asserting that *Roe* is settled law and should be respected. As a consequence, the Court invalidated all of *Akron*'s regulations. Lee did persuade Justice O'Connor, however, of the value of the "undue burden" approach, and she articulated it in her dissenting opinion. She wrote: "[i]n my view, this 'unduly burdensome' standard should be applied to the challenged regulations throughout the entire pregnancy without reference to the particular 'stage' of pregnancy involved."[12] In a passage destined to be repeated, O'Connor illustrated the complete illogic of *Roe's* trimester analysis: "the Roe framework [is] clearly on a collision course with itself. As the medical risks of various abortion procedures decrease, the point at which the State may regulate for reasons of maternal health is moved further forward to actual childbirth. As medical science becomes better able to provide for the separate existence of the fetus, the point of viability is moved further back toward conception."[13]

There was no escaping O'Connor's assessment of medical technology. But she, like Rex Lee, was playing the lawyer's game—perpetuating, to use the Noonan terminology, the legal mask that depersonalizes the unborn child. In retrospect, it is understandable that Lee's "Solomonic" course would satisfy no one. The lesson of Solomon is that splitting the baby kills it; a course properly rejected by the true and loving mother. Creating a legal path in which killing the unborn is precluded only if it is not "unduly burdensome" has very little constitutional basis, let alone moral appeal.

Charles Fried

That the Department would abandon Lee's moderate course was left to Lee's successor as Solicitor General, Charles Fried. Lee resigned in May 1985 to pursue a more lucrative law practice in support of his large family and also to return to his beloved BYU. Fried was not immediately appointed Solicitor General, and there is some speculation that it was his brief in the next abortion case, *Thornburgh v. American Coll. of Obst. & Gyn.*,[14] that earned him the post. Fried, himself, reports that "[t]he brief, filed in mid-July 1985, put me in a leadership position in the Department."[15]

Before coming to the Department as Rex Lee's deputy earlier in 1985, Fried had spent virtually his entire legal career in the academy. A contracts and jurisprudence teacher at Harvard, he fled Nazi-controlled Czechoslovakia in 1938 as a child, spending two years in England before coming to the United States at the age of five. Before teaching at Harvard, Fried clerked for the younger Justice Harlan. Unlike Lee, Fried did not seem to personally share the President's moral abhorrence to abortion. An unidentified Harvard colleague was quoted after Fried's *Thornburgh* filing as being perplexed, saying: "[Fried] has consistently said that he thought the court made a principled and fine decision in legalizing abortion and that the states should not have jurisdiction for regulating it."[16] When this friend reportedly asked Fried if the administration knew of his liberal abortion position, Fried supposedly smiled saying "Well, I've never written it down."[17]

Having much affinity for Charles as a person and respect for his scholarly ability, I am resistant to concluding that his *Thornburgh* brief was wholly opportunistic. He observed one autumn day as we strolled down Constitution Avenue toward the National Art Gallery for lunch that he had been briefly baptized a Catholic to facilitate his escape from the horror of Nazi killing. In context, I am sure he was telling me this because of my own Catholicism and association with Notre Dame, but in retrospect, the remark means more to me. To Charles, who reported that he was never a practicing Catholic, baptism was an expedient—to be sure, an important one—in his exit from Prague. But whatever the motivations of Charles' family, baptism brings a spiritual grace and blessing. Perhaps, more than Charles knew, there was a Divine hand in the preservation of a solitary and scared child of 3 from the clutches of Nazi imprisonment and death. Might he, 47 years later, standing before a powerful legal forum return that blessing on countless unborn children?

Whatever his source of inspiration, Fried's brief in *Thornburgh* was a significant indictment of *Roe*. Fried argued: "[t]he textual, doctrinal and historical basis for *Roe v. Wade* is so far flawed and, as [the prior cases] illustrate, is a source of such instability in the law that this Court should reconsider that decision and on reconsideration abandon it."[18] Having said that, the brief left open the possibility that the Court might still want to adopt Rex Lee's suggested deferential approach to abortion regulation. In particular, the brief attempted to argue that *Akron* signaled a departure, even from *Roe*, in its hostility toward state regulation of abortion. Nevertheless, Fried's brief in *Thornburgh* made it plain that the mere adoption of Lee's suggested middle or deferential approach would not fully solve the problem. The brief stated: "candor compels us to state our conviction that *Akron* is a symptom, not the source, of the problem. . . . Because the parameters of the inquiry are indeterminate, courts are disposed to indulge in a free-ranging, essentially legislative process of devising regulatory schemes. . . . The result has been a set of judicially-crafted rules that has become increasingly more intricate and complex, taking courts away from what they do best and into the realm of what legislatures do best."[19]

As direct as Fried's argument was in *Thornburgh*, it still fell well short of the recognition of the humanity of the unborn child. Fried had been pressed to take the view that from conception, the unborn child has a constitutionally protected right to life, like any other person, under the fourteenth amendment. He refused. Perhaps it was his prior antipathy toward right-to-life issues. Perhaps it was a reluctance to press his internal staff still smarting over Lee's resignation and the perception that Fried would be more conservative. Fried later recalls that "[Meese] liked the idea that we had attacked *Roe* not on the President's right-to-life grounds." Maybe so. As mentioned earlier, Meese did not have much familiarity with natural law, and the nonlegally trained wordsmiths around him were more apt to emphasize the severe problem of judicial law-making in *Roe* rather than its basic inhumanity.

Once again, however, the attempt to even partially remove the legal mask over the killing of the unborn was rebuffed. The salient features of the Pennsylvania Abortion Control Act at issue in *Thornburgh* required that doctors provide women seeking abortion with information about the risks of the procedures as well as alternatives. After the first trimester, doctors were required to record and report the basis for their conclusion that the child was not viable. When viability was a possibility, a second physician was required to be present to care for the child. In a strongly worded opinion, Justice Blackmun, the inventor of the abortion right, along with four other justices invalidated these provisions as an attempt "to intimidate women into continuing pregnancies."[20]

Significantly, Chief Justice Burger abandoned his support for *Roe*. He wrote: "[E]very Member of the *Roe* Court rejected the idea of abortion on demand. The Court's opinion today, however, plainly undermines that important principle, and I regretfully conclude that some of the concerns of the dissenting Justices in *Roe*, as well as the concerns I expressed in my separate concurrence, have now been realized. [I]f . . . today's holding really mean[s] what [it] seem[s] to say, I agree that we should reexamine *Roe*."[21] Once again, the original dissenters disavowed the Blackmun claim that *stare decisis* mandated adherence to *Roe*. Justice White observed that "decisions that find in the Constitution principles or values that cannot fairly be read into that document usurp the people's authority. . . . For this reason, it is essential that this Court maintain the power to restore authority to its proper possessors by correcting constitutional decisions. . . . "[22] Moreover, said White, "that flaws in an opinion were evident at the time it was handed down is hardly a reason for adhering to it."[23]

Despite the new dissenter and the powerful dissenting language of Justice White, *Thornburgh*'s reaffirmation of abortion was harsh, almost defensive. Even abortion supporter, Professor Laurence Tribe observed a "degree of gratuitous, unnecessary hostility" in the tone of the Court.[24] In truth, the judicial emperors had been told that they had no clothes, and they didn't like it. When neither text nor history nor morality could sustain the killing of the unborn, all that was left was assertion—the assertion of raw judicial power. Such is never becoming.

The Solicitor General as "Handmaiden" to the Court

Charles Fried took the Court's harsh words as a signal to lie low. Speculating that he would not ask the Court to again reverse *Roe*, Fried stated that "[t]here is such a thing as making a pest of yourself."[25] Fried's reluctance may have also been traceable to his sensitivity to the increasing accusation that he had "politicized" the office of Solicitor General. Fried was caught in a bind on this having been selected, in part, because of Rex Lee's perceived reluctance to forcefully present the President's view of the Constitution to the Court. Lee had argued that the Solicitor General had a "special duty" to the Court. Fried was now saying this, too, although the exact origin and contours of this duty were unclear. As early as his confirmation hearing, Fried cryptically opined that "although we are advocates, though we are the government's lawyers, we are also handmaidens to the Supreme Court."[26]

Fried's sensitivity to arguing from the conservative perspective may have been heightened by the publication of a book entitled *The Tenth*

Justice.[27] In the book, author Lincoln Caplan assailed Fried for abandoning his special duty or "dual responsibility" to both the Court and the executive branch. Caplan, too, never identifies the source of this special duty, other than to recount the unquestioned accuracy and high technical quality with which the Court historically has regarded the work of the Solicitor General. The most stinging criticism in the Caplan work came from unidentified sources, including some anonymous Supreme Court Justices. One Justice was alleged to have said that Fried's submissions were "hardly the mark of a reasoned approach to the law. It's ideology, pure and simple. It's an assault on settled practices."[28]

In a magazine article, Caplan attributed the dual responsibility theory to Justice Emeritus Lewis Powell. Powell disavowed Caplan's comments in a letter to Fried in which he wrote: "I do not know Caplan, and he did not interview me.... Of course, I have not agreed with all of your arguments, but... I thought your arguments before the Court were scholarly and quite well delivered."[29] Caplan responded that he had talked with Powell on the phone. Chief Justice Burger, however, also wrote Fried saying that statements attributed to him were "never made."[30] Caplan again responded that he had a reliable source who "told me he had heard Burger say" the disputed comments.

The hearsay was getting pretty thick. But regardless of who said what to Caplan, this dual responsibility notion needs to be settled. It would be difficult for Lee, Fried, or Caplan to deny the ample history of past solicitor generals being sensitive to the constitutional views of their presidents. Roosevelt's lawyers were vocal in disputing the application of the Constitution by the Court to the New Deal. Harry Truman instructed the Solicitor General in arguments made against private racial restrictive covenants.[31] As Caplan, himself, records, Eisenhower took a special interest in *Brown v. the Board of Education* and school desegregation and Carter intervened directly in the handling of a reverse discrimination case.[32]

Close examination suggests that the dual responsibility notion is simply a false premise. As John O. McGinnis, my deputy in OLC, has since written in response to Fried's account of his service, "[a]s a matter of constitutional law the Solicitor General is not independent from the President and is wholly independent from the Court."[33] McGinnis points out that this does not mean that the Solicitor General does not have a special role before the Court. He does. But the uniqueness of that role derives from the fact that the Solicitor General's principal client, the President, has himself taken an oath to uphold the Constitution. McGinnis writes: "[b]ecause of the President's constitutional responsibilities the Solicitor General is fundamentally unlike private litigants: he cannot enter into litigation as if into an echo chamber where the Court precedents are the only sounds, but must vigorously, albeit respectfully, inject into the proceedings the Executive Branch's distinctive interpretation at every opportunity."[34]

Fried did not fully see it that way. He reports in his book that he resisted federalism and state interests, not because Fried thought the federalism imbalance the Court had created was constitutionally correct, but because he favored federal deregulation efforts on economic efficiency grounds.[35] Fried also describes how he resisted my efforts and that of John Bolton, the head of the civil division, to uphold criminal sentencing guidelines, but only if they could be sustained with an argument faithful to the separation of powers. Fried states that we were "less interested in regularizing sentences than in the philosophical and constitutional issues."[36] You bet. As Fried himself said on another occasion, in Supreme Court litigation, it is not whether you win or lose, but that you "told the [constitutional] truth."[37] Keeping a scorecard on victories, said Fried, was "a mug's game." Well, Fried won the sentencing guideline case, but, in his own words, "[t]he opinion was a disaster."[38] Justice Scalia wrote in dissent, "I think the Court errs, . . . because it fails to recognize that this case is . . . about the creation of a new branch [of government] altogether, a sort of junior-varsity Congress. It may well be that in some circumstances such a branch would be desirable; perhaps the agency before us here will prove to be so. But there are many desirable dispositions that do not accord with the constitutional structure we live under. And in the long run the improvisation of a constitutional structure on the basis of currently perceived utility will be disastrous."[39]

Webster: To File or Not to File—Why Is This a Question?

Of course, another instance of Fried's independence from the constitutional views of the President has already been mentioned: his avoidance of the President's right-to-life view that unborn children are persons under the Constitution. In the last abortion case of the Reagan era, it seemed for awhile that Fried wanted to avoid not just this view, but the abortion issue altogether. In *Reproductive Health Service v. Webster*, the eighth circuit had invalidated a variety of Missouri abortion restrictions, including a statutory section that declared life to begin at conception, another than prohibited public funds, employees, and facilities from being used to perform abortions or for abortion counseling, and a requirement that a doctor conduct tests and make findings to determine the viability of the unborn child.[40] Missouri appealed to the Supreme Court, and in so doing, asked the Court to reconsider *Roe*.

When Brad Reynolds (William Bradford Reynolds), Stephen Markman, and I met with Fried to discuss the case, we were startled at his resistance to filing an amicus brief in support of the Missouri appeal. Fried had already made known his intention to leave the Department and return to Harvard in January 1989, and there was a sense that he just didn't "need" another abortion argument this late in his tenure. Fried argued that the Court knew our view from *Thornburgh*. This was true, but there were several new faces now on the Court. Rehnquist had been elevated to Chief Justice upon Warren Burger's retirement, and Scalia and Kennedy had been appointed. In addition, even before the new appointments, the Court since *Thornburgh* had decided *Bowers v. Hardwick*[41] declining to extend the contraception-abortion-privacy line of cases to include a right of homosexual sodomy. In particular, *Bowers* strongly argued against the practice of discovering fundamental rights "not readily identifiable in the Constitution's text." Fried fell back on etiquette, saying that it was unusual for the United States to file at the jurisdictional stage. Maybe, but the United States had always done so when there was a strong federal interest. Fried's staff disputed even this, notwithstanding the obvious federal interest in correct constitutional interpretation and the effect an adverse holding in *Webster* could have on federal abortion restrictions, including recently issued federal restrictions on abortion counseling that were being litigated in the federal appellate courts.

Lingering in the background of our discussions with Fried was the fact that no one knew the prospective administration's thinking on abortion. In late October 1988, most of us felt reasonably confident of Bush's election, but many feared that he might return to his pre-Reagan moderate-to-liberal views on abortion. Filing at the jurisdictional stage to have *Roe* reconsidered would set the course for the postelection brief on the merits and the later oral argument. The Solicitor General's staff called this concern an "institutionally inappropriate" reason to file. I called it realism, and not forfeiting one ounce of the responsibility entrusted to us to assist even an outgoing lame-duck President fulfill his duty to "take care that the laws be faithfully executed."

Fried took our arguments under advisement. The election came and went, and with the November 10 deadline for filing approaching, there was great silence from the east end of the fifth floor where the Solicitor General resides. It was highly unusual for there to be so little communication among the principal decision makers of the Department. It certainly was unusual after the long discussions we had with Fried on this particular issue. But, in truth, these were unusual times. Meese had left in August and Thornburgh's management approach was, charitably, mysterious. Like any sizeable organization, and certainly like most major law firms, Meese had daily management meetings with the heads of the divisions. This kept the Attorney General abreast of the ongoing work in the Department and gave him a chance to direct it at an early stage. It also kept the Department aware of important developments in overlapping subject areas. As Fried himself would often point out to reporters who rumored that one person or another dominated litigation strategy, Justice under Meese was "collegial."

Under Thornburgh, Justice was imperial. Morning meetings were canceled. Access to the Attorney General, by heads of divisions (and even the White House Counsel at times), was minimal. No one met to coordinate efforts, or, importantly, to make sure that one part of the vast Department was not working at cross purposes with another. Virtually all communications to the Attorney General were filtered through one of three staff members Thornburgh had brought with him from Pennsylvania. To make matters worse, there was the distinct feeling that none of these staff people ever wanted to hear about the work of the divisions. If I had to describe their attitudes when matters of some importance were said to need the Attorney General's personal attention, it was one of annoyance.

On one occasion I was presented with a highly classified national security matter that it would have been irresponsible not to have brought to the Attorney General's immediate attention. Rarely did I use my direct intercom line, with either Meese or Thornburgh, but this was such an occasion. On an open or unsecured phone line, I could not discuss the substance of a classified matter, but I could get the Attorney General's attention to then meet him next door in his office or another secure room. Thornburgh answered the line, and I suspected from his tone that I had just violated every rule of Thornburghian etiquette. No, he didn't want to hear about it, thank you; just tell Robin (Robert S. Ross Jr.), one of the three guarding Pennsylvanians. With all due respect, I said, I wasn't sure I could do that since I did not believe Robin had yet received the requisite security clearance. "Robin is my eyes and ears in all things," said Thornburgh. Thankfully, I had better luck getting the attention of the criminal division and the general counsel of the CIA.

This was the way of the future. It was most uncomfortable, and unworkable. But it had to be dealt with because there *were* important constitutional issues to address and decisions to be made. Brad Reynolds broke the abortion silence by drafting a brief in the *Webster* case. Obviously, this was jumping the gun since no one knew whether we were going to file at the jurisdictional stage. Diplomatically saying "[s]ometimes it helps the decision process to see the actual arguments set forth in writing," Reynolds presented his draft to the Attorney General, through one of the Pennsylvanians of course, and a close circle of others, including Fried and myself.

Still the silence continued. Finally, the day before the deadline, I called Fried to learn his decision. "I know what it is," Fried said, "but I am duty bound not to tell you." It was hard to fathom that our good working relationship, if not friendship, could be treated in this manner. I was personally disappointed and professionally offended, and I told Charles so. More than that, I was seriously concerned that we had forfeited our constitutional responsibility and would not urge the Court to note probable jurisdiction in *Webster* and reconsider *Roe*.

Happily, I was wrong. Fried did file a brief on November 10, and the Court took the case, signalling that it would again reconsider *Roe*. In retrospect, I regret the exchange I had with Fried. The iron curtain secrecy that enshrouded the early Thornburgh Justice operation, both within and without, was not Fried's doing. He was merely being the good soldier. How very unfortunate, though, that the Thornburgh management style was breeding distrust among those who had so long worked together, not always in agreement, but always with respect and candor. Don't misunderstand me. I respect Dick Thornburgh, then and now. However, the vast interests of the Department could not be successfully managed by funneling everything through three, even well-meaning, political associates.

By the time the Court granted probable jurisdiction in *Webster* in January 1989, George Bush was the President-elect, Brad Reynolds had been gone from the Department for about a month, and my lovely wife, Carolyn, had blessed our family with our fourth and fifth children—two girls born December 2. When Charles Fried joined our family and the OLC lawyers and staff at my home several weeks later for a Christmas gathering, he delighted in cradling one, and sometimes both, of these new lives in his arms. Appropriately, we didn't speak much about business that evening, including the drafting of the merits brief in *Webster*, though anything I could have said would have surely paled into insignificance by the gentle statement made by these two innocents.

After the New Year, our focus returned to brief writing. Before leaving the Department, Reynolds had suggested that the Department's brief concentrate on showing the similarity between *Bowers* and *Roe*—demonstrating that just as there was no fundamental right to homosexual sodomy, so, too, there was no fundamental right to kill unborn children implicit, to use the Court's phraseology, in the "concept of ordered liberty." Initially, the Solicitor General's staff did not want to brief the issue of overturning *Roe* at all. Rather, the staff argued, an effort should be made to merely defend the specific abortion regulations at issue as compatible with the *Roe* framework. If the Court wants to overturn *Roe* in the process, reasoned the staff, it could do so on its own initiative. This was a bogus argument. All knew, including the Solicitor General's staff, that the Court seldom acts on its own without adequate legal argumentation, both oral and written.

Since Brad Reynolds had left the Department, the usual support for unborn life in the civil rights division had become somewhat weakened. Thornburgh designated James Turner, a career lawyer, to become acting head of the civil rights division. Turner suggested that if *Roe* was wrong, the Department should spell out what protection a woman would have from "unreasonable" state regulation of abortion. In this regard, Turner implied that abortion regulation should be required to pass a level of judicial scrutiny higher than that applied to other regulation. Further, Turner continued, the review of abortion restrictions should be designed to ensure that they are not premised on religious teaching.

To me, this was utter backsliding. I advised William Bryson, who was acting Solicitor General following Charles Fried's departure for Cambridge, that the central contention of our merits brief ought to be overruling *Roe*, "root and branch," as they say. After all, in taking the case, the Court had granted review on all of the questions presented by Missouri, including the reconsideration of *Roe*. Having worked this long to put the question before the Court, it would be foolish not to suggest the correct answer. Agreeing with Reynolds' previously-stated analysis that was now being championed by his former deputy, Roger Clegg, I argued that "[t]he same analytical framework (applied in *Bowers*), [when] applied to abortion, mandates the reversal of *Roe*." I also pointed out how Turner's suggested approach would merely perpetuate abortion. "The adoption of any special, intermediate standard of scrutiny for abortion regulations," I argued, "not only would be contrary to those precedents, but also necessarily implies the existence of a constitutionally protected abortion right: otherwise no such standard would be justified." Finally, I rejected out of hand, Turner's claim that protecting unborn life could be the imposition of a religious view. "If . . . there is some notion that abortion statutes may not be based on moral choices by the electorate, which choices are themselves influenced by the Nation's religious traditions, then the Turner [position] is in conflict with many decisions of the Court, including *Bowers*. There, the Court rejected a similar argument, stating that '[t]he law . . . is constantly based on notions of morality. . . .' "

As finally drafted, the merits brief tracked the approach originally suggested by Reynolds and seconded by myself. The brief attacked *Roe*'s two fundamental assumptions: "that there is a fundamental right to abortion and that the States do not have a compelling interest in protecting prenatal human life throughout pregnancy."[42] It was pointed out that abortion could not draw any support from the text of the Constitution or from history. Moreover, the assumption that the state does not have a compelling interest in prenatal life throughout the pregnancy, rather than as *Roe* held only in the final trimester, was not borne out by the manner in which compelling interests had been previously located in judicial cases. The brief illustrated that "[t]he tenor and contemporaneous understanding of the anti-abortion laws enacted from the mid-Nineteenth Century up to the time of the decision in *Roe v. Wade* leave little doubt that they were directed not only at protecting maternal health, but also at what was widely viewed as a moral evil comprehending the destruction of actual or nascent human life."[43]

In the hours before it was sent to the printer, Tom Merrill, the Deputy Solicitor General coordinating the final draft of the merits brief, kindly gave me an opportunity to make a few changes that I hoped would remove the legal mask from the humanity of the unborn child. Whenever possible, we deleted from the brief the "potential life" terminology of Justice O'Connor. Instead, as in the passage above, we settled on the terminology of "prenatal life." This was a subtle effort to convey that in "potentiality" one could not find an excuse for murder. In addition, the prenatal terminology was linked to our argument that the state's interest was compelling throughout the term of the pregnancy. While not the unequivocal declaration of unborn humanity that I would have liked, the brief argued: "[t]he assumption that a State's asserted interest in protecting prenatal life is qualitatively different at different periods of pregnancy is debatable at best. . . . [E]ven if there is a core of common sense in the notion that a State's legitimate interest in prenatal life 'grows in substantiality' along with the development of the fetus, it does not follow that this interest should not be regarded as *compelling* throughout pregnancy. An interest may be sufficiently weighty to be compelling in the constitutional sense even if subsequently it takes on even greater urgency."[44]

As the merits brief was drafted, it was not clear who was going to make the oral argument in *Webster*. Bryson would be superbly qualified to argue almost any case before the Court, but it would be somewhat unusual for an acting official to argue a case with this high profile. There was public speculation that Judge Kenneth Starr, a former special assistant to Attorney General Smith and then a judge on the D.C. Circuit, was interested in the Solicitor General's job, and so he too was a possible advocate. However, the speculation over Starr, who ultimately was named by Bush to be his Solicitor General, also suggested that the Solicitor General's post might be used by Starr as a stepping stone to the Court. In light of the Bork confirmation battle, however, arguing an abortion case might well prove to be another type of stone—namely, a millstone. As winter became spring, it was announced that Charles Fried would be brought back on a one-time basis to make the argument.

Not everyone was happy. On the right-to-life side, the reception to Fried's return was lukewarm. In contrast, things were hot among the proabortion forces. Even 50 lawyers within the Department publicly protested the effort to reverse *Roe*; opposing "any Government interference with this basic right." As might be expected, the *New York Times* gave this protest prominent play in a Sunday edition in late March.[45] The hand-wringing and bombast notwithstanding, the preparation for the oral argument continued a pace. In late April, Fried participated in the usual moot court preparation round at the Department and coordinated his thinking with Missouri Attorney General William Webster. Webster would argue the technical aspects of the statute and Fried would make the arguments against *Roe*.

At the actual argument, Webster softened or blurred the effect of a number of the statutory provisions. The preamble's statement that "[t]he life of each human being begins at conception," Webster contended, was without substantive effect and "doesn't affect anyone." On that interpretation, the Court held it was the mere precatory expression of a "value judgment." Similarly, Webster argued that the state limitation on the use of public funds to encourage or counsel abortion affected only those who administered state funds, not the recipients of the funds. There was thus no one before the Court who was sufficiently affected by the statute for the Court to render a decision. The Court dismissed the issue as moot. The validity of abortion counseling limitations would now have to await the litigation over the federal government's own restrictions on such counseling. Finally, as to the state provision that required a doctor to make findings with regard to gestational age, fetal weight and lung maturity before performing an abortion, Webster argued, and the Court accepted, that such findings would not be required in all circumstances, "including when the physician's reasonable professional judgment indicates that the tests would be irrelevant to determining viability. . . ."[46]

The viability testing provision applied to an unborn child of 20 or more weeks. Because this was earlier than the 24 week point that *Roe* indicated would permit the state to assert an interest in the life of the unborn child, *Roe*'s trimester analysis was arguably before the Court. Three justices (Rehnquist, White, and Kennedy) thus took the occasion to state that the *Roe* trimester analysis was incompatible with the Constitution. Justice Scalia wrote separately to suggest that, without trimesters, *Roe* was effectively overruled, and that it was unwise not to state that explicitly. Four justices thus were disposed to "effectively" overrule *Roe*. Justice O'Connor was not. While she upheld all of Missouri's restrictions, she believed that they were consistent with *Roe*.

None of the justices were willing, however, to find that the unborn child is a person. Despite my tinkering with the brief language, the Court insisted on calling the child "potential life." In his portion of the oral argument, Fried—also departing somewhat from the emphasis of the brief as written—fell back on his *Thornburgh* argument that abortion was not a natural extension of the contraception cases like *Griswold v. Connecticut*.[47] Fried described *Griswold* as prohibiting a "concrete intrusion" in marital intimacy, while *Roe* was an "abstract right." When Justice O'Connor asked Fried if in a future century we had a serious overpopulation problem, "has a [state] right to require women to have abortions after so many children?" Fried properly responded in the negative.

Nevertheless, that what Fried thought denied O'Connor's hypothetical was not the "termination of future life," as even Fried now was calling the unborn child, but the "violently . . . laying hands on a woman." At this point, it was quite evident that Fried was not arguing against abortion. In his book, Fried recalls his argument saying that he looks forward to when, "having one day abandoned *Roe*, the Court may reasonably distinguish between statutes forbidding abortions outright and statutes requiring a delay of a few days . . . or between statutes regulating abortion services and statutes punishing women who undergo abortions."[48]

This is not the day to which I look forward. Justice White toward the end of Fried's argument asked, if there is a human life involved, is there "some problem about the state permitting abortions?" Fried responded: "Oh no, I think there is not." In my judgment, informed by the natural law foundation of our Constitution, the answer must emphatically be, "Oh yes, I think most certainly there is."

Abortion Counseling

As indicated, the Court did not address restrictions on abortion counseling in *Webster*. But there were federal limitations afoot. In 1970, Congress enacted Title X of the Family Planning Services Act. That statute expressly precludes any federal funds from being "used in programs where abortion is a method of family planning."[49] This statutory language first came to my attention in 1987 when an heroic woman, Jo Ann Gasper, at the Department of Health and Human Services (HHS) in charge of supervising the distribution of family planning funds, issued a directive to clinics that no clinic that performed abortions or did abortion counseling was an eligible recipient of federal funds.[50] According to some reports, Mrs. Gasper may have issued this directive without the proper approval from HHS Secretary Bowen, and for this she was dismissed from her post.[51] Pro-life forces were enraged, and both Chris Cox, then an associate White House Counsel (and now a very well-regarded congressman from California), and I were intrigued.

What we discovered upon our examination was that HHS had been wrongly administering the law for 17 years. Mrs. Gasper had somewhat overstated her case by proposing to deny federal funds even to organizations that carefully separated federal and private money and used only the latter for abortion services; nevertheless, she was precisely right that federal law prohibited the use of federal money for abortions or abortion counseling. Our investigations turned up the fact that the Government Accounting Office in conducting audits of the family planning clinics was also concerned that federal money was being used contrary to the statute.

I called Ron Robertson, the general counsel of HHS, and asked him to come by my office to give me some background on the Title X program. What I learned I could hardly believe. Here was an express prohibition on the use of federal money for abortion services, including counseling, and HHS by regulatory guideline was not only failing to honor it, they were *requiring* that grant recipients counsel for abortion. The guidelines provided that: "pregnant women should be offered information and counseling regarding their pregnancies, . . . and referral upon request [for]: . . . pregnancy termination."[52] Robertson's staff lawyers produced some Carter administration legal opinions that meandered about with the wholly unsatisfying rationalization that abortion counseling was all right so long as it was "non-directive" or so long as it did not have the immediate effect of promoting an abortion. There was no basis for this in the law. As I wrote Chris Cox at the end of July 1987: "the legislative history makes clear that any activity that promotes abortion as a method of family planning is prohibited. . . . [Moreover, I] have serious doubts that counseling for abortions as a method of family planning would even pass muster under [HHS'] 'purpose or principal effect' test. The principal and foreseeable effect of counseling on abortions as a method of family planning is that some women will choose abortion as such a method. Indeed, it is impossible to discern what other effect such counseling could have or could be intended to have."

In response to my opinion, Chris Cox and Ken Cribb, who had gone over to the White House as a domestic policy advisor after serving as Ed Meese's special assistant, convened a meeting in the West Wing. Again, I outlined the statute and HHS' misapplication of it, and after some lengthy discussion, we settled on the course of having HHS issue new regulations that would faithfully follow the law by prohibiting the use of federal money for abortion counseling or advocacy and require family planning clinics that supplied abortion services with their own funds to clearly segregate such activity from that supported by the federal taxpayer. Following the meeting, Cox and I sat down and drafted some remarks for the President on the subject. The next day in a briefing at the White House, the President stated: "[a]t present, the co-existence of abortion with federally supported family planning service fosters the view that abortion is an acceptable and government-sanctioned method of family planning. . . . I have directed the Secretary of Health and Human Services to publish in the Federal Register new guidelines that will [correct this misimpression]. . . ."[53]

Drafting the guidelines would be an arduous process. While the President had spoken, and the HHS Secretary was in general agreement, there would be plenty of resistance within HHS. Ron Robertson pulled me aside and said, "You know, we will be counting on Justice to defend us when the litigation begins." I reassured him that we would be there. As it turned out, I was not being entirely—or at least personally—truthful. For about a month, I had been wrestling with the fact that one of my dearest friends and colleagues back at Notre Dame, Father Michael McCafferty, had lost an 18-month battle with cancer at the age of 40. When I was leaving for the Justice post, I could tell that Mike was understanding, but disappointed. "Are you coming back?" he queried with his usual directness. The subscript of that question was "Isn't Our Lady's school good enough for you any more?" When I mentioned to him that I had spent the morning in Sacred Heart Church on campus praying over the wisdom of my decision to leave teaching for government service, he knowingly looked me in the eye, shook my hand, and said he would await my return. Well, a fate neither he nor I understood interceded. Nevertheless, I felt I had to make good on my promise to return sooner rather than later.

In August, I was back at Notre Dame teaching what would have been Father Mike's constitutional law class. Back at the Department, OLC's John McGinnis was laboring with HHS to finish the draft of the abortion counseling regulations. They were drafted with tremendous care, promulgated in September, and subject to immediate attack. As might be expected, it was said that limiting abortion counseling was an infringement on the supposed fundamental right to abortion. More interestingly, the abortion counseling regulations were assailed as "gag rules" in violation of the first amendment right of free speech. That was clever political rhetoric, but it was fundamentally untrue. As the regulations very carefully outlined, the new rules applied only to the use of federal funds, not private resources. No one was "gagged"; grant recipients were merely required to observe the intended purpose of the federal money. Just as grants for library books could not be spent on videotape players, so too, grants for preventive family planning could not be used to kill the offspring that was not prevented.

OLC kept in fairly close contact with me over the coming months. When Chuck Cooper, then head of OLC, came out to Notre Dame at my invitation to watch the Irish "roll" over the Tide of Alabama (Chuck is a devoted Alabama graduate), our weekend discussions convinced me to return to Justice, and I did at the end of the spring term. I had kept my promise to Mike, and with Ed Meese and Chuck Cooper's concurrence, was being given an opportunity to return to the nation's premier constitutional law firm. By that time, or shortly thereafter, the lower courts had divided over the validity of the abortion counseling regulations. In November 1989, the second circuit upheld the regulations in *Rust v. Sullivan*,[54] finding that neither the abortion right nor free speech were offended. The second circuit's decision was not unanimous; Judge Amalya Kearse, who the press later reported to be on Bush's short list to replace Thurgood Marshall, thought it was insufficiently deferential to the abortion right in *Roe* and created anti-free-speech zones. The gag order characterization had successfully misled at least one federal judge.

The Supreme Court granted review in *Rust*, and the case was closely watched, because it would provide the first meaningful opportunity for David Souter, Bush's first Court appointment replacing the liberal activist William Brennan, to disclose his views on the abortion issue. Solicitor General Kenneth Starr, who had been exempted from the *Webster* argument, made the argument for the United States. Correctly, he outlined how the abortion "right" could not possibly be offended by the regulations, since the government is under no obligation to subsidize the exercise of that "right," or indeed, any fundamental rights. The Court majority, including Souter, fully accepted that proposition.[55] As I would later write in the *Wall Street Journal*, "the Bill of Rights is a safeguard against federal power, not an invitation to raid the federal treasury."[56]

The more difficult argument was over the first amendment. If read literally, the amendment had no application since it prohibits government censorship; it says absolutely nothing about the government taking a particular policy view itself, or through its programs. Laurence Tribe, representing the pro-abortion view, structured his oral argument around the proposition that the regulations coerced a pro-life viewpoint on clinics receiving federal funds. But that argument painted with a roller rather than a brush. As Starr's brief made plain: "[t]he government regulations limit the *Title X project's* activities, but they do not prevent a Title X grant recipient, its employees, or its clients from advocating and pursuing other objectives outside the Title X project itself."[57] Importantly, the Court understood the difference between a gag order and a condition on a gift of money. The government need not be viewpoint neutral in the setting of policy. In the Court's words, "[w]hen Congress established the National Endowment for Democracy to encourage other countries to adopt democratic principles, it was not constitutionally required to fund a program to encourage competing lines of political philosophy such as Communism and Fascism."[58]

The last point has considerable significance well outside the abortion context. In the last year or so, a great many artists have been pouting that certain members of Congress have had the audacity to insist that federal art subsidies granted by the National Endowment for the Arts not be used for bizarre, often obscene, performances. *Rust* clearly fortifies Congress' ability to set minimal levels of civic morality. Regrettably, the Bush White House has since vacillated and softened its objection and supervision of much of this filth.

PORNOGRAPHY

Speaking of filth, there is little question but that another factor weakening the American family is the widespread availability of pornography. At the President's direction, the Attorney General convened a commission on pornography. The Commission was asked to "determine the nature, extent, and impact on society of pornography in the United States, and to make specific recommendations to the Attorney General concerning more effective ways in which the spread of pornography could be contained, consistent with constitutional guarantees."[59] Made up of lawyers, doctors, psychologists, and other prominent community figures concerned with child abuse, the commission released a 1,000 page report and over 92 recommendations. The commission confirmed the great social destruction insidiously brought by pornography. Because its primary purveyor is organized crime, pornography opens dangerous channels to drug dealing, prostitution, and illegal gambling. As with past studies, the commission verified the empirical connection between pornography and violent sexual assault. Even more shocking was the direct coercion of young children in the burgeoning market for child pornography.

In reviewing the commission's work, a troubling fact was discovered: "[t]he Federal Government is one of the single largest distributors of sexually explicit material, some of which may be legally obscene. The General Services Administration licenses 526 shops in federal buildings. ... The military operates 413 major retail stores and thousands of smaller retail outlets throughout the world."[60] A White House working group recommended that the President put the federal government out of the smut business by issuing an executive order "prohibiting the distribution and sale of obscenity and child pornography, as well as restricting minors' access to indecent or sexually explicit materials, on federal lands and in federal stores, both military and civilian."[61]

The President turned to OLC for the drafting of the order, and we supplied one carrying out the working group's recommendation. Specifically, the order would rid federal establishments of obscenity and child pornography and prohibit the display or dissemination to minors of sexually explicit material. Word of the proposed executive order reached Senator Bill Armstrong of Colorado. Armstrong strongly agreed that pornography demeaned women and undermined the moral authority of the family. The Senator, however, thought our draft order did not go far enough; in his view, all sexually explicit material, including *Playboy* and the like, should be excluded from federal stores. As distasteful as much of this material is, this type of so-called soft-porn would generally not be held obscene under Supreme Court standards. Because we knew that Armstrong's well-motivated, but more sweeping proposal would engender immediate litigation, we tried to convince him that our draft order following the recommendations of the family working group was the sounder course.

Armstrong would have none of it. Late one day, he asked that I meet him at his Senate office to discuss the issue. I took with me Daniel Troy, an OLC attorney-advisor who had specialized in broadcast and free speech matters before coming to Justice. For the next two hours, Dan and I outlined the difficulties we saw with Armstrong's approach. One of the largest stumbling blocks to Armstrong's proposal was the Court's prior opinion in *Southeastern Promotions Ltd. v. Conrad*,[62] where the Court found a first amendment violation when a municipal theater refused to allow the musical "Hair" to be performed. Other more recent decisions also suggested problems: the *Lakewood*[63] case, invalidating a city's discretion over the placement of newsracks on public property, and *Pico*,[64] where a plurality of the Court expressed concern with a school board's decision to remove certain books they felt inappropriate from the school library. The meeting with Armstrong ended inconclusively, but amicably.

Armstrong persisted. Repeated calls by Armstrong to White House Counsel A. B. Culvahouse meant repeated calls by Culvahouse to me. After each conversation, I reexamined the issue. At the time, I felt it was a very close call. There was a reasonable argument that as a proprietor, rather than a regulator, the government must of necessity choose to sell some publications and not others, and this should not be thought to violate the first amendment. Logically, if one thought of a federal bookstore at the Gettysburg Memorial, few would think the government obliged to sell books there unrelated to the Civil War. I was also much taken with the dissent of then-Justice Rehnquist in *Southeastern Promotions*. Rehnquist asked: "[m]ay an opera house limit its productions to operas, or must it also show rock musicals? May a municipal theater devote an entire season to Shakespeare, or is it required to book any potential producer on a first-come, first-serve basis? These questions are real ones in light of the Court's opinion, . . ."[65] Nevertheless, despite its intuitive appeal, no other member of the Court joined Rehnquist. I stuck to the view that it was wiser to issue the executive order that, without question, would be constitutional.

Before I knew it, I was in the Oval Office with the President to my left, and the White House Counsel directly across the highly polished, drop-leaf coffee table. On the other side of the President was, guess? Right—Senator William Armstrong. The President listened patiently to the Senator's argumentation. It was as good and persuasive as it had been with me privately. By and large the President remained cordially silent as Armstrong proceeded. However, if I was reading the President's mind correctly, he was saying something like: "Well, Bill, all of us can agree with what you say, but we have to stay within the constitutional boundaries the lawyers lay out for us." When Armstrong finished the essential thrust of his presentation, the President pulled from his coat pocket the executive order we had previously drafted and began to say that he was prepared to sign it that afternoon. Armstrong abruptly spoke out saying that order was "worse than nothing." That startled the President, and strategically, it probably cost Armstrong the debate. His objection to an order that accomplished virtually all of his objectives, and the entire goal outlined by the family working group seemed like a definite overreach to the President. All I had to do to was mop up with a few references to the uncertainty in the Supreme Court cases.

I won that legal discussion that afternoon, and I should not have. It is reasonably plain to me now that the "government as proprietor" argument is the correct one. Just as the Court would later decide in the *Rust* abortion counseling decision that the government may make a value judgment favoring childbirth over abortion and implement that judgment by the allocation of public funds, so too, the government could make the value judgment that some publications, even publications within the ambit of the first amendment, could be excluded from government stores. The late folk-singer, Steve Goodman, once lightheartedly sang about what life would be like if it were on videotape: "you could replay all the good parts, and erase all the bad." Senator Armstrong, if you're watching, I would rerun this one in your favor.

AIDS

One of the findings of the commission on pornography highlighted by the family working group was that "pornography and the anonymous sexual promiscuity it encourages contribute directly to the spread of sexually transmitted diseases, including AIDS."[66] The tragedy of acquired immune deficiency syndrome or AIDS is now well known to the American public. Because it is almost always fatal and there is no known cure, there was much concern, and some initial hysteria, over the way in which the disease is transmitted. Rumors, some emanating from the scientific community, that the disease could be spread by casual contact led to children with AIDS being excluded from schools, nursing homes and hospitals refusing to treat AIDS patients, and even the homes of some AIDS victims being burned.

This was the state of play when Ron Robertson, the general counsel of HHS, asked OLC to supply an opinion on the application of section 504 of the Rehabilitation Act[67] to individuals with AIDS. Enacted in 1973, this section of the Rehabilitation Act was most notably intended to prevent discrimination against handicapped individuals. AIDS was not well known outside the medical community in the early 1970s, and even if some member of Congress had heard of it, there is no direct evidence of how Congress thought section 504 would apply. Nevertheless, by executive order, the responsibility for coordinating the enforcement of section 504 had been delegated to Justice, and Robertson's request for advice merely accelerated that consideration.

It was not an easy issue. Chuck Cooper took the matter up personally. Cooper naturally consulted with Brad Reynolds because the civil rights division would later have the day-to-day enforcement tasks of an OLC opinion on this issue. Within OLC, Cooper relied on the research ability of an able young attorney-advisor named Gary Lawson. For months, Cooper and Lawson "noodled" (as Cooper benignly called lengthy drafting sessions) over the issues presented.

To give a proper legal answer, Cooper reasoned, the medical science had to be understood, even if the state of that science was imprecise or incomplete. First, could AIDS be transmitted by casual contact? Cooper and Lawson found that there was "no epidemiological evidence of transmission . . . through casual contact with or proximity to infected persons."[68] Nevertheless, they proceeded to upset the medical community by stating that "[i]t has been suggested, however, that conclusions of this character are too sweeping. Harvard researcher Prof. William Haseltine, for instance, was recently reported to have declared that '[a]nyone who tells you categorically that AIDS is not contracted by saliva is not telling the truth. . . . There are sure to be cases . . . of proved transmission through casual contact.' "[69] When Dr. Robert Windom, assistant secretary of health, read the Cooper opinion, he stated that he was "outraged because the opinion seemed to directly contradict AIDS guidelines issued by [the Center for Disease Control] and all informed medical research."[70]

It seemed to me at the time, and since, that Cooper's recital of medical information was entirely balanced. How many times have you received a categorical "yes" or "no" answer from a doctor? With a disease as little understood as AIDS, medical knowledge about transmission must necessarily be thought of as tentative, subject to change. In point of fact, as presently understood, the disease is transmitted by "blood to blood" exposure with an infected person. Thus, as an initial matter, this most prominently occurs in homosexual anal intercourse and the reuse of contaminated needles, especially, as one might suppose, in illegal drug use settings. Tragically, AIDS can also be transmitted from mother to child during pregnancy. Of course, as a secondary matter, infection can occur in numerous other contexts: a hemophiliac child receiving a blood transfusion with contaminated blood supplied to a blood bank or in the doctor-patient context of oral or invasive surgery, where either doctor or patient is infected.

In reality, the outcry—largely from homosexual quarters—over Cooper's opinion resulted less from the medical information he cited, than from the fact that he used the uncertainty over AIDS transmission to deny protection against discrimination to AIDS-infected individuals. Section 504 bars discrimination against a person "solely by reason of his handicap." To Cooper, this meant that if a person was excluded from a program or activity receiving federal financial assistance, not because of his handicap, but because of a reasonable or unreasonable fear of contagion, there was no violation of the statute. Chuck's opinion read:

[S]ection 504 simply does not reach decisions based on fear of contagion—whether reasonable or not—so long as it is not in truth a pretext for discrimination on account of handicap. An employer, for example, who makes hiring decisions based on an unreasonable concern about contagion is no different from an employer whose hiring decisions rest on any other unreasonable basis that lies outside section 504's limited reach. To illustrate this point, consider an employer who has the bizarre belief that persons with curly hair make better employees than persons with straight hair. Section 504 does not prohibit the employer from making hiring decisions based on this wholly unreasonable basis. Straight hair is not a handicap; nor is discrimination against such persons conceivably a pretext masking discrimination against the handicapped.[71]

As legal arguments go, Cooper's opinion was plausible. Chuck bolstered his conclusion by pointing out the long history of state and federal regulation of contagious diseases. Moreover, in the face of this expansive regulation, the legislative history of the Rehabilitation Act, was silent. Cooper said this was "as revealing as Sherlock Holmes' famous dog that did not bark in the night."[72] "If section 504 applied to discrimination based on communicability, the entire, long-established body of state and federal law dealing with communicable diseases would be called into question in unforeseeable ways."[73] This is good common sense, but as a legal matter, arguments from legislative silence are not particularly strong. That Chuck knew as much could be judged by the placement of the argument at the end of his opinion.

The fire storm of controversy over the Cooper opinion was partially traceable to press misreading, suggesting that Cooper had rendered a medical judgment about transmissibility when he had not. The reaction may have been especially hostile because about a month earlier, someone in the civil rights division had leaked an internal working draft produced by that division which outlined the opposite conclusion. But "anonymous sources" were not running the Department. Brad Reynolds clearly supported Cooper's legal conclusion. Moreover, shortly thereafter, Charles Fried incorporated Cooper's arguments in an *amicus* brief filed in *School Board v. Arline*,[74] a case dealing with the firing of a school teacher because of her susceptibility to tuberculosis.

When *Arline* was decided, however, the Court appeared to squarely reject the core of the Cooper argument:

We do not agree . . . that, in defining a handicapped individual under section 504, the contagious effects of a disease can be meaningfully distinguished from the disease's physical effects on a claimant in a case such as this. Arline's contagiousness and her physical impairment each resulted from the same underlying condition, tuberculosis. It would be unfair to allow an employer to seize upon the distinction between the effects of a disease on others and the effects of a disease on a patient and use that distinction to justify discriminatory treatment.[75]

In a footnote, the Court clouded the holding's applicability to AIDS. The Court seemingly declined to answer the precise question with which Chuck had been presented: "This case does not present, and we therefore do not reach, the questions whether a carrier of a contagious disease such as AIDS could be considered to have a physical impairment, or whether such a person could be considered, solely on the basis of contagiousness, a handicapped person as defined by the Act."[76]

Did *Arline* overrule the Cooper opinion? Despite the Court's ambiguous footnote, it was popularly thought to do so. However, *Arline* should not be characterized as a stinging rebuke to Cooper. The opinion clearly must be chalked up to the fact that reasonable minds can differ. The Court had no more legislative history to support its position than Chuck Cooper had for his. Cooper said that nothing in the legislative history precludes taking contagiousness in consideration; the Court stated "[n]othing in the legislative history . . . suggest[ed] that Congress intended [Cooper's] result."[77] Well, if there is nothing in the legislative history, and there is nothing explicitly in the statute, it is hardly unreasonable to ask judges not to create something out of nothing. That is, if Congress wanted to make the exclusion of contagious individuals an act of discrimination, they should have said so explicitly. Thus, judicial restraint lay behind Cooper's approach, and it prompted OLC's two alums on the Supreme Court, Rehnquist and Scalia, to dissent.

Since the Court expressly declined to reach the application of the Rehabilitation Act to those with AIDS, White House Counsel A. B. Culvahouse wrote Cooper and asked him to "revisit the question . . . in light of the Supreme Court's decision." Cooper had little stomach for it, and he asked Mike Carvin, who had recently come over from civil rights, to look into the issue. Shortly thereafter, however, Cooper and Carvin would leave the Department with the original AIDS opinion unamended and the White House request still pending.

The task then fell to me to complete the "revisitation." I, too, came to the effort reluctantly. While I was not involved in the writing of the original opinion, as I indicate above, absent the Supreme Court's coin flip, the statute could be reasonably construed either way. In addition, I had, and have, enormous respect for the legal ability of Chuck Cooper. Even though I would have deleted part of Cooper's medical discussion and changed the tone of the analysis somewhat and been reluctant to liken a fatal disease to an analogy about straight or curly hair, I was not initially sure where Cooper and I differed.

Paul Colborn of my staff, who had been working with Carvin on the issue before he left, helped me sort things out. To avoid medical misstatement, we arranged a meeting with C. Everett Koop, the Surgeon General. As Surgeon General, Koop was the head of the Public Health Service, which has the curious distinction of being uniformed civilians. Koop strode into our meeting in full uniform, a feature which seemed to accentuate his Captain Ahab-like appearance and booming voice. Koop and I had met before. While members of the same administration, we testified on opposite sides of proposed legislation to limit tobacco advertising. Koop naturally was all for it for the obvious medical reasons. I did not dispute the likelihood of cancer in the least, but I was very much opposed to conceding that Congress had the constitutional power to limit speech about a legal product. As far as I was concerned, if tobacco is dangerous to one's health, Congress ought to have the courage to ban the product, not paternalistically censor what we read and hear about it. The advertising restriction never passed, but it continues to be debated. Since my testimony, the Supreme Court has, unwisely in my judgment, returned to treating commercial speech as less worthy of constitutional protection.

At our AIDS meeting, Koop was as forthright and clear as medical knowledge permitted. He reiterated the limited contexts of transmissibility casting considerable doubt on any research suggesting the possibility of casual contact infection. But this was not my principal interest. Unlike Cooper, and after *Arline*, I felt the issue of transmissibility had less to do with whether a person was statutorily within the scope of the definition of a "handicapped individual" than with the important, but analytically secondary, issue of whether a handicapped individual was "otherwise qualified" or could be "reasonably accommodated" within an employer's work force, a school, or other covered context. This reading of the statute was confirmed by the Civil Rights Restoration Act of 1987,[78] in which Congress, with knowledge of both *Arline* and the Cooper opinion, redefined an individual with handicaps in the employment context to exclude an individual with a contagious disease *only if* such individual "would constitute a direct threat to the health or safety" of others or was unable to do the job.

Thus, the Court in *Arline* (and Congress) directed that an individual who was both handicapped *and* contagious was protected against discrimination. The nettlesome issue of whether contagiousness alone was enough was left open. It was readily apparent that someone with full-blown AIDS was handicapped and contagious, but what I wanted to know from Koop was whether someone in the early stages of AIDS, a so-called asymptomatic carrier of the virus, could in any way be said to be handicapped or impaired in a major life activity. If an asymptomatic carrier was impaired, the Court had wrongly assumed that AIDS did not give rise to both "physical impairment and contagiousness," and thus, while proclaiming not to have answered the AIDS question, it may have actually done so.

At our meeting and in a follow-up letter that became important to the legal outcome, Koop stated: "much has been learned about HIV infection [the medical name that included the AIDS virus] that makes it inappropriate to think of it as composed of discrete conditions such as ARC [AIDS-Related Complex] or 'full blown' AIDS. HIV infection is the starting point of a single disease which progresses through a variable range of stages. In addition to an acute flu-like illness, early stages of the disease may involve subclinical manifestations, i.e., impairments and no visible signs of illness. The overwhelming majority of infected persons exhibit detectable abnormalities of the immune system. . . ."[79] What Koop was telling me was, effectively, that asymptomatic infection was, itself, a medical impairment, even though it was outwardly undetectable. If that medical impairment was also a legal one—that is, if it substantially limited a major life activity—the affected person would be protected against discrimination.

Back at the office, Paul Colborn and I again worked through the statute, its legislative history, and the medical information. We concluded that major life activities of asymptomatic carriers might well be substantially affected. In particular, we reasoned that "[i]n light of the significant risk that the AIDS virus may be transmitted to a baby during pregnancy, HIV-infected individuals cannot, whether they are male or female, engage in the act of procreation with the normal expectation of bringing forth a healthy child."[80] Moreover, because the Act as amended included within the definition of handicapped persons, those who were regarded by others as impaired whether they were or not, it might well be possible for an asymptomatic carrier to fall within the statute by demonstrating that this perception of handicap led to a denial of work or other substantial limitation of life activity.

In the end, we concluded that symptomatic and asymptomatic HIV-infected persons were protected under the Rehabilitation Act. With the better information from the Surgeon General, that impairments existed throughout the course of the disease from start to finish, the AIDS issue had effectively been answered by *Arline*. We wrapped up the opinion cautioning, however, that even though HIV-infected individuals were within the terms of the Act, that did not mean that federal employers or federally-conducted or financed programs could not, in individual circumstances, exclude an HIV-infected individual. In particular, if that individual posed a threat to the health or safety of others or was unable to perform the job or satisfy the requirements of the program, the person could be excluded if there was no reasonable way to accommodate the health and safety or performance concerns. In essence, individuals—even those with AIDS—had to be judged on their merits or risks, not stereotypes or generalized fears.

When I completed work on the opinion, Dick Thornburgh had been Attorney General for less than one month. I had no idea how he might react. I informed one of the Pennsylvanians, Robin Ross, whose immediate reaction was to accompany me into the Attorney General's office to hear me lay out my reasoning. When I had finished, Thornburgh asked if it was a difficult decision to reach. I said it was, both because of the complexity of the statute and the medical information, and personally because I did not like having to abruptly depart from the thinking of my former colleague, Chuck Cooper. Thornburgh indicated that he understood, and I was pleased by his apparent support. I left a copy of the opinion with him to read.

Had I been totally candid with Thornburgh, the AIDS opinion was difficult for another reason. I was troubled that the opinion might be mistakenly viewed as a federal endorsement or sanctioning of homosexual practice. AIDS was then perceived as a homosexual disease. Indeed, it still largely is. Substantial moral and religious teaching instructs that homosexuals have the same intrinsic moral worth as any other person; however, it also strictly forbids homosexual practice, regarding it as a physical and spiritual dysfunction for which counseling should be sought and compassionately provided. Certainly, moral concern prompted the family working group's concern that unlimited pornography might encourage promiscuity, and in turn, AIDS. As a *normative* matter, the elimination of barriers to federal jobs and benefits for practicing homosexuals might be said to run counter to both morality and sound family policy if such were perceived as a condonation of homosexual practice. Taking the relationship between law and morality seriously, I privately wrestled with this moral dilemma. Ultimately, I concluded that ridding federally-supported activities of discrimination against individuals with a disease, even if that disease is largely visited on homosexuals, did not condone homosexual practice. The fact that a significant number of those with AIDS are entirely innocent victims of infection from transfusions or health care activity bolstered my thinking. Had I been unable to reach this moral conclusion, I would have recused myself from the entire issue. With my private moral doubts settled, however, I simply emphasized as legal counsel, my job was to interpret the *law*, not to make *policy*.

In early October 1988, Thornburgh and Culvahouse advised that I was to conduct a news conference to announce my AIDS opinion. This was not the usual routine for OLC opinions, but this one had higher visibility than most. The first question from the assembled media was why it took nearly a year for OLC to fall in line with the Supreme Court. I responded, as I discuss above, that there was more involved than the Court's decision, since the Court had expressly declined to decide the AIDS issue. I also pointed out that it was only the month before that the President, himself, requested the Attorney General to consider the recommendations of his AIDS Commission. It was that Commission that had asked for reconsideration of the Cooper opinion. I also referenced the recent nature of the very helpful medical information provided by the Surgeon General.

A few reporters tried to get me to repudiate the Cooper opinion, calling it a reversal or overruling. I insisted that my opinion merely "superseded" Cooper's. My opinion, after all, had the benefit of the Supreme Court's opinion in *Arline*, Congress' passage of the Civil Rights Restoration Act of 1987, and the subsequent medical clarification of Dr. Koop. Some at the news conference thought the opinion reflected the transition from Meese to a "kinder, gentler" Thornburgh. There was the following colloquy between me and Rita Braver of CBS News:

Braver: I think that some people are going to inevitably believe that this is a change in politics, as well as policy within the Department and that we now have a Justice Department that is perhaps more interested in the suffering of some of the people or groups that perhaps the old Justice Department didn't want to take on and help in the same way that maybe this Justice Department does. Is there a difference?

Kmiec: I think the Office of Legal Counsel always approaches its task to give as good faith an interpretation of the law as possible. That is solely my interest. And so, as to the other matters, I really can't speak.[81]

Perhaps capturing some of the normative and public concern with homosexual practice, another reporter demanded to know "Why is it good to extend protection to people with AIDS?" And "Why is it good to include this group with people in wheelchairs and crutches . . . ?" I answered again: "That's really not my function. The function as to whether or not this was good or bad public policy was Congress'. We have fairly interpreted the statute."[82]

So we did. Chuck Cooper was quoted in the paper the following day that he did not disagree with my conclusion and might have reached the same result in light of the subsequent developments. I appreciated that vote of confidence from my former colleague. Apparently, the view was not unanimous among my conservative friends. Some months later, as President-elect Bush went about filling positions, more than a few insiders told me that my AIDS opinion was hurting my chances for continuation into the next administration among some members of the transition team. Even Chuck Cooper later suggested that I "may have shot myself in the foot." I have no idea if this was true. I can honestly state that I did not give the matter of my federal service *any* consideration in rendering the AIDS opinion as I did, or when I did. Nor if I had it to do over again would any part of the opinion change. In thinking about it now, however, I am amused by the thought that I might be the only person "handicapped" by an AIDS legal opinion—at least, that is, in terms of a major life activity—namely, federal employment. There is also some personal irony, I suppose, if these rumors were true, in a Reagan conservative being done in by the "kinder, gentler" Bush.

EDUCATION

During the Reagan years, efforts to strengthen student performance concentrated on increasing parental involvement and family educational choice. Today, in almost every community the public school system is a legal monopoly. As most every parent knows, students are assigned on the basis of local address, or if a busing order is still in effect, race. If the school assignment happens to be a good one, fine; if not, you're stuck. Parents can voice their concerns for needed improvements at school meetings, but since school funding is allocated by government agents sometimes at distant locations, parental concerns may not be directly, or promptly, addressed. Affluent parents can cut through this difficulty by "voting with their feet" and sending their children to the best private school available. But for those parents who cannot afford the double-payment of school taxes and tuition, their voting feet are in concrete blocks.

The absence of choice breeds parental non-interest and resignation. Disinterest is devastating to educational achievement, as the work of James Coleman at the University of Chicago has consistently demonstrated. Indeed, Coleman finds that the "social capital" of a close parent-student-teacher relationship is far more important to student achievement than whether the school has a new chemistry or language lab.[83] And a free choice among schools strengthens this relationship. The family working group report found that "[i]n Harlem, New York City, test scores rose markedly when choice was introduced to the public schools. A Brookings Institution study concluded that responsiveness to the market is the key to making schools effective."[84] The working group also noted that the public was overwhelmingly supportive of introducing more choice by providing parents with tuition vouchers that could be spent on any public or private school.

With such persuasive evidence and public support, why haven't vouchers become commonplace? Two reasons: one political, one legal. The political concern is seen in the grip the National Education Association and other teachers' unions have on the course of public education in Congress, state assemblies, and local school districts. Curiously, these unions seemingly extol parental involvement, but nevertheless work mightily to deny parental choice. As one writer put it: "the very group of professional educators which fears voucher-waving parents keeps imploring those same parents to visit schools, supervise homework, and generally take a greater interest in their children's education. Are most parents intelligent and concerned, or aren't they?"[85]

Good question. The question goes unanswered, however, because the teachers' unions quickly roll out the policy objection that the public schools cannot compete with private schools because they have a legal duty to educate everyone. Better students, it is charged, will leave the public schools making them the "dumping ground" for problem children. This union complaint can be answered in several ways, the most obvious of which is that it is highly insulting to public schools and public school teachers. Were public schools and teachers required to compete for tuition vouchers, there is every reason to believe that many of the public schools would be the schools of choice, especially if the individual schools were freed of centralized managerial decrees that preclude these schools from developing their separate institutional strengths. In any event, the policy objection is pure speculation. Indeed, frequently those most interested in vouchers are the parents of inner-city children.[86] It is highly likely that these same parents, once empowered with a voucher, will motivate their children toward the best available school, public or private.

To directly avert the argument that voucher-plans overlook the needs of the disadvantaged, Secretary of Education William Bennett introduced the Equity and Choice Act of 1985. This was not a new federal spending program. Rather, it reconstituted, in voucher form, chapter I of the Elementary and Secondary Education Act which already provided $3.2 billion annually for the remedial instruction of impoverished children. Under Bennett's plan, instead of the schools receiving this subsidy, parents would. The recipient parents could then "spend" the voucher at any public or private school that provided "efficient and effective" remedial instruction.

Once again, the stale policy arguments against vouchers generally were leveled at the Bennett plan. Given the plan's focused nature on the disadvantaged, however, such argumentation was now wholly unsatisfying. Which brings us to the legal objection to vouchers: they are said to "establish religion" contrary to the first amendment, which provides, in part, that: "Congress shall make no law respecting an establishment of religion, . . . " If you do not immediately see how providing vouchers for educational choice establishes religion, score one, and proceed to the next chapter. Regrettably, however, the Court has been stuck on this question for the last half century. Since some, perhaps many, of the private schools that might be favored with vouchers are religiously affiliated, the syllogism underlying the difficulty is: the government has provided the voucher, the voucher has ended up supporting a religiously affiliated school, therefore, the government has "established" a religion. The argument is a bit of a strain even on its face, but I am told that if you stare at it long enough, it is said to make sense.

When Bennett's proposal was forwarded to me for constitutional review, the first thing I discovered was that even OLC had previously cast doubt on the constitutional validity of earlier voucher plans. I was determined to start from the ground up. I asked Margaret Love, a hardworking career OLC lawyer to assemble, and help me digest, all of the relevant Supreme Court cases. They were a mess. As Justice Rehnquist once wrote for a majority of the Court itself:

It is not at all easy . . . to apply this Court's various decisions construing the [Establishment] Clause to governmental programs of financial assistance to sectarian schools. Indeed, in many of these decisions we have expressly or implicitly acknowledged that 'we can only dimly perceive the lines of demarcation in this extraordinarily sensitive area of constitutional law.'[87]

It is very much a wavering "line of demarcation" between the acceptable and unacceptable. The Court has upheld congressional support for parental reimbursement for parochial school transportation,[88] the lending of textbooks to private schools,[89] release time for public school students to attend religious instruction at religious schools,[90] funds for secular purposes at religious institutions of *higher* education,[91] and general tax exemptions for property used for religious purposes.[92] In contrast, other quite similar government involvement has been found to be an impermissible religious establishment and invalidated: for example, state grants for religious schools or parents who send their children to them,[93] reimbursements for state-required record keeping,[94] and support for public school teachers working after hours in religious schools teaching remedial reading.[95] The school cases made such little sense that when the Court seemingly held that textbooks, but not maps, could be made available to religious schools with public money, Daniel Patrick Moynihan, now Senator from New York, reportedly quipped: "What about atlases or books of maps?"[96]

The school cases are merely part of the Court's larger confusion in the religion clause area. Recent cases find the Court, for example, approving of government support for a menorah display, but not a nativity scene.[97] The constitutional difference supposedly was that the menorah was accompanied by a 46-foot Christmas tree and a sign bearing the Mayor's name and his "salute to liberty," while the privately-donated nativity scene was on the steps of the courthouse with the traditional angelic banner proclaiming, "Gloria in Excelsis Deo." Of course, even the mention of voluntary school prayer as an option for students during a moment of silence has been struck down.[98]

The Court has supplied this bollixed "wisdom" pursuant to an often mechanically applied three-prong test that it fashioned in *Lemon v. Kurtzman*.[99] Under the test, government assistance must have a secular purpose, the effect of neither advancing nor inhibiting religion, and not foster excessive government entanglement with religion. As the above examples demonstrate, however, the test is wholly unpredictable, and largely subjective. It has increasingly met with dissatisfaction even by members of the Court.[100] Justice Rehnquist has posited that the test is "a constitutional theory [that] has no basis in the history of the amendment it seeks to interpret, is difficult to apply and yields unprincipled results."[101]

Justice Rehnquist's mention of constitutional history identifies the location where a map out of this judicial distortion may be found. As Rehnquist reports, "[t]he actions of the First Congress, . . . confirm the view that Congress did not mean that the Government should be neutral between religion and irreligion."[102] On the same day as Madison introduced the Bill of Rights, including the establishment clause, Congress approved land grants for private schools in the Northwest Territory. The purpose of these grants was aptly captured by the recital that "religion, morality, and knowledge, being necessary to good government and the happiness of mankind, schools and the means of education forever should be encouraged."[103] Revealingly, those on the Court who insist on separating church and state in ways never intended, have acknowledged that their reading of the establishment clause is contrary to its original purpose. In the prayer case, for example, Justice Stevens asserted that even if the original intent of the establishment clause was merely to preclude a government preference for one religion over another, "the Court has unambiguously concluded that . . . the First Amendment embraces the right to select any religious faith or none at all."[104] But should the Court's unambiguous conclusion matter if it is divergent with the Constitution as written?

As I write this, the Supreme Court has accepted for review the case of *Lee v. Weisman.*[105] In this case, a rabbi opened and closed a middle school graduation ceremony with a reference to God, asking Him for blessing on the students, their families, and their nation. Based on the *Lemon* test, the district and appellate courts found the prayer an unconstitutional establishment of religion. In the district court, *Lemon* was said to lead to the inescapable conclusion that "God has been ruled out of public education as an instrument of inspiration or consolation."[106] The school principal has turned to my former OLC colleague, Chuck Cooper, to try to rid the Court of this sour taste of *Lemon.* As Cooper masterfully argues in his Supreme Court brief, the framers did not "intend to deprecate or restrain religious expression in the life of the nation. The Establishment Clause was not intended to operate as some sort of constitutional gag order, enjoining public officials and their invitees to omit any reference to God from civil ceremonies."[107] What the history of the establishment clause reveals is a concern with the coercion of religious belief, not the acknowledgment of religion. As long as government actions do not establish an official religion nor coerce participation in religious activities, they do not transgress the Constitution clause.

The practical effect of returning to the original understanding would likely not sanction school prayer in a classroom setting where attendance was mandatory, but it would just as surely not preclude a moment of silence in which a voluntary prayer could be made or prayers at graduation ceremonies. Nativity scenes, menorahs and other religious symbols could be as freely displayed by government or on government property as James Madison, the author of the establishment clause, could ask for the "guidance of that Almighty Being whose power regulates the destiny of nations, whose blessings have been so conspicuously dispensed to this rising Republic, and to whom we are bound to address our devout gratitude for the past, as well as our fervent supplications and best hopes for the future."[108]

But what about tuition vouchers or financial assistance for the secular purposes of religious schools? When Bill Bennett sent his proposed legislation over for OLC review, I concluded that his proposed delivery of vouchers to parents for their discretionary application to either public or private school was constitutional. My analysis, of course, had to accommodate the *Lemon* test, but that was largely possible by a small exception that had been sliced from *Lemon*. In *Mueller v. Allen*,[109] the Supreme Court approved a tax deduction under Minnesota's tax code for educational expenses, including tuition, incurred in any school, public, private, or religious. That the tax deduction was available to all, in public or private settings, and allocated pursuant to parental, not state, choice allowed the Court to conclude that, even under *Lemon*, this financial assistance did not have the purpose or effect of advancing or inhibiting religion. As the Court stated, "public funds be[came] available only as a result of numerous, private choices of individual parents of school-age children."[110] The *Mueller* rationale was later confirmed in *Witters v. Washington Department of Services for the Blind*,[111] upholding the ability of an individual student to apply state vocational assistance to a private, sectarian school. Again, the Court relied upon the fact that the aid "ultimately flows to religious institutions . . . only as a result of the genuinely independent and private choices of aid recipients."[112] The Bennett plan sufficiently followed this model to dispel any prior OLC doubts.

Would it have mattered if the Bennett plan had proposed to give aid directly to private, religious schools for secular educational purposes like remedial reading and math? The Court's *Lemon* decisions would likely find this direct assistance invalid, but in my judgment, that is constitutional error. The government's interest in supporting education generally amply separates even assistance given directly to a school from any claimed religious establishment. Quite simply, no one is being coerced by such assistance into a particular religious practice or worship.

It might be argued that there is a form of coercion in the raising of public revenue and its allocation to a private, religious school. This has some logical appeal since it cannot be denied that taxation and public spending involve a level of coercion. However, it is a level of coercion that we modernly tolerate for good constitutional reason. As a taxpayer I may be distressed that my tax dollars are going to support large federal bureaucracies or the B-1 bomber or the strategic defense initiative. My constitutional remedy for this is the ballot box, not federal court. To grant me or any other taxpayer standing to litigate congressional funding decisions generally would totally subvert the separation of powers. Contrary to some highly contradictory, almost intellectually embarrassing, case law,[113] taxpayers ought not be allowed to transmute the federal courts into minilegislatures for the purpose of redebating and reallocating public funds.

History fully supports keeping funding decisions out of federal court even when the taxpayer objection is premised on the establishment clause. It is true that Madison and Jefferson expressed strong opposition to and helped defeat an Assessment Act[114] which would have taxed persons for the Christian sect of their choice. But this is a different case. As Justice Harlan observed in dissenting from the Court's expansive grant of taxpayer standing: "[i]f this case involved a tax specifically designed for the support of religion, as was the Virginia tax opposed by Madison in his Memorial and Remonstrance, I would agree that taxpayers have rights under the religious clauses of the First Amendment that would permit them standing to challenge the tax's validity in the federal courts. But this is not such a case, and appellants challenge an expenditure [for secular educational purposes in religious schools], not a tax. . . ."[115]

As Harlan's dissent reveals, the Assessment Act was a direct support of religion, not of secular educational endeavors that happen to be conducted by religious organizations. That Madison and Jefferson's opposition was aimed at the problem of coerced payment for religious activity, and not the support of secular educational functions that happen to be performed by religious schools, is evident from the terms of Jefferson's Religious Freedom Act that followed the defeat of the Assessment Bill. The Freedom Act provided: "[N]o man shall be compelled to frequent or support any religious worship, place, or ministry whatsoever, . . ."[116] The Act did not provide that the government should sever all ties with religion or religious bodies. If that were true, it would make mockery of the Act's preamble, where Jefferson recites: "[w]hereas Almighty God hath created the mind free; that all attempts to influence it by temporal punishments or burthens . . . are a departure from the plan of the Holy author of our religion, who being Lord of both body and mind, yet chose not to propagate it by coercions on either, as was his Almighty power to do. . . ."[117]

As in other areas of constitutional jurisprudence, returning to the principles of the original understanding would eliminate the tangles of false and unhelpful reasoning. Insofar as the *Lemon* test has not totally precluded support for the secular educational activities of religious organizations, it has retained a seed of that understanding. But, as indicated before, the twists and turns of *Lemon*'s applications cannot be justified. Discarding *Lemon* in favor of the true establishment clause principle against the establishment of an official religion or the coerced participation in religious activity would restore the intended coherence to this area of the law.

Bill Bennett's tuition voucher proposal, despite our constitutional clearance, never saw the light of legislative day. He made several efforts, but the stranglehold of the education unions could not be loosened. Whether greater parental choice through vouchers, or similar arrangements, will yet materialize is difficult to predict. The parental interest remains strong, and there have been some favorable state and local efforts. George Bush, however, seems to be of at least two minds. As an education advisor to his election campaign during the period of 1987 when I was back at Notre Dame, I know that the mere mention of Bill Bennett or vouchers would send Bush regulars scurrying for cover. President Bush seemed to candidly reveal similar feelings in response to a young boy's question during a White House visit in March 1989:

> *Q*: Hello, Mr. President . . . I go to a private school, . . . [b]ut yet part of the taxes which [my parents] pay to the Federal Government go[es] to the public school system. . . . Should they get a tax break on that?
>
> *The President*: No they shouldn't. . . . I have been intrigued with the concept of tuition tax credits [the equivalent of vouchers]. And some say, well, should that include parochial schools? And I've said yes, but the problem again is that we are—and that gets really to your philosophical underpinning of your question—we can't afford to do that. So I think that everybody should support the public school system. And then, if on top of that, your parents think that they want to shell out, in addition to the tax money, tuition money, that's their right,. . . .[118]

This response distressed many of the President's usual supporters, including myself. Since then, President Bush's second Secretary of Education, Lamar Alexander, has outlined encouraging education reform proposals showing a reawakened sympathy for giving some federal education money directly to parents for allocation to public or private schools. That tip of the hat toward parental and family interests has generated the usual teachers' union opposition. It remains to be seen whether the primary role of parents in their children's educations will be acknowledged, and the dubious policy and constitutional objections to that reaffirmation of family discarded.

NOTES

1. *Major Policy Statements of the Attorney General: Edwin Meese III 1985–1988* 176 (1989).

2. President's Legislative and Administrative Message, 23 *Weekly Comp. Pres. Doc.* 91 (Jan. 25, 1988).

3. Office of Policy Development, *Report to the Domestic Policy Council on the Family* 11 (1988). [Hereinafter "OPD Report"].

4. 410 U.S. 113 (1973).

5. Reagan, *Abortion and the Conscience of the Nation*, 9 Human Life Review 7–9 (1983).

6. H. Kelsen, *The Pure Theory of Law* 95 (2d ed. 1967).

7. Noonan, *The Root and Branch of Roe v. Wade*, 63 Neb. L. Rev. 668, 675 (1984).

8. Reagan, *supra* note 5, at 7.

9. 462 U.S. 416 (1983).

10. *No Friend of the Court*, N.Y. Times, Aug. 4, 1982, at A22, col. 1.

11. McClellan, *A Lawyer Looks At Rex Lee*, 1 Benchmark 1, 3 (Mar.–Apr. 1984).

12. 462 U.S. 416, 453 (O'Connor, J., dissenting).

13. *Id.* at 458.

14. 476 U.S. 747 (1986).

15. C. Fried, *Order and Law* 34 (1991).

16. Romano, *Solicitor General Takes on Critics*, Wash. Post, Jan. 7, 1985, at A8 (quoting a person "who has known Fried intimately during his tenure at Harvard" but who "asked not to be identified").

17. *Id.*

18. Brief for U.S. at 7, *Thornburgh v. American Coll. of Obst. and Gyn.*, 476 U.S. 747 (1986) (No. 84–495).

19. *Id.* at 20–21.

20. *American Coll. of Obst. and Gyn.*, 476 U.S. at 759.

21. *Id.* at 782–83, 785.

22. *Id.* at 787 (White, J., dissenting).

23. *Id.* at 788.

24. Lauter, *A Tone of Impatience Noted in Abortion Decision*, Nat'l L.J., June 23, 1986, at 5 (quoting Tribe).

25. *Id.*

26. *Confirmation Hearings on the Nomination of Charles Fried, Hearings Before the Committee on the Judiciary*, 99th Cong., 1st Sess. 485, 486 (1985).

27. L. Caplan, *The Tenth Justice* (1987).

28. Caplan, *An Exchange of Views: Has the Solicitor's Office Become Politicized?*, Legal Times, Nov. 2, 1987, at 22.

29. Lauber, *An Exchange of Views: Has the Solicitor's Office Become Politicized?*, Legal Times, Nov. 2, 1987, at 22.

30. *Id.*

31. Elman, *The Solicitor General's Office, Justice Frankfurter, and Civil Rights Litigation, 1946–1960: An Oral History*, 100 Harv. L. Rev. 817, 818 (1987). The case was *Shelley v. Kraemer*, 334 U.S. 1 (1948).

32. Caplan, *supra* note 27, at 31–54.

33. McGinnis, *Principle versus Politics: The Solicitor General's Office in Constitutional and Bureaucratic Theory*, at 7 (forthcoming book review essay 799 in 44 Stan. L. Rev. 1992).

34. *Id.* at 7–8.

35. C. Fried, *supra* note 15, at 187.

36. *Id.* at 165.

37. Lauter, *A Champion of the Reagan Agenda*, Nat'l L.J., Jan. 27, 1986, at 1.
38. C. Fried, *supra* note 15, at 169.
39. 488 U.S. 416–22 (1989).
40. 851 F.2d 1071 (8th Cir. 1988).
41. 478 U.S. 186 (1986).
42. Brief for the U.S. at 6, *Webster v. Reproductive Health Services*, 492 U.S. 490 (1989) (No. 88–605).
43. *Id.* at 16.
44. *Id.* at 15–16.
45. Wines, *Justice Dept. Lawyers Assail Anti-Abortion Effort*, N.Y. Times, Mar. 26, 1989, at 19. col. 1.
46. 492 U.S. 490, 514 (1989).
47. 381 U.S. 479 (1965).
48. C. Fried, *supra* note 15.
49. (Family Planning Services Act) 42 U.S.C. § notes 300a–6 (1991).
50. *Insubordination Cited in Firing of HHS Official*, L.A. Times, July 4, 1987, at 20, col. 6.
51. *Id.*
52. Department of Health and Human Services, *Program Guidelines for Grants for Family Planning Services* 13 (in effect as of July 30, 1987).
53. Remarks at White House Briefing, 23 *Weekly Comp. Pres. Doc.* 879 (July 30, 1987).
54. 889 F. 2d 401 (2d Cir. 1990).
55. 111 S. Ct. 1759 (1991).
56. Kmiec, *The Abortion Counseling Decision Is Right*, Wall St. Journal, May 30, 1991, at A18.
57. Brief for the Respondent Department of Health and Human Services at 12, *Rust v. Sullivan*, 111 S.Ct. 1759 (1991) (emphasis in the original).
58. 111 S. Ct. at 1773.
59. United States Attorney General's Commission on Pornography *Final Report* 215 (1986).
60. OPD Report, *supra* note 3, at 11.
61. *Id.*
62. 420 U.S. 546 (1975).
63. 486 U.S. 750 (1988).
64. 457 U.S. 853 (1982).
65. 420 U.S. at 572–73 (Rehnquist, J. dissenting).
66. OPD Report, *supra* note 3, at 10.
67. 29 U.S.C. 794 (1988).
68. Memorandum for Ronald E. Robertson, General Counsel, Department of Health and Human Services, from Charles J. Cooper, Assistant Attorney General, Office of Legal Counsel 12 (June 20, 1986).
69. *Id.* at 12–13, citations omitted.
70. Abramson, *The AIDS Opinion; Reagan Agenda Pushed to the Max*, Legal Times, Aug. 4, 1986, at 1.
71. Cooper Opinion, *supra* note 68, at 34.
72. *Id.* at 44.
73. *Id.*

74. 480 U.S. 273 (1987).
75. *Id.* at 282.
76. *Id.* at 282 and n.7.
77. *Id.*
78. 20 U.S.C. § 1681 (1991).
79. Letter from C. Everett Koop to Douglas W. Kmiec 1–2 (July 29, 1988).
80. Memorandum for Arthur B. Culvahouse, Jr., Counsel to the President, from Douglas W. Kmiec, Assistant Attorney General, Office of Legal Counsel 10 (September 27, 1988).
81. Press Conference, 9–10 (October 6, 1988) (transcript available from the Department of Justice).
82. *Id.*
83. *See, e.g.*, Coleman, *The Creation and Destruction of Social Capital: Implications for the Law*, 3 Notre Dame J. L. Ethics and Pub. Pol'y 375 (1988).
84. OPD Report, *supra* note 3, at 26.
85. Kidder, *Tuition Vouchers: Should Parents Set School Policy?*, Christ. Sci. Monitor, April 8, 1985, at 21.
86. Henry, *School Choice OK, If Public*, South Bend Tribune, August 22, 1991, at A6 (reporting that "[t]he voucher plan found its strongest support among minorities and urban residents, 57 percent in each group.").
87. *Mueller v. Allen*, 463 U.S. 388, 393 (1983).
88. *Everson v. Board of Educ.*, 330 U.S. 1 (1947).
89. *Board of Educ. v. Allen*, 392 U.S. 236 (1968).
90. *Zorach v. Clausen*, 343 U.S. 306 (1952).
91. *Tilton v. Richardson*, 403 U.S. 672 (1971).
92. *Walz v. Tax Comm'n*, 397 U.S. 664 (1970).
93. *Committee for Pub. Educ. v. Nyquist*, 413 U.S. 756 (1973).
94. *Levitt v. Committee for Pub. Educ.*, 413 U.S. 472 (1973).
95. *Grand Rapids v. Ball*, 473 U.S. 373 (1985).
96. Will, *The Court's Moral Microscope*, Wash. Post, June 9, 1986, at D7.
97. *Allegheny County v. ACLU*, 492 U.S. 573 (1989).
98. *Wallace v. Jaffree*, 472 U.S. 38 (1985).
99. 403 U.S. 602 (1971).
100. *Allegheny County v. ACLU*, 492 U.S. 656 (Kennedy, J., concurring, calling for substantial revision of the doctrine); *Roemer v. Board of Public Works*, 426 U.S. 736, 768 (1976) (White, J., concurring and stating that he was as dissatisfied with the *Lemon* test from the time it was first decided).
101. *Wallace v. Jaffree*, 472 U.S. 38, 112 (1985) (Rehnquist, J., dissenting).
102. *Id.* at 100.
103. *Id.*
104. The Northwest Ordinance, 1 Stat. 50.
105. *Lee v. Weisman*, 111 S.Ct. 1305 (1991).
106. 728 F. Supp. 68, 70 (D. R.I. 1990).
107. Brief for the Petitioners at 13–14, *Lee v. Weisman*, 111 S.Ct. 1305 (1991) (No. 90–1014).
108. *Inaugural Addresses of the Presidents of the United States from George Washington, 1789 to George Bush, 1989* 25, 28 (Bicentennial ed. 1989) (first inaugural address of James Madison, March 4, 1809).

109. 463 U.S. 388 (1983).
110. 463 U.S. at 399.
111. 474 U.S. 481 (1985).
112. *Id.* at 487.
113. *Compare Flast v. Cohen*, 392 U.S. 83 (1968) (finding taxpayer standing to challenge a spending grant to finance remedial reading and arithmetic classes in public and private, including religious, schools) *with Valley Forge Christian College v. Americans United for Separation of Church and State Inc.*, 454 U.S. 464 (1982) (finding no taxpayer standing to challenge the allocation of surplus federal property to a Christian college).
114. *See Everson v. Board of Educ.*, 330 U.S. 1, 72–74 (1947) (Rutledge, J., dissenting) (Bill contained in appendix).
115. 392 U.S. 83 at 125–26 (Harlan, J., dissenting).
116. 5 *The Founders' Constitution* 84, 85 (P. Kurland and R. Lerner eds. 1987) (citing the Virginia Act for Establishing Religious Freedom [1785]).
117. *Id.* at 84.
118. 24 *Weekly Comp. Pres. Doc.* 448 (March 29, 1989).

5

Work: Securing Economic Liberty

Constitutional argumentation sometimes tends toward the abstract. Were I to extol the importance of economic liberty, few would disagree, but few would be very excited either. Only when it is understood that the economic liberties secured under the Constitution have a significant impact on matters very close to home—literally—do we have our attentions focused.

Take the cost of a family home. When President Reagan took office, it was after a decade in which the cost of housing rose dramatically—approximately 176 percent.[1] Now, not all of this increase was attributable to government regulation, but a fair share was. A presidential commission found: "[e]xcessive regulation raises housing costs by restricting available land, imposing unnecessary requirements in site development and construction standards, and lengthening the time needed to obtain regulatory permits. . . . Although the cumulative effect cannot be precisely determined, all the studies have a common finding: regulations increase costs—as much as 25 percent of the selling price in some cases."[2] Is all this costly regulation necessary? More relevantly for present purposes, is all of it constitutionally authorized?

Economic liberty also affects whether one can open a new business and whether, once that business is operating, contracts can be entered into with the reasonable expectation that they will not be supplanted by public regulation. If, for example, government can change the rules at any time for buying and selling widgets, and those rule changes can be retroactively applied to existing businesses and contracts, few of us would ever be willing to risk our life savings in the widget business.

THE HISTORICAL IMPORTANCE OF ECONOMIC LIBERTY

Now the cost of the four-bedroom ranch and widgets sounds distinctly modern and quite far from the bicentennial eloquence we normally associate with the Constitution. But it is not. There is substantial documentation suggesting that protecting economic liberty was a foremost concern of the founders.[3] The founders made this concern manifest in two provisions of the Constitution, principally the taking and contract clauses. The fifth amendment's taking clause provides that "private property shall [not] be taken for public use, without just compensation."[4] Textually, the taking clause appears to be only a limitation on Congress; however, the Court has found that it was intended to be incorporated as a limitation against the states as well pursuant to the due process clause of the fourteenth amendment. Appearing in article I, section 10, the contract clause provides that "no state shall pass any law impairing the obligation of contracts," and thus, by its terms, limits only state action. Occasionally, federal courts imply a similar limitation against Congress under fifth amendment due process. Putting aside the not insignificant problem of incorporation,[5] it was the "deletion," or at least the judicial dilution, of these two great clauses which concerned Attorney General Meese. Meese stated, "[J]udicial deletion of economic rights from the Constitution is a species of activism every bit as deplorable as the unwarranted manufacture of new, so-called civil rights."[6] The Court was treating economic liberty as second-class or unimportant, failing to perceive its constitutional and logical importance to the exercise of personal liberties. Propertyless individuals or those whose business endeavors are subject to unlimited government discretion are unlikely to be very critical of public figures or very active in the community.

Property as a Natural and Positive Law Concept

Just about every colonial or state constitution that preceded the American Constitution referenced the importance of property. Indeed, it can be persuasively argued that one of the essential purposes of our new government was the protection of property. As a right derived from the natural law, the founders believed that it could not be surrendered. Thus, the 1776 Virginia constitution provided that: "all men are by nature equally free and independent, and have certain inherent rights, of which, when they enter into a state of society, they cannot by any compact, deprive or divest their posterity; namely, the enjoyment of life, liberty, with the means of acquiring or possessing property, and pursuing and obtaining happiness and safety."[7] In *Vanhorne's Lessee v. Dorrance*,[8] the Court observed that the state constitution of Pennsylvania expressly declares that property "is a right not *ex gratia* from the legislature, but *ex debito* from the constitution. It is sacred; . . . The constitution is the origin and measure of legislative authority. It says to legislators, thus far ye shall go and no further."[9]

This suggests that the founders saw property as a pre-societal claim, and absolute. But this was only part of the story. First, the individual founders in their personal transactions relied upon state and colonial definitions of property, thus conceding—at least somewhat—that positive law, and not just nature, played a role in the conferral of a property right. Second, after the Constitution and Bill of Rights were ratified, a more qualified understanding of property might be derived from the constitutional document as a whole. The Constitution contains *both* an explicit protection of property in the fifth amendment *and* delegated regulatory power to Congress in article I and reserved power in the states under the tenth amendment. It could not be fairly said, therefore, that property ownership completely immunized the owner from such authorized regulation.

There is obvious tension between the view that "property is absolute" and not subject to regulation or diminution, even by compact, and the view that property is wholly defined by the legislature. Sometimes the tension appeared in the same case. In *Vanhorne's Lessee*, for example, the issue was whether one group of settlers had title in preference to another. Both it seemed had "acquired" the property, and Justice Patterson affirmed the "natural, inherent, and unalienable" right to acquire property,[10] but also the fact that "[t]he rights of private property are regulated, protected and governed by general, known and established laws."[11]

One way in which the framers tried to analytically bridge this tension was by emphasizing the common law limitation on property that went by the Latin maxim *sic utere tuo ut alienum non laedas* or "enjoy your property in such a manner as not to injure that of another person." In essence, this meant that uses of property that constituted a harm or a nuisance were not part of the natural right to property, and thus, could be subject to legislative regulation. The trick, of course, was then to differentiate a regulation that precluded harms from one that extracted benefits, or took property contrary to the fifth amendment.

Another way in which the natural law of property was reconciled to the positive law of property was by drawing a distinction between rights of acquisition and rights of use. This was the path taken by constitutional delegate James Wilson in his *Lectures on Law*.[12] Wilson explains that the tension between the natural and positive law aspects of property is traceable to Blackstone's characterization of private property as an absolute right along with life and liberty and Blackstone's simultaneous treatment of the incidents of ownership (use) as a right to things, which was necessarily qualified. This distinction partially overlaps with the no-nuisance limitation on property, since nuisances commonly arise only in matters of use, not ownership. But Wilson's explanation does not perfectly match the no-nuisance limitation. If the dividing line for valid government regulation is the prevention of nuisances, that would mean that both ownership and all non-nuisance uses could not be regulated by government. In contrast, drawing the line based on Wilson's distinction between ownership and use would leave all uses, even some no-nuisance ones, subject to government regulation. Perhaps recognizing this, Wilson put possession on the ownership side of the line—that is, the side free of government regulation.

These natural law and positive law aspects of property remain difficult to untangle, but it is important to recognize their presence and their difference. The natural law part is arguably not subject to government regulation; the positive law part is qualified, or as Chief Justice John Marshall pointed out "the creature of civil society and subject in all respects to the disposition and control of civil institutions."[13] Knowing which aspect of property is involved in a given case will never be scientifically precise. Nonetheless, sorting out these different aspects is at the philosophical core of every property dispute between citizen and government. Only when the natural and positive law aspects of property are fully understood can the economic liberty of the Constitution be fully provided.

The Multi-Faceted Nature of Property

But let's add a further difficulty: the concept of property itself. Nonlawyers readily think of property as "things"—the farm, that chair, and so forth. Legally, however, property is far more expansive; it includes expressions of ideas, designs, chemical formulas, and a host of other intangible items that can have great value. The farm itself consists not just of the surface and the corn or farmhouse attached to it, but the subsurface and air-rights, and certain rights to water and access. Giving legal definition to these more intangible aspects of property requires that the mind accept property not as a thing that can be physically held or trod upon, but as a dynamic relationship among individuals with regard to certain economic assets. As might be expected, all of us, judges included, occasionally fail to perceive the manifold ways in which property may be said to exist in these intangible ways. This failure of perception compounds the problem of effectively guaranteeing economic liberty under the Constitution. To the extent that intangible property is not accurately perceived to exist, government may be regulating in ways that violate the natural law of property or its positive protection under the taking and contract clauses.

ECONOMIC LIBERTY AND JUDICIAL DEFAULT

The elusive nature of property as a concept, notwithstanding, it is an important device for ensuring economic, and derivatively, personal liberty. It is property that protects an individual from redistributive majorities, or "factions" as Madison called them.[14] It might be thought, therefore, that the Court in applying the taking and contract clause guarantees would apply heightened scrutiny to any proposed limitation of them.

In fact, however, as any student of constitutional law can verify, the protection of property and contracts had been all but judicially erased from the face of the Constitution. Interestingly, this may have resulted from an equally illicit judicial attempt to strengthen property and contract rights. At the turn of the twentieth century, the Supreme Court regularly used the due process clause to invalidate all manner of state regulation dealing with economic matters from property use to the wages, hours, and conditions of employment. This judicial practice was far more sweeping than even the natural law of property could authorize, and therefore, insufficiently respectful of the government's regulatory power. Ultimately, an economic depression, a president frustrated by judicial undoing of his proffered "new deal" regulatory solutions, and a threat to "pack the Court," led to the abandonment of what has since been frequently referred to as the discredited *Lochner*[15] substantive due process view.

In the substantive due process cases, the Court almost never referred to the taking or contract clauses, let alone had a proper jurisprudential understanding of natural law. Nevertheless, Mother's admonition against traveling in bad company proved true, and when substantive due process was abandoned, so were these explicit protections of the Constitution. Rather than applying careful or heightened scrutiny to economic regulation, the Court has placed economic liberty on the lowest plane of constitutional protection, deferring almost entirely to legislative judgment.

The Modern Taking Cases

This was the state of the law when several important taking cases came before the Court during my tenure in OLC. While conservative legal scholars might be generally thought to be inclined toward the free market and economic liberty, even they—over time—had become skeptical of any judicial review of the legislative process. In other words, even conservatives were confusing the judicial activism that occurred under some virulent forms of substantive due process with the constitutionally justifiable intervention of the court under the taking and contract clauses against majoritarian abuse. As the Attorney General observed at an economic liberties conference that he convened in 1986: "[none of us are] fans of unfettered and arrogant judicial power... But I think we all recognize that there is an equal danger in raw, unbridled majoritarianism. Both excesses are equally to be feared for either one, when allowed to go unreined, will lead to the end of the rule of law and the loss of liberty, ..."[16]

Most of the taking cases have arisen in the context of land use restrictions. In an early case, Justice Holmes tried again to reconcile the "absolute-but-qualified" nature of property, when he wrote: "while property may be regulated to a certain extent, if regulation goes too far, it will be recognized as a taking."[17] Other than finding a specific subsidence regulation that abrogated the landowner's coal interests to be a taking, however, Justice Holmes never said how far was too far. Shortly thereafter, the Court upheld the most common form of land use regulation—zoning—in *Euclid v. Ambler Realty*,[18] but a close reading of the case suggests that the Court used the "no-nuisance limitation" to distinguish between valid and invalid regulation. Expressly citing the *sic utere* maxim mentioned earlier, Justice Sutherland observed that the particular uses being regulated there "[came] very near to being nuisances."[19] Two years after *Euclid*, the Court found a taking in the misapplication of a zoning ordinance where commercial property had been erroneously categorized as residential.[20] This case suggested that the Court would use the taking clause to fairly determine if regulation was actually furthering a substantial government interest, or was merely a makeweight.

Shortly after this, however, the Court went silent for almost 50 years. It had been chastened by its substantive due process rebuke to defer to legislative judgment in matters of economic regulation. In *U.S. v. Carolene Products*, the Court opined that "the existence of facts supporting legislative judgment is to be presumed, for regulatory legislation affecting ordinary commercial transactions is not to be pronounced unconstitutional unless... it is of such a character as to preclude the assumption that it rests on some rational basis...."[21] In other words, if the government could have rationally decided that its regulation might further its regulatory interests, that is the end of the matter. It doesn't matter if the regulation, in fact, does *not* further those interests, and it almost never matters that great economic losses are suffered by individual landowners.

While the Supreme Court slept, the notion took hold in lower federal courts and in state courts that the dividing line between acceptable and unacceptable government regulation had more to do with the economic effect of the regulation than whether the government was regulating within the scope of its authority. This "impact notion"—especially when combined with the almost total deference to legislative judgment—struck the balance far too greatly on the side of government regulation. The belief that the government can regulate at will so long as it leaves the landowner with some amount of value that might be called reasonable is a false one. It fundamentally overlooks the importance of keeping government out of some areas of private activity. As Justice Rehnquist once observed in dissent, "it is the character of the invasion [taking], not the amount of damage resulting from it, . . . that determines the question of whether it is a taking."[22]

When the Court awakened, a 1978 opinion by Justice Brennan all but declared the taking clause to be moribund. In *Penn Central Transportation Co. v. New York*,[23] the Court upheld a landmark preservation ordinance that precluded the owners of the Grand Central terminal from building an office tower similar in size to most of the surrounding structures. In essence, New York said, we like the look of your property, and we insist that you leave it unchanged. Now, I am all for landmarks. But, in fairness, I cannot think of any constitutional justification that allows government to require that you maintain one in an unaltered condition for my benefit. It is as if your neighbor took a liking to your backyard garden and insisted that you continue to grow the exact same flowers and vegetables year after year. The neighbor that leaned across the back fence with that command might well be thought to be on some sort of hallucinogenic substance.

When the owners of the terminal argued that the government had exceeded its constitutional authority in requiring them to confer this uncompensated benefit on the city, and pointed out that the Court's prior cases had suggested that harm-prevention, not benefit-extraction, was the legitimate basis for government land use regulation, Justice Brennan performed a bit of revisionist magic. Valid exercises of government power, claimed Brennan, do not depend upon the " 'noxious' quality of the prohibited uses but rather on the ground that the restrictions were reasonably related to the implementation of a policy . . . expected to produce a widespread public benefit."[24] And, of course, since the Court will defer to the legislative judgment on what produces a "public benefit," landowners should not expect to win any taking cases.

Justice Brennan did outline a list of "ad hoc" factors that he posited might hypothetically convince a Court that a taking of property by regulation had occurred. These factors focus on the economic impact of regulation, rather than on the government's right to regulate in the first place, and they suggest that unless the property is rendered, what the Court describes as, economically nonviable, the landowner need not bother filing his complaint. Since the Court had refused to review cases that resulted in upward of an 80 percent reduction in value,[25] the Court apparently meant what it said.

But just suppose there is some unfortunate soul whose property has been rendered economically nonviable, can he step right up to the government pay window and ask for a certified check? Not exactly. The California Supreme Court held, for example, that the only remedy a landowner is entitled to upon demonstrating the near-impossible standard of economic nonviability is invalidation of the regulation. This meant that the landowner received no compensation for the period of time that the regulation was in effect and being litigated.[26] While it might be possible in a few cases to obtain a monetary remedy in court pursuant to federal statute, by and large, the invalidation-only remedy was no remedy at all. Litigation would drag on for five, six, sometimes, ten years. Even if the landowner survived the litigation costs and won invalidation of the regulation, he had another surprise waiting for him: nothing, absolutely nothing, precluded the government from enacting just a slightly less restrictive regulation and starting the process all over again.

Advocating a Constitutional Remedy for Regulatory Takings

Before coming to Justice, I had done extensive academic research and writing on the taking problem. In 1983, I had occasion to talk with Solicitor General Rex Lee about the issue, and I strongly urged that the United States enter an appropriate *amicus* to the effect that the mere invalidation of overzealous regulation without compensation was not a remedy faithful to the fifth amendment and the taking clause. Lee was sympathetic, but it took a while for the Court to face the issue. Case after case presenting the remedy issue to the Court in the early 1980s were found deficient on one procedural pretext or another.[27]

In 1986, the United States entered a brief following the course that I had urged upon Rex Lee. Almost with exasperation given the Court's previous nondecisions, the brief flatly stated: "the merits of this case are important and deserve resolution."[28] Further, the Department made the very important argument that "[b]ecause regulation of land may constitute a 'taking,' within the contemplation of the Fifth Amendment, and because a temporary appropriation of land likewise can constitute a 'taking,' it would seem to follow inexorably that a regulatory restriction on the use of land that is only of temporary duration may also, in appropriate circumstances, constitute a 'taking' that implicates the Just Compensation Clause."[29] The prose in that argument was somewhat tortured, and I thought, needlessly qualified. Having only recently come to OLC, I didn't know why. However, after years of silence in the face of the Court's slighting of economic liberty, it was significant, in itself, for the Department to recognize the regulatory taking problem. That said, the Court declined—again—to reach the merits of the remedy issue.[30]

First English: Providing a Constitutional Remedy

In late June 1986, the Court noted probable jurisdiction in yet another case raising the taking remedy issue. In *First English Evangelical Lutheran Church v. County of Los Angeles*,[31] a summer camp had been destroyed by flood and the county enacted a permanent moratorium barring any construction on the property. As pleaded, it was a total taking, and the landowners asked for just compensation. The county moved to strike the request for compensation on the basis that invalidation was the only available remedy. The trial court granted the county's motion, thus isolating for legal consideration the remedy issue. Whether the regulation was warranted, whether particular development proposals or some other might still be found acceptable, whether some administrative exception might be granted, all of these extraneous questions were separated from the discrete issue of what, if any, remedy the federal Constitution requires when property is taken by regulation. In short, the Court could no longer dodge the issue.

I promptly urged Solicitor General Fried to file a brief on behalf of the church. Surprisingly, my advice met with Fried's immediate resistance. I now understood the tentative, convoluted prose in the earlier filing. Perhaps, I thought, his reluctance was traceable to the posture of the case. In essence, the injury issue was being skipped over to settle the constitutional principles for remedy. To answer this, I reminded Fried that the entire mess had started in the very same way. "The California Supreme Court determined that as a matter of *federal* constitutional law monetary relief is never appropriate for a regulatory taking in the context of a case in which the underlying taking was [also] never proven. This constitutional error deserves to be corrected," I wrote, "separate and apart from whatever view the Court ultimately adopts with reference to the definition of a regulatory taking."[32]

Hank Habicht, the head of the land and natural resource division, joined my effort with an excellent memorandum in support of the church and in favor of reaching the remedy issue. His assistance was most welcome, since picking up on Fried's opposition, the Solicitor General's staff had already circulated the exact opposite analysis favoring the county. Unbelievably, the staff took the California Supreme Court position that invalidation, not just compensation, should be the remedy for regulatory takings. The promise of "just compensation" in the Constitution was merely a condition precedent to the exercise of government power, the staff argued. In other words, the Constitution really didn't mean what it said. Fried's lawyers also insisted that damages were inappropriate because there had not been an express waiver of sovereign immunity. (Unlike the rest of us, the government has to consent to be sued.) This would have been a plausible argument had Habicht not reminded Fried that the just compensation spoken of in the fifth amendment is not damages at all, but indemnification, or the payment of fair market value for the property interest taken. An old case, *Jacobs v. United States*,[33] seemed to strongly make Habicht's point:

> [The right of just compensation] was guaranteed by the Constitution. The fact that condemnation proceedings were not instituted and that the right was asserted in suits by the owners did not change the essential nature of the claim. The form of the remedy did not qualify the right. It rested on the Fifth Amendment. Statutory recognition was not necessary. A promise to pay was not necessary. Such a promise to pay was implied because of the duty to pay imposed by the Amendment. The suits were thus founded upon the Constitution of the United States.[34]

Fried dismissed it all. *Jacobs*, he said, was a case premised on the Tucker Act, and therefore, sovereign immunity had been waived by statute. Fried thus revealed his principal objection to be conceding that the Constitution could ever confer any direct right of compensation absent authorization from Congress. Fried did not like the fact that the Court had previously implied a cause of action under the fourth amendment for a grossly unlawful search,[35] and he was concerned that filing in support of just compensation under the fifth amendment would increase the likelihood of more implied damage actions. This was a baffling and lame line of argument. Whether or not the Court was wrong to *imply* a cause of action for tort damages under a wholly separate part of the Constitution hardly justified ignoring the explicit promise of just compensation elsewhere.

Fried would not be persuaded. The arguments became more intense, and on Fried's part, more byzantine. He now took to arguing that California had not really opined on the meaning of the federal Constitution at all, but merely adopted the view that as a matter of state law, California officials were not authorized to undertake unconstitutional takings, and when they made them, they had to give them back. Well, yes they did, but that surely didn't answer the point that the *federal* Constitution expressly mandates that they also pay just compensation for any period of time in which they had taken the property by regulation. Fried was willing to concede that a landowner could file an action for damages under federal statute (section 1983), but not the Constitution. By *ipse dixit*, he proclaimed, "The just compensation clause is not self-executing."

The lawyers who handled land and natural resource matters on a day-to-day basis could not disagree more strongly with Fried. Even Secretary of Interior Hodel wrote Fried to recommend strongly that the United States support the church and its position in favor of constitutionally-required compensation. Hodel acknowledged that taking claims might increase the cost of his department, but he observed: "fairness demands that the government pay when it takes private property. Just compensation means that no one individual is to be forced to bear the burdens of government that rightfully should be borne by the whole public."[36] In that sentence, Hodel had captured the essence of the fifth amendment's property protection and its importance. It, however, did not convince Fried.

Recognizing the stalemate, Attorney General Meese convened a meeting in which all sides were represented and the arguments recounted here, and others, were explored in extraordinary detail. In addition, Alden Abbott, who at the time was a lawyer in the Office of Legal Policy and had become something of a taking clause historian, nicely demonstrated why the importance of property as a natural right justified the type of special protection that just compensation represented. It was reasonably evident that the Attorney General was skeptical of Fried's position. Habicht and I—together with the Attorney General's special assistants, Ken Cribb and Steve Calabresi—hoped that Meese would overrule Fried. But Ed Meese was wiser than that. He knew Fried would be greatly offended if his superior so openly countermanded him. He also knew that it would add fuel to the cries that the Solicitor General's office had become "politicized."[37] That Fried would have viewed it this way is evident by his later writing in which he reports that he wanted "to quit over the whole thing."[38]

Meese also stayed his hand, I believe, because he concluded that the Court was on the verge of correcting the constitutional error of the California Supreme Court, regardless of what Fried wanted to argue. In this the Attorney General was exactly right. The Solicitor General disregarded our counsel and filed on the side of the county regulators with the argument that the fifth amendment does not directly provide for monetary compensation. The Court completely rebuffed the Solicitor General's argument. In a 6–3 decision, the Court wrote:

> The Solicitor General urges that the prohibitory nature of the Fifth Amendment, combined with principles of sovereign immunity, establishes that the Amendment itself is only a limitation on the power of the Government to act, not a remedial provision. The cases cited in the text, we think, refute the argument of the United States that "the Constitution does not, of its own force, furnish a basis for a court to award money damages against the government."[39]

Moreover, the Court agreed with the proposition that the invalidation remedy was constitutionally inadequate where the improper regulation had already been in effect. The Court wrote: "[t]hese cases reflect the fact that 'temporary' takings . . . are not different in kind from permanent takings, for which the Constitution clearly requires compensation."[40] The Court highlighted the inadequacy of Fried's invalidation-only position by noting that the regulation had been imposed in 1979, and "the merits of [the Church's] claim had yet to be determined. The United States has been required to pay compensation for leasehold interests of shorter duration than this."[41]

No one likes to lose, and Fried was gracious in defeat. A half hour after the Court announced its decision in early June 1987, Fried dropped by my office to acknowledge that the Court had seen things my way. He seemed relieved in a way, and at the time I interpreted it to mean that he had been genuinely divided—almost of two minds on the issue. The Court having denied the path he took, he could now cheerfully admit to the important reaffirmation of the compensation element of the taking clause. Since then, Fried has reflected differently. In his recent book on his experience as Solicitor General, Fried records: "[i]t was the merits that bothered me. I doubted the wisdom of giving the courts a powerful new engine for redistributing to sympathetic plaintiffs possibly vast sums of money at the expense of the public."[42]

This new reflection is most troubling. Fried's role as Solicitor General was not to exercise his discretion as to which parts of the Constitution to enforce. If the fifth amendment provides for just compensation, it was not for Charles Fried to use the cloak of his office and the pretense of constitutional argument to implement his contrary policy choice. Moreover, the remainder of Fried's recent public reflection makes matters worse. He justifies his argument against just compensation with the comment that he was alerted to the fact that "Justice Brennan had once expressed sympathy for the interim-damages argument."[43] From this he apparently concludes that the position must be wrong. Now, admittedly I, like many other conservative legal scholars, have disputed much of Justice Brennan's constitutional interpretation. However, it is surely anti-intellectual to believe that every opinion issued above a Brennan signature is automatically incorrect. And Fried's reflection gets even darker. The reason he gives for avoiding any association with a Brennan position is that were compensation recognized for "the concerns of businesses and property owners," it would rather quickly be carried over "to secure the expectations of welfare beneficiaries, government jobholders, and the like."[44] Whoa! This is not only being selective in the choice of which constitutional provision to enforce and stereotyping by judicial author, it is also deciding who is entitled to equal treatment under law. Fried's explanation is that he was being "[l]oyal to what [he] conceived to be the heart of the Reagan Revolution . . . [namely,] that tax cuts and budget reductions were the only effective and systematic way to control the leveling tendencies of the welfare state."[45]

It is my belief, or at least fervent hope, that Charles Fried did not give substantial thought to the writing of those passages. If he were to have truly conceived of his job in this ugly fashion, then the charges of "politicization of the Solicitor General" have been proven by admission. The Solicitor General's oath is to the Constitution, and the Constitution extends its protection to big business and welfare recipient alike. It is the President's responsibility to fashion tax and budget policies under the Constitution; it is not the Solicitor General's function to remake the Constitution to advance his conception of the President's policies. Certainly, that is what Ronald Reagan expected from Charles Fried.

This is not to say that a plausible legal and constitutional argument cannot be drawn between the natural right conception of property in the Constitution and the privilege of government benefits, be they welfare or any other form of largesse. Fried does reference the Court's acceptance of this distinction.[46] Nevertheless, I remain dismayed by the passages quoted, and that even in retrospect, Fried would find that the correct interpretation of the taking clause to be a matter of "relative unimportance."[47] To the everyday citizen, who builds his or her life around the ownership and use of property, and within that property, finds private space to which the government may not enter or interfere, it is an issue of utmost importance.

First English is a landmark achievement for the original understanding of economic liberty in the Constitution. It is regrettable, but of no great moment, that it was not effectively advanced by the Department. As Meese suspected, the Court had seen the error on its own. This was, as I note, reason enough for the Attorney General not to override Fried in the *First English* matter. Yet, Meese had an additional motivation. The Attorney General knew that there was a case to come before the Court very shortly that would not just raise the issue of remedy, but also the underlying issue of when a regulatory taking occurs. Meese made it plain to Fried that he expected a carefully drawn brief in favor of economic liberty. Fried got the message.

Nollan—The Court Revisits the Original Understanding of the Taking Clause

Jim and Marilyn Nollan had saved to purchase property along the California coast. The Nollans wanted to replace the dilapidated beach cottage on the property with a three-bedroom home, similar in size and design to neighboring houses. The government said they could have their building permit, but only if the Nollans granted the public a right of way over their beach area. By at least one estimate, this right-of-way, or easement, would occupy one-third of their property. The Nollans challenged the easement requirement, won in trial court, and built their home. When the state court of appeal reversed demanding that they turn over an easement, the Nollans appealed to the Supreme Court.

Charles Fried thought this an easy case. He writes in his book that it involved "a traditional taking of a traditional property interest."[48] Maybe so, and it was heartening to have Charles on the right side. But those of us who had been following economic regulation, and in particular land use regulation before the Court, knew that the outcome of the case was no sure thing. First off, there was the deferential standard of review applied to economic regulation. The coastal commission that imposed the permit requirement would surely rely on the many post-New Deal cases to the effect that the Court should defer to any rational basis put forth by the commission. Second, the economic impact of this regulation was not the type of total wipeout demanded by the Court's "economic nonviability" standard. Third, finding for the Nollans in this case would cast doubt on a great variety of land use regulations which require property owners to build day-care centers, municipal theaters, schools, firehouses, and highway interchanges, as a condition of development approval. Exactions of this type upon land development had become a handy replacement for property taxes that were increasingly being placed by state and local voters under legal limitation. In short, it was exactly as Madison feared: redistributive majorities imposing disproportionate burdens on individual property owners.

Applying the original understanding and natural law principles examined earlier, the imposition upon the Nollans could not be justified. The Nollans were not a source of harm; rather, they were merely seeking to build a family home. Were constitutional delegate James Wilson available for consultation, I am certain he would conclude that the Nollans were merely exercising their natural right to acquire and possess property—a right that no social compact could require them to forfeit. Perhaps it was this strong natural rights predicate that allowed Fried, as he put it, to "strengthen[ ] the brief that came up in the usual course of business from the Attorney General's people."[49]

As one of the "Attorney General's people," I was delighted to have Fried's added strength. When I met with Don Ayer, Fried's deputy, and Richard Lazarus of Fried's staff, to work through their later draft of the brief, however, I was concerned that it had become a bit schizophrenic. The brief now argued that the case should be remanded, rather that decided by the Court, on the theory that the lower courts had misapplied the Court's taking standards. There was no reason for this timidity. The facts were clear from the record, and now was the time to push for a clean, Supreme Court rethinking of the prior taking cases. In addition, the order of the later draft was somewhat backward, with the weakest argumentation leading off. That said, the final copy of the brief filed with the Court did ultimately warm to its subject and clearly provided an avenue for returning the Court to the original understanding of the taking clause.

Putting aside the unhelpful *ad hoc* factors of the Court's prior cases, we argued in the brief that the ultimate constitutional issue would be determined by "whether the [permit] condition is rationally related to a *legitimate* governmental goal *and* whether the terms of the condition are reasonably proportional both in character and degree to the burdens imposed by appellants' development."[50] Note carefully what was imbedded in that argument. First, there was a return to government accountability. If government was to regulate, it had to have a meaningful justification. Yes, this meant heightened judicial scrutiny. But, this was not judicial activism. As mentioned before, illicit judicial activism occurs both when constitutional rights are made up *and* when explicit constitutional guarantees are ignored. Heightened judicial scrutiny here is warranted by the constitutional guarantee against takings. Second, there was a recognition of the fact that government regulation of property is most justified when it is aimed at addressing problems caused by the landowners being regulated. Moreover, in rectifying the harms caused by a landowner, regulation must be proportionate.

In deciding the case, the Court appeared to rely greatly on our arguments. Thankfully, it also agreed with my initial assessment that there was no need for a remand. Rather, the Court found the easement requirement to be a taking since it could not reasonably be said to substantially advance a legitimate governmental interest. The governmental interest suggested by the coastal commission was the reduction in "psychological" blockage to the beach that would be caused by the construction of the Nollans' new home. Justice Scalia told the commission to lie down on its psychological couch. The condition utterly failed, said the Court, to advance the government's interest because creating an easement to facilitate the flow of people already on the beach can have nothing to do with the psychological mindset of those seeking access to the beach. In this, the Court was applying heightened scrutiny. Importantly, the Court explicitly tied this heightened scrutiny of the government's justification to the explicit protections of the fifth amendment, thereby answering the charge that it was resurrecting the conservative judicial activism that previously masqueraded under substantive due process during the *Lochner* era.

The difference between substantive due process scrutiny and the heightened scrutiny of *Nollan* is sometimes said to be that, in the former, the Court second-guesses the propriety of the government's end or objective, whereas, in the latter, the Court's interest is in the fit between regulatory end and means. As a rough description, this is not bad, however, in one respect, it is misleading. True, the *Lochner* Court had no business making legislative policy decisions dealing with wages and hours and the like as a matter of due process. However, because the taking clause, in itself, is a substantive limit on the scope of government authority, occasionally the Court will be called upon to review where that substantive authority begins and ends. This, too, is captured in the *Nollan* opinion, but more obliquely. On the one hand, the Court observes that past cases have made it clear that "a broad range of governmental purposes and regulations"[51] falls within the government's authority. This is appropriate judicial restraint under a scheme of separated power. On the other hand, in carrying out this "broad range" of objectives, the government must not "single out" one landowner " 'to bear public burdens which, in all fairness and justice, should be borne by the public as a whole.' "[52] This is a modern recognition that part of property predates the Constitution and is not subject to regulation. It is also an acknowledgement that the protection of property must be balanced with the avoidance of harm. Regulation that proportionately addresses a harm caused by a given landowner is beyond constitutional question. Regulation that attempts to extort from a landowner a benefit that, in itself, may be a good thing, must be paid for.

Nollan's return to the original understanding of the taking clause was so lucid and so completely at odds with the meandering of the Court's prior taking cases that those who had become accustomed to thinking of private property as just another inconvenience on the way to public nirvana have gone into a period of denial. Efforts have been made to limit it to its facts or to disparage it as "conservative judicial activism,"[53] but don't be fooled. *Nollan* is a faithful return to the economic liberty secured by the written Constitution. On this one, Charles Fried can be justifiably proud to have helped the Court find its way after being truly lost for over 50 years.

The Taking Executive Order

Following the Court's decisions in *First English* and *Nollan*, the question was raised whether the federal government's regulatory house was in order. In other words, was the federal bureaucracy acting consistently with the fifth amendment in its own decision making as a matter of course, or was it imposing unjustified regulatory costs in the expectation that few citizens would have the wherewithal to file suit? The President's Task Force on Regulatory Relief thought at first that the individual legal counsel within the various departments might be relied upon to bring their respective departments into line. On reflection, however, it became clear that presidential direction was needed.

In January 1988, President Reagan included the following in his legislative and administrative message to Congress:

> It was an axiom of our Founding Fathers and free Englishmen before him that the right to own and control property was the foundation of all other individual liberties. . . . In the wake of the [*Nollan* and *First English*] decisions, this Administration is now implementing new procedures to ensure that federal regulations do not violate the Fifth Amendment prohibition on taking private property; or if they do take a citizen's property for public use, to ensure that he receives constitutionally required compensation.[54]

The first administrative step consisted of the President's issuance of Executive Order 12360 in March 1988.[55] Modeled after prior executive orders that require executive agencies to assess the costs and benefits of regulatory actions generally, the new order mandated that executive agencies be guided by the *Nollan* and *First English* principles in their internal decision making. In particular, almost all proposed federal actions, be they administrative or legislative, that implicated the regulation of private property for the purpose of protecting health or safety were to be accompanied by a taking impact assessment (TIA). This TIA must identify the health risk, show that the proposed government action substantially advances the purpose of avoiding or mitigating the risk, demonstrate that the proposed restrictions do not disproportionately burden any single landowner, and estimate the potential cost of the regulation in the event it was later judicially found to be a taking. The order expressly provided that the TIA was an internal deliberative document, thereby promoting as much candor as possible. While neither the order nor the TIA created any private right of enforcement, the extent of compliance by an agency with the executive order might well affect a court's subsequent assessment of the reasonableness of regulation.

Roger Marzulla, who succeeded Hank Habicht as head of the land and natural resources division, deserves most of the credit for the careful drafting of the executive order and its subsequent implementation. When I first met Roger, I was greatly impressed by his quick, analytical mind and his comprehensive knowledge of environmental law, but I was a bit disconcerted by an inability to achieve eye contact with him. He would pace about his office and move things around on his desk, but seemingly avoided ever looking at me. As it turned out, the explanation was simple: he was blind. If anyone ever needs an example of great personal and professional success overcoming a significant physical handicap, and almost treating it with disdain as a minor inconvenience, look no further than Roger Marzulla.

OLC's function in reviewing the executive order for the President, and my personal concern in reviewing the Attorney General's guidelines that later issued as a result of the order, was to ensure that the federal government was fully meeting its constitutional obligation. Upon examination, it turned out that Marzulla had chosen to hold the federal government to an even higher standard. For example, in section 3[b] of the order, federal agencies were directed to be alert to possible takings when regulations "substantially affect" the value of private property, not just when regulation renders property economically nonviable under the Court's ungenerous standard. The order also mirrored, and perhaps extended, *Nollan*'s requirements that government regulation substantially advance a legitimate health and safety purpose and not be a disproportionate burden. Quite simply, the executive order asks whether the regulated landowner caused the problem he is being asked to remedy. As Marzulla reflected: "[t]he [o]rder embraces [the *Nollan*] approach without forgetting the origins of regulatory authority in the nuisance exception."[56]

There have been some complaints within government that the TIA requirement is just so much more paperwork. If not conscientiously undertaken, it might be. But the questions asked pursuant to the executive order certainly promote sound management and fiscal policy. Whether good answers are supplied largely depends on personnel. The internal analysis prompted by the order should not only reduce monetary taking claims against the federal government, which in the 1987 fiscal year were over $20 million, but also instill greater respect for an executive branch working to stay within the rule of law. In brief, the executive order reflected how Roger Marzulla defined his personal objectives as the federal government's chief environmental litigator: "[w]e can have a clean and healthful America, which, at the same time, respects traditional constitutional liberties. And that, in the end, is the true genius of our governmental system."[57]

The Contract Clause

A similar tale of constitutional misinterpretation could be told here about the contract clause. The clause, it will be recalled, precludes the state from passing a law "impairing the obligation of contracts." As John McGinnis and I have written elsewhere, properly interpreted, the clause was intended to "prohibit all retrospective, redistributive legislation which violates vested contractual rights by transferring all or part of the benefit of a bargain from one contracting party to another."[58] Nevertheless, asserting that the clause is "not to be read literally,"[59] the Court has allowed for the abrogation of private contract by government regulation whenever it is "reasonable and necessary."[60]

As in the taking cases, there has been a longstanding confusion between enforcement of the contract clause and substantive due process.

The contract clause protects vested contractual rights; substantive due process illicitly invites the Court to question the policy wisdom of legislation. The contract clause does not deny a legislative body the power to prohibit private parties from entering into certain contracts in the future (after a law's date of enactment); substantive due process invalidation results in a type of unconstitutional preemption of even prospectively-applied legislation. The contract clause exists in constitutional text and history; substantive due process is in neither. The two paths of constitutional analysis could not be more different. As I observed at the Attorney General's conference on economic liberty in 1987, while both the contract clause and the discredited substantive due process are ostensibly aimed at the same objective, substantive due process is an imposter that, in the name of protecting economic liberty, has weakened it.

There were few litigation opportunities to raise the correct interpretation of the contract clause during Ed Meese's tenure as Attorney General. Perhaps now that the taking clause has been nudged back toward its original path, the opportunity will not be far behind.[61]

NOTES

1. President Reagan's Commission on Housing, Final Report 180 (1982).
2. *Id.* at 181.
3. *See* B. Siegan, *Economic Liberties and the Constitution* (1980).
4. U.S. Const. amend. V.
5. The Court's "incorporation doctrine" is the subject of much debate, with some scholars contending that it is a substantial departure from the original understanding. *See* R. Berger, *The Fourteenth Amendment and the Bill of Rights* 11–13 (1989). It is beyond my purposes in this book to fully examine this debate, but suffice it to say for present purposes, that I am inclined from the history toward the view of the late Justice Hugo Black that the first eight amendments were intended to be incorporated against the states by the due process clause of the fourteenth amendment. *Adamson v. California*, 332 U.S. 46 (1947) (Black, J., dissenting). I do not agree, however, with Justice Black's characterization of the natural law as "an incongruous excrescence on our Constitution." It is unfortunate that Black chose to liken the majority's "selective" incorporation theory to natural law, since they are not the same. As understood by the framers, natural law related to fundamental precepts of life, liberty, and property, it did not provide answers dependent upon contingent facts, such as whether "fairness" is offended by permitting the prosecution to comment on the defendant's failure to take the witness stand.
6. Meese, opening remarks at the Economic Liberties Conference, June 14, 1986, in *Major Policy Statements of the Attorney General*, 141 (1989).
7. Virginia Colonial Constitution of June 12, 1776, *reprinted in* B. Schwartz, *The Bill of Rights: A Documentary History* (1971).
8. 2 U.S. (Dall.) 304 (1795).

9. *Id.* at 311.
10. *Id.* at 310.
11. *Id.* at 312.
12. 2 *The Works of James Wilson* 296, 302 (J. D. Andrews ed. 1896).
13. 3 U.S. 211 (1796).
14. *See* J. Nedelsky, *Private Property and the Limits of American Constitutionalism* 22–23 (1990).
15. *Lochner v. United States*, 461 U.S. 931 (1983).
16. *Major Policy Statements of the Attorney General* 140 (1989) (Opening Remarks to the Economic Liberties Conference by Meese).
17. *Pennsylvania Coal v. Mahon*, 260 U.S. 393, 415 (1922).
18. 272 U.S. 365 (1926).
19. *Id.* at 395.
20. *Nectow v. City of Cambridge*, 277 U.S. 183 (1928).
21. 304 U.S. 144, 152 (1938).
22. *Penn Central Transportation Co. v. City of New York*, 438 U.S. 104 at 149–50 (Rehnquist, J., dissenting). Rehnquist made the statement quoting *United States v. Cress*, 243 U.S. 316, 328 (1917), which in the original quotation inserts in the ellipses the phrase "so long as the damage is substantial." Rehnquist did not specifically comment on this limitation, and taken literally, it might be read to disavow the very statement that Rehnquist was making; namely, that the taking issue is determined more by whether the regulation was authorized than whether it left the landowner with some remaining economic value. In all likelihood, the caveat is probably nothing more than a judicial device to screen out *de minimis* cases.
23. 438 U.S. 104 (1978).
24. 438 U.S. at 134 n.30.
25. *HFH ltd. v. Superior Court,* 15 Cal. 3d 508, 542 P.2d 237, 125 Cal. Rptr. 365 (1975), *cert. denied* 425 U.S. 904 (1976).
26. 447 U.S. 255 (1980).
27. *See Agins v. Tiburon*, 447 U.S. 255 (1980) (issue could not be addressed where development plan had not been submitted); *San Diego Gas and Electric Co. v. City of San Diego*, 450 U.S. 621 (1981) (Court drew a ridiculous distinction saying California did not hold that a zoning ordinance could never be a taking; it simply limited the remedy to nonmonetary relief); *Williamson County Regional Planning Commission v. Hamilton Bank of Johnson City*, 473 U.S. 172 (1985) (finding the case insufficiently "ripe" since the landowner had not applied for administrative variances from the regulation or asked for compensation from the state); *MacDonald, Sommer and Frates v. County of Yolo*, 477 U.S. 340 (1986) (rejection of one plan doesn't mean the county wouldn't accept some other).
28. Brief for the United States at 16, *MacDonald, Sommer and Frates v. County of Yolo*, 477 U.S. 340 (1986) (No. 84–2015).
29. *Id.* at 20.
30. *MacDonald, Sommer and Frates v. County of Yolo*, 477 U.S. 340 (1986).
31. 482 U.S. 304 (1987).
32. Memorandum for the Solicitor General from D. W. Kmiec, dated 3 (August 19, 1986).
33. 290 U.S. 13 (1933).

34. *Id.* at 16.
35. *Bivens v. Six Unknown Named Agents of Federal Bureau of Narcotics*, 403 U.S. 388 (1971).
36. Letter from Donald Paul Hodel, Secretary of the Interior, to Charles Fried, Solicitor General of the United States, 1 (August 29, 1986).
37. See the discussion in Chapter 6.
38. C. Fried, *Order and Law* 185 (1991).
39. 482 U.S. 304, 316 n. 9 (1987).
40. *Id.* at 318.
41. *Id.*
42. C. Fried, *supra* note 38, at 184.
43. *Id.*
44. *Id.* at 185.
45. *Id.*
46. *Schweiker v. Chilicky*, 487 U.S. 412 (1987).
47. C. Fried, *supra* note 38, at 185.
48. *Id.*
49. *Id.*
50. Brief for the United States at 21 *Nollan v. California Coastal Commission*, 483 U.S. 825 (1987) (No. 86–133).
51. 483 U.S. 825, 835 (1987).
52. *Id.* at 836 n.4. (citing cases).
53. *See, e.g.*, Farber, *"Taking" Liberties: Conservative Judicial Activism*, 198 New Republic 19 (June 27, 1988).
54. Marzulla, *The New 'Takings' Executive Order and Environmental Regulation—Collision or Cooperation?*, 18 Environmental Law Reporter 10254 (1988) (quoting the President's letter).
55. Exec. Order No. 12,630, 53 Fed.Reg. 8,859 (1987).
56. Marzulla, *supra* note 54, at 10259.
57. *Id.* at 10260.
58. Kmiec and McGinnis, *The Contract Clause: A Return to the Original Understanding*, 14 Hastings L.Q. 525, 526 (1987).
59. *See, e.g.*, *Keystone Bituminous Coal Association v. DeBenedictus*, 486 U.S. 470, 504 (1987).
60. *United States Trust v. New Jersey*, 431 U.S. 1 (1977) (this case is viewed as reviving the clause, but given the Court's reasonableness qualifier, the clause is still semiconscious at best).
61. The Supreme Court was urged to return to the original understanding of the Contract Clause in *General Motors* v. *Romein*, Case No. 90–1390, argued December 10, 1991.

6

Neighborhood: The Revival of Federalism

No one was more committed to federalism than Charles J. Cooper, my predecessor as head of OLC. How many other people have the tenth amendment, which reserves the power not delegated to the federal government to the states, framed on their wall? Raised and educated in Alabama with a strong sense of southern pride, it might be said that he has an inbred sense of "state's rights." But don't be misled by that label. Cooper, himself, would very likely not see federalism and state's rights, as the term is loosely used today, as perfectly synonymous. Chuck well understood that the constitutional convention had overcome the hapless league of friendship of the Articles of Confederation. Under the Constitution, some power had been expressly and exclusively given to the central government; other authority was to be shared. But significantly and often overlooked, some subjects were reserved for the states. To Cooper, federalism was important not just because it produced experimentation and diversity, not just because it allowed for more direct political interaction between citizen and government, but also because it was a key element of the entire federal structure. Like the separation of powers, it had been carefully calibrated by the founders to secure individual liberty.

But whatever the original calibrations, it was clear to Chuck Cooper, and to any honest appraiser of constitutional doctrine, that federalism was a principle in decline. States were often the demeaned supplicants for federal funds—the subordinate administrative units that carried out federal commands. No longer were they truly "sovereign states." This grieved Cooper greatly, and it was a concern that the President, a former governor, shared deeply. In his inaugural, remember, Ronald Reagan unequivocally stated his "intention to curb the size and influence of the federal establishment and to demand recognition of the distinction between the powers granted to the federal government and those reserved to the states or to the people."[1] Reestablishing a meaningful dividing line between federal and state authority meant, as in other areas, reexamining the original understanding of the Constitution.

THE ORIGINAL UNDERSTANDING OF FEDERAL-STATE RELATIONS

When the delegates assembled in Philadelphia in 1787, the immediate concern was to address the failure of the Articles of Confederation. Under this loose "compact resting on good faith," there was no meaningful national government. The enforcement of national laws rested largely within the discretion of the several states. Moreover, the states were increasingly antagonistic to one another, erecting costly trade barriers. The severity of the confederation's problems enabled Madison, Randolph, and others to quickly change the terms of the debate. Instead of patching up the old confederation or "confederal" system, a new one with a "supreme Legislative, Executive and Judiciary" would be created. The resulting system embodied by the Constitution was later described by Madison as "neither a national nor a federal Constitution, but a combination of both."[2] He explained that "[t]he proposed government cannot be deemed a *national* one; since its jurisdiction extends to certain enumerated objects only, and leaves to the several States a residuary and inviolable sovereignty over all other objects."[3]

The strongest adherents of state authority were suspicious. James Winthrop, for example, argued that "[i]t is a mere fallacy . . . that what rights are not given are reserved."[4] Sam Adams and the antifederalists thought that the explicit powers of the national government would subsume the states. These arguments did not go unheard and several states voted for the Constitution, *but only* on the condition that a bill of rights would be provided, including the express reservation of power to the states. As Chuck Cooper would observe in a federalism report for the President:

> [f]or the generation of men and women who lived during the founding years of the republic, States mattered. After all, the States preceded the Constitution. The delegates who wrote the Constitution were delegates from the States and votes at the Constitutional Convention were cast by States. The Constitution was ratified by delegates in conventions in the States. The States provided the primary source of identification and political loyalty for most citizens. The federal character of the Constitution was designed to ensure that the States continued to matter.[5]

What Happened?

It would be impossible to describe states as having the same importance to the men and women of 1992. We worry over the completion of our federal tax return and rather quickly prepare state forms that we view as secondary. Our focus is on the election of senators and congressman, with far less thought to gubernatorial and other state offices. Some of this change is of our own doing: the sixteenth amendment and the national income tax centralized economic resources; the seventeenth amendment made senators popularly elected, instead of selected by state legislatures. Economic depressions and external conflict brought us together as one nation in both legal and emotional ways that are hard to set aside.

There has also been considerable judicial misconstruction. The necessary and proper clause, which provides that Congress may "make all laws which shall be necessary and proper for carrying into execution"[6] its expressly delegated powers, rather quickly became an open-ended invitation to expand the terms of those powers.[7] Jefferson feared such broad interpretation, predicting that it would "swallow up all the delegated powers and reduce the whole to one power."[8] He was not far wrong.

The most expanded, if not distorted, power of Congress is that dealing with commerce. The congressional power to "regulate commerce... among the several states" was scarcely discussed at the constitutional convention, but when it was, its purpose was limited to the control or abolition of state barriers to trade.[9] Madison in correspondence explicitly denied that the commerce power was "to be used for the positive purposes of the general government,"[10] but that is exactly what it has modernly become. At first, Supreme Court opinion remained reasonably faithful to the original understanding, invalidating federal regulation that addressed matters that preceded commerce, such as the manufacturing process.[11] In contrast, decisions within the last 50 years have authorized federal action whenever activities may in any way be said to "affect" interstate commerce. Thus, a farmer's production of wheat for home consumption, even though trivial in size and impact, could be prohibited because the aggregate or class of such activity might be deemed of national consequence.[12] From this, it was just a short step for the Court to accept the commerce power as the equivalent of a national police power to be used for regulation promoting any desired social policy whether the activity was commercial or not.

The judicial expansion of the commerce power to authorize virtually any federal restriction did not stop with the regulation of private citizens; it extended even to the states as entities. In *Garcia v. San Antonio Metropolitan Transit Authority*,[13] the Court denied that the tenth amendment placed any limit on the federal commerce power and upheld the congressional regulation of wages and hours of state employees. The states were told that if they didn't like it, they should write their congressman. In essence, states were relegated to the status of lobbyists seeking to influence federal legislation. Justice Sandra O'Connor, who had served on the Arizona appellate court before being appointed to the U.S. Supreme Court by President Reagan, said that after *Garcia* "all that stands between the remaining essentials of state sovereignty and Congress is the latter's underdeveloped capacity for self-restraint."[14]

The judicial expansion of the federal commerce power was probably enough to undo constitutional federalism. To worsen matters, the federal government occasionally bribes the states to forfeit their sovereign authority. Article I, section 8 of the Constitution authorizes Congress to "pay debts and provide for the common defence and general welfare." This spending power was construed throughout much of our history as simply empowering Congress to make expenditures to carry out its expressly delegated power. Again, toward the middle of this century, the Court concluded that Congress could make any expenditure limited only by the vague requirement that it be for the "general welfare."[15] With that expansive interpretation in hand, Congress proceeded to condition the receipt of federal funds by the states. At first, these conditions were limited to the purposes of the money, but now it is commonplace to find the imposition of unrelated conditions. Highway funds have been conditioned with prohibitions on political activity by state employees, education money is encumbered with affirmative action requirements, and public-works funding is conditioned on minority set-asides. All of this conditional funding has been upheld by the Court.[16]

Despite the strings, state officials seldom can afford to pass up federal money. Higher federal taxes have made it difficult for states to raise their own tax levies. More directly, refusing to accept a federal condition means a loss of money that was at least partially raised from a state's own citizens. Furthermore, for a state, as for the rest of us, it is always tempting to spend now, pay later. Money-in-hand for roads or schools or airports looks mighty tempting when local taxes do not immediately need to be raised for them.

One last judicial misadventure undermining federalism is the tendency of federal courts to find state laws to be impliedly preempted by federal statute. The concept of preemption is derived from the supremacy clause which provides that the Constitution and "[l]aws . . . made in pursuance thereof"[17] are the supreme or governing law of the land. Not surprisingly, the unwarranted judicial expansion of the commerce and spending powers has, in itself, increased the likelihood of conflict between federal and state law. This problem is magnified when the Court "finds" preemption even when Congress has not provided for it. Here, the Court is basing its opinion on slender inferences in the legislative record. Often this evidence is conflicting or ambiguous. Nevertheless, the Court has opined that preemption is appropriate where the federal law "touch[es] a field in which the federal interest is so dominant that the federal system [must] be assumed to preclude enforcement of state laws on the same subject."[18] As the federalism report observed, this "malleable" standard allows the Court "unilaterally to decide which 'federal interests' are so 'dominant' that *any* federal regulation of the same subject will preempt *all* state regulation."[19]

Redressing the Federalism Imbalance

The President and the Attorney General sought to redress the federalism imbalance by establishing a government-wide working group on federalism. Chuck Cooper was this working group's initial chairman, and I followed. Our instruction was to "develop 'a basic, administration-wide strategy' for ensuring that federal law and regulations are rooted in 'basic constitutional federalism principles.' "[20] The working group made recommendations for all branches of government.

To Congress, the working group urged that new legislation be assessed for its federalism impact and any effort to directly regulate the states in their own operations be avoided altogether. Beyond this, it was recommended that grant monies not be used to impose unrelated conditions on the states and any federal intent to preempt be stated explicitly. Relatedly, if Congress extended rule-making authority to federal agencies, it was counseled to generally not include the power to preempt state law by agency rule. To the federal courts, other recommendations were made. For example, it was suggested that diversity jurisdiction be limited and a greater exhaustion of state administrative and judicial remedies be required before federal litigation. In making these recommendations to the other branches, the working group, and chairman Cooper, knew they would likely be ignored. A big-spending Congress was fully comfortable dictating every last detail of state activity its unlimited source of money could buy. Prospects for reform of federal court jurisdiction were equally remote.

Greater receptivity was expected, and received, from the President. In April 1986, the President issued a statement of federalism principles to guide the Cabinet. One of these principles stated: "[i]n the absence of clear constitutional or statutory authority, the presumption of sovereignty should rest with the individual states. Uncertainties regarding the legitimate authority of the national government should be resolved against regulation at the national level."[21]

To make sure that the presumption in favor of federalism was given effect, the President issued an executive order in late October 1987. The order restated the federalism principles and directed executive departments and agencies to "closely examine the constitutional and statutory authority supporting any Federal action that would limit the policymaking discretion of the States, . . ."[22] Whenever possible, the President wanted his departments to "[r]efrain . . . from establishing uniform, national standards for programs. . . ."[23] In regulation and litigation, the executive departments were to avoid preemption, unless it was expressly provided by Congress or the exercise of state authority would directly conflict with federal law. Within each department a federalism official was to be appointed for the purpose of preparing federalism assessments to accompany executive proposals with "sufficient federalism implications."

Within the Washington special-interest establishment, the President's executive order was greeted complacently. However, lobbyists quickly grasped that the order might have a dramatic impact if it was taken seriously. When OMB started using the order to send regulations back to the drawing board, self-serving squeals started to be heard from every quarter used to employing federal regulation to raise the costs of a competitor or to disadvantage one region of the nation over another. To these special interests, the order was "self-censorship"; it was "assailed" for the possibility of regulations being more narrowly drafted.[24] This was just fine with state and local governments. A spokesman for local communities commented that "[r]ealistic regulations coming from Washington could save small governments thousands of dollars a year, in some cases as much as the community received from revenue sharing."[25]

FEDERALISM IS NOT NECESSARILY CONSERVATIVE

It is important to recognize that federalism is structural, not substantive. Allowing state and local governments to carry out their constitutional prerogatives also means affording them the freedom to enact policies that, from a conservative perspective, may be entirely wrongheaded. This was not hidden by the Attorney General. Speaking to the annual Conservative Political Action Conference, sponsored by several national conservative organizations, including *Human Events*, the Young Americans for Freedom and the *National Review*, Meese warned that federalism "will not please everyone. . . . [F]ederalism will give states the freedom to make choices with which we, as conservatives, may very well disagree."[26] Two of many issues that gave truth to the Attorney General's observation were state and local South African divestment statutes and California's costly food labeling requirements, known as "Proposition 65."

South African Divestment

The President was dead set against divestment as a means of ending the heinous practice of apartheid. He had no quarrel with penalizing South Africa in carefully selected ways to express our abhorrence of its codified system of racial segregation, but he could not understand how targeting the labor intensive industries upon which black South Africans relied for bare existence would help matters. In vetoing Congress' Comprehensive Anti-Apartheid Act of 1986, President Reagan asked:

> Are we truly helping the black people of South Africa—the lifelong victims of apartheid—when we throw them out of work and leave them and their families jobless and hungry in those segregated townships? Or are we simply assuming a moral posture at the expense of the people in whose name we presume to act?[27]

Congress voted overwhelmingly to override the President's veto. Tip O'Neill, the Speaker of the House, told the President that he was "disappointed that you continue to give credence to the last-ditch argument of the South African government that economic sanctions will, in the words of its ambassador, 'do serious and long-term damage to those it seeks to help.' It is ludicrous for the defenders of apartheid to use the victims themselves as their final shield against international sanctions."[28] In retrospect, now that apartheid has been seemingly abolished by the South African government, the congressional policy course to ban imports of South African iron, steel, uranium, coal, sugar, and other agricultural products as well as textiles appears to have been vindicated by subsequent world events. Yet, who is to say what the sanctions meant in the individual lives of the 23,000 black farm laborers during the period the sanctions were in effect. The question of individual sacrifice for the greater good is as old as history and philosophy itself. Having this individual sacrifice imposed through the sanctions of an affluent nation surely compounds the moral difficulty.

Some 20 states and over 100 municipalities separately resolved this difficult philosophical question against the President and in accordance with the general prosanctions view of the Congress. However, the approach the state and local governments took did not always coincide with the substantive course that Congress set for itself. While Congress banned imports, new investment, and landing rights, states and localities most frequently required the divestment of their employee pension funds from companies doing business with South Africa or prohibited a city or state from entering into contracts with companies having investments, licenses, or operations in South Africa. As a policy matter, the President was no more supportive of these state initiatives than he was of the sanctions enacted by Congress. However, just as Attorney General Meese had cautioned, there would be times when the states would enact policies with which we didn't agree. If federalism was to mean anything, it could not be a doctrine of mere convenience.

Despite the President's disposition toward federalism, a number of Justice Department and administration officials argued strenuously that this was an occasion to displace the states. Since 1985, the State Department had been arguing that state divestment laws interfered with the execution of foreign policy committed to the President. In addition, these measures were thought to impede foreign commerce, another matter within the exclusive preserve of the federal government. Abraham Sofaer, the legal advisor to the State Department, reminded us that it was the policy of the Administration to encourage U.S. firms to use their influence to promote change in South Africa and to remain in that country. Because the state and local measures are designed primarily to discourage U.S. firms from conducting business in South Africa, Sofaer argued, these actions directly conflict with U.S. foreign objectives.

Richard Willard, the head of the civil division, agreed with Sofaer and felt strongly that the United States ought to challenge these state and local laws. Willard was less troubled by the judicially created federalism imbalance than either Chuck Cooper or myself. As one of the Department's chief litigators, Willard's perspective was more congenial to accepting the law as he found it. If the Court had read federalism out of the Constitution, so be it; that could be put to good use in cases where we opposed state policy. In this regard, Willard had been separately urging, also over our federalism objections, that the federal government preempt local tort laws that allow for no-fault recoveries and excessive awards of punitive damages. Willard made three arguments against state and local divestment laws: they intrude into the exclusively federal responsibility for the conduct of foreign policy; they improperly burden foreign commerce; and they are federally preempted. These were substantial arguments. Close analysis suggested to OLC, however, that they were not dispositive.

It is true that the Constitution can be reasonably read as making foreign affairs the exclusive preserve of the federal government. In *The Federalist*, James Madison observes that "[i]f we are to be one nation in any respect, it clearly ought to be in respect to other nations."[29] Moreover, the Supreme Court has stated that "the President alone has the power to speak or listen as a representative of the nation.... [He exercises] the very delicate, plenary and exclusive power... as the sole organ of the federal government in the field of international relations...."[30] If this weren't clear enough, the Constitution provides that "[n]o state shall enter into any treaty, alliance, or confederation...."[31]

Yet, only once has the Court invalidated a state statute based on the federal government's foreign affairs authority. In *Zschernig v. Miller*,[32] the Court invalidated an Oregon probate statute that precluded nonresident aliens from inheriting property in the United States unless the reciprocal courtesy was extended to Americans in the alien's country. *Zschernig* was a different case than South African divestment, however. So far as the Court was concerned, the flaw in *Zschernig* was the fact that the state courts made persistent inquiries into the actual administration of foreign laws and in so doing questioned the veracity of foreign officials. The Court stated: "As one reads the Oregon decisions, it seems that foreign policy attitudes, the freezing or thawing of the 'cold war' and the like are the real desiderata."[33] In the case of South African divestment, no state official was conducting investigations or making assessments of foreign officials. In point of fact, the burden of these statutes fell on U.S. firms, and only indirectly on South Africa. In this, the divestment statutes were more like the California probate statute upheld in *Clark v. Allen*,[34] which also required the reciprocity of a foreign nation, but without any disparaging inquiries into a foreign nation's administration of their laws.

The probate reciprocity cases in themselves also differed from divestment statutes in another critical way. No state is required to adopt probate reciprocity, but states must decide where to invest state funds. As we pointed out, a state might decline to invest in a firm doing business in South Africa because there was a risk of revolution, and that decision would have the identical impact on South Africa as a decision premised on the moral opposition inherent in a divestment statute. It could not be tenably argued that states were constitutionally forbidden from making their own investment decisions.

As to foreign commerce, Willard admitted that his argument was premised on more unsettled terrain. Nevertheless, he argued that divestment statutes constitute a direct burden on foreign commerce by creating distinct disincentives, if not outright prohibitions, against investment in firms doing business in South Africa. Moreover, he posited that there were no strong local interests that could justify such burdens. Willard did concede that the Supreme Court in domestic commerce cases had applied a different standard where the state was acting as a market participant, rather than a regulator, but he did not believe this exception would apply with full force in the foreign commerce context.

In direct opposition to Willard, OLC relied on the market participant exception. This exception simply acknowledged that "[n]othing in the purposes animating the Commerce Clause prohibits a state, in the absence of congressional action, from participating in the market and exercising its right to favor its own citizens over others."[35] In this, the Court likened a state making investment decisions to any other private party, who, of course, had complete freedom to decide with whom to deal.[36]

Under a divestment statute, the state was declining as an investor to deal with certain firms; it was not using its sovereign power to compel those firms, however, not to deal with South Africa.

Willard suggested that, even were it applicable, the market participant exception had been recently narrowed by the Court's decision in *Wisconsin Department of Industry, Labor and Human Relations v. Gould.*[37] There the Court held that a federal labor statute precluded Wisconsin from announcing that it would refuse to deal with persons or firms that had violated labor law three times in a five year period. *Gould's* merits can be disputed, but more importantly, we pointed out that its holding was inapposite to a state divestment statute unless it was preempted by federal law. As the Court noted in *Gould*, "what the Commerce Clause would permit States to do in the absence of [the federal labor law] is thus an entirely different question from what the States may do with the Act in place, . . ."[38]

The final argument made by Richard Willard was preemption. At first, Willard premised his argument on the Export Administration Act[39] or the President's executive order that, even prior to Congress' Anti-Apartheid Act, had imposed selective sanctions on South Africa.[40] These were clearly insufficient. If original understanding was to be our guide, when a state is acting in an area that historically has been the province of state decision, a Court should not find preemption absent the "clear and manifest" intent of Congress.[41] The Export Act permits the President to control exports for reasons of national security, foreign policy, and short supply. It has nothing whatsoever to do with the proprietary decisions of the states, or for that matter, even private parties. The executive order was an even weaker basis for preemption, insofar as it required firms doing business in South Africa to abide by the so-called Sullivan principles, which precluded racial decision making. The order could not be construed to require firms to do any business in South Africa, nor could the order be said to require states or individuals to invest, or stay invested, in firms that do.

The passage of the Anti-Apartheid Act, however, was argued to preempt. This position was pressed by Secretary of State George Shultz directly on the Attorney General. Shultz was frustrated by the fact that, despite his entreaties, Justice had not intervened in a single case to challenge the state and local measures. Justice, of course, was divided on the issue with Willard urging intervention, and OLC taking the position that while we don't like the states' policies, it is their decision to make. Nothing in the text, structure, or legislative history of the Anti-Apartheid Act convinced us to change this posture. As mentioned earlier, the Act basically prevented private parties from importing certain goods from South Africa, buying Kruggerands, or arranging direct airline flights. There was nothing in the Act precluding private parties from doing more, that is, disinvesting altogether. Thus, there was no basis from which to infer that states could not similarly disinvest their own resources.

One provision of the Act, section 606, did deal explicitly with state and local divestment laws. This section addressed the issue of whether *federal* funds could be cut off from a state or local government that implemented its divestment statute. In one New York matter, OLC had advised the Secretary of Transportation that he was obligated by law to withhold federal highway funds when New York City applied its local divestment statute to undermine competitive bidding. Bidders who engaged in business with South Africa had been excluded. This OLC ruling prompted Senator D'Amato to introduce section 606 to suspend the legal obligation of the Transportation Secretary or other federal officials to reduce or deny federal funds in such circumstances for 90 days. D'Amato had tried unsuccessfully to preclude the denial of federal funds permanently on account of state or local divestment laws. Neither of D'Amato's efforts, however, stated or implied that Congress was preempting state and local divestment statutes as they applied to *state*, as opposed to *federal*, funds. Indeed, the very fact that Congress passed D'Amato's more limited amendment demonstrated that it was aware of state and local divestment statutes and had chosen not to broadly preempt.

Senator Lugar was perhaps the strongest advocate for preemption on the Senate floor, but even he did not affirmatively argue that the Act accomplished this. When Senator Pell of Rhode Island pointed out to the Indiana senator that Pell's state had made the decision to divest from its public portfolio securities of companies which continued to do business with South Africa, Senator Lugar declined to opine that such state action was precluded by the Act. Lugar stated only: "I think the answer to his question is that Rhode Island might be able to continue enforcing its law and it might not be able to continue. That would be up to a court to decide and would be an interesting case."[42]

OLC had thus answered Willard's arguments to displace state authority. That our legal answer was directly contrary to the President's policy is a tribute to both OLC's integrity generally and the strength of its commitment to federalism. That the President and the Attorney General never sought to set aside OLC's legal decision on policy grounds is a profound tribute to them personally.

The Department advised the Secretary of State that it did not believe any of the pending cases were appropriate for intervention. In particular, the Department declined to enter a Baltimore case in which the city had mandated that its pension system divest from banks or companies doing business "in or with" South Africa. Maryland's highest court upheld the validity of those ordinances unanimously, against the same foreign affairs, commerce, and preemption arguments that OLC had rejected internally.[43] The U.S. Supreme Court denied further review.[44]

Taking Federalism (Too) Seriously?

Staying the federal preemptive hand against state and local South African divestment laws was a test of principle. But a more difficult one lay ahead. In November 1986, California voters approved an initiative known as Proposition 65, imposing warning requirements on any product—produce, processed food, cosmetics, drugs, etc.—that contained carcinogenic or reproductively toxic substances above a "no significant risk level." At first, the Governor of California listed only 29 chemicals requiring warnings, but the list soon grew to include widely available substances, such as formaldehyde, alcohol, and lead. The burden for compliance with Proposition 65 fell on the manufacturer, not the retailer. Compliance could be achieved through a variety of means, including product labels, cash register receipts, shelf labeling, signs, or combinations of these methods.

As reasonable sounding as any health measure could be, Proposition 65 had a number of serious policy difficulties. First, "no significant risk" was defined at a very low level, thereby insuring that many products commonly assumed to be without risk would need warning labels. Second, California was unlikely to be the only state interested in a warning label requirement. If more states followed California's lead, there might quickly be a crazy-quilt of regulations, not only confusing consumers, but also jeopardizing their health to the extent that consumers then refrained from the use of needed products or medicines. Health might also be jeopardized if consumers focused on insignificant state information to the exclusion of information that federal health officials felt was especially important. Third, Proposition 65 was potentially very costly. It meant a separate distribution system for products headed for California, and even then, if a Nevada bottle of aspirin found its way across the desert, that in itself might lead to manufacturer liability.

These were not insignificant concerns. Indeed, were I a policy maker, I would find them dispositive against the wisdom of Proposition 65. Perhaps because of these problems, the Governor of California issued an interim exemption from the state labeling requirements for foods, drugs, cosmetics, and medical devices regulated by the federal Food and Drug Administration (FDA). This exemption, however, did not keep the National Food Processors Association and an army of business lobbyists from trying to convince the FDA, and any one else that touched the issue, that federal preemption of Proposition 65 was warranted now and forever.

The lobbying associated with Proposition 65 was the most intense I witnessed during my federal service. Since OLC's function is to provide legal counsel to the Attorney General and executive agencies, it was the long-standing tradition of the office not to meet with outside interests. We were not policy makers, but lawyers. We would either do our own legal research or consult the research of one of our "client" agencies. Because OLC is both an advisor, and, by executive order, the final arbiter of legal disputes within the executive branch, I felt it was extremely important for the integrity of our decision-making process to be maintained. Private fortunes may be won or lost on OLC's interpretations of law, and under no circumstances, did I want to subject myself or my lawyers to outside pressure. Nor did I wish to create even the remotest appearance that private, expensive lawyering or "connections" at the White House could influence our legal thinking.

Proposition 65 did occasion calls to my office from the manufacturing and industry concerns. As best I could, I tried to have Lawan Robinson, the most savvy and efficient secretarial assistant any lawyer could ever ask for, deflect these calls to the policy arms of the Department, or elsewhere in the administration. This would have normally included the Office of Legal Policy (OLP) or Brad Reynolds, the counselor and gatekeeper to the Attorney General. Brad immediately informed me that he had some personal financial interests in food companies, and thus, as a matter of ethics, he had to recuse himself from the entire issue. The issue did not attract OLP, and thus, the hordes of well-paid industry spokesmen were deflected outside the Department of Justice. This did not make them happy. After all, wasn't Ronald Reagan *their* President?

Enter federalism. The President's executive order directed all federal agencies to construe a federal statute to preempt state law "only when the statute contains an express preemption provision."[45] Could this be said of Proposition 65? Generally no. Except for the express preemption in several poultry and meat inspection acts administered by the Department of Agriculture, there were no explicit prohibitions of state labeling requirements. This meant that if the industry demand for preemption was to be satisfied under the President's executive order, there would have to be "firm and palpable evidence compelling the conclusion that . . . the exercise of State authority directly conflicts with the exercise of Federal authority under the Federal statute."[46] But there was no present conflict. California was enforcing Proposition 65 in virtually all respects in conformity with FDA policy. In fact, there was very little FDA policy on labeling, since the FDA had only selectively required warning labels in the past. It could not be meaningfully argued that it was impossible to comply with both federal and state law, since, as presently administered, it was either the same, or, in a few instances dealing with reproductive toxicity, the state was more strict. Moreover, unless the FDA was prepared to announce a general, regulatory policy against all state warnings except those authorized by it (an announcement that, itself, would have cut deeply against the grain of the federalism executive order), Proposition 65 was not standing as an obstacle to the accomplishment of any federal purpose.

You can bet that the business-types did not like this message either. In fact, their public commentary suggests that they viewed OLC as "federalism aliens," infected by a decidedly impractical constitutional disease. A representative for the food processors lamented: "[w]e've tried to point out to them what Proposition 65 means: 'Do you realize this was pushed by [state Assemblyman] Tom Hayden [and] and NRDC [Natural Resources Defense Council Inc.]?' . . . But the more conservative elements in the Reagan Administration have said to us, 'If that's what the voters of California want to do, let them do it.' And that comports with their federalism philosophy. I think it shows why federalism as subscribed to in this Administration can't be a purist sort of philosophy."[47] Here, again, however, the Attorney General's caution against thinking of federalism as a doctrine of convenience seemed to OLC to be a wholly sufficient rebuttal.

In late July 1988, the Attorney General asked me to outline the situation for him in writing in preparation for a Domestic Policy Council (DPC) meeting that would take up the issue. I did, and I recommended that the FDA open an informational rule-making proceeding to gather information and comments on California's administration of Proposition 65. Only at such time as subsequent developments put the state administration of its warning label statute in conflict with federal objectives, should the FDA specifically preempt Proposition 65. This moderate "wait and see" course, I reasoned, best coincided with the President's admonition against sweeping preemptive federal action under broad rule-making authority. In his executive order, the President instructed that preemptive rules should be, issued when such preemptive regulatory authority was authorized by Congress, and then, only after consultations had been undertaken with state officials to avoid the conflict altogether. If the conflict could not be avoided, the President's unequivocal direction was that "[a]ny regulatory preemption of State law shall be restricted to the minimum level necessary to achieve the objectives of the statute. . . ."[48]

Riding over to the White House with the Attorney General, it was clear to me that Meese thought the policy underlying Proposition 65 was unwise. The possible commerce and health implications of divergent warning label requirements made no more sense to him than to me. Yet, he shared the President's commitment to federalism. After all, Ed Meese had once been Ronald Reagan's chief of staff in the administration of the California government. He knew the importance of leaving states free to experiment with different regulatory courses. Some state courses would fail, but, as the framers saw it, this was the advantage of federalism: at least the failure would not then be national. And where states succeeded, of course, the federal government could then base any need for national action on the best of the state models.

Nevertheless, I confirmed for the Attorney General that, absent the President's executive order, the FDA had ample regulatory authority immediately to preempt Proposition 65 specifically, or all state warning label requirements if that was the course the DPC wanted to pursue. Given the potential breadth of FDA's general authority, preemption could be pursued even absent a present conflict between federal and state law. However, respecting the President's federalism executive order, it was my view that any FDA regulatory preemption should be deferred until the federal-state conflict could be demonstrated, and then, preemption ought to be limited to California's actions, not to the states generally.

At the DPC meeting, the Attorney General asked me to outline the federalism principles and the possible legal bases for preemption. While the press reported that Agriculture Secretary Dick Lyng and the Attorney General supported preemption, and HHS Secretary Otis Bowen (a former governor and medical doctor) opposed, my recollection is somewhat different. I recall Meese's role strictly as a facilitator of discussion. As DPC chairman, Meese wanted both sides heard fully. Perhaps the public perception of his role was confused because he, like I, was of two minds on the subject, with the legal and policy perspectives being in sharp disagreement. In any event, the DPC as a body did not recommend an immediate, wholesale regulatory preemption or even the specific preemption of Proposition 65. Instead, it created a working group to identify any conflicts between state laws and federal programs that might warrant preemption.

Dr. Frank Young, the head of the FDA, was the chairman of this working group. Young narrowed the DPC's charge to a consideration of "possible conflicts posed by California's implementation of Proposition 65." In so doing, Young knocked off the table, perhaps inadvertently, what industry most wanted: one, national, uniform rule on labeling. In advising Young's working group, I again noted—as I had for the Attorney General and the DPC—that the FDA had authority to preempt all state warning laws or specifically Proposition 65; however, to be consistent with the President's federalism executive order, any preemption effort should await "firm and palpable evidence" of federal-state conflict. Tom Moore, a member of the President's Council of Economic Advisors, was commissioned to study the cost impact of Proposition 65. He did, and in early December 1988, he recommended that the federal government reject the preemption pleas of the food manufacturers and other industry groups. As of that time, Moore concluded, the cost of Proposition 65 to the manufacturers had not been excessive.

None of this was playing very well with the industry lobbyists who were becoming more and more shrill. Nevertheless, given my legal advice and Moore's economic analysis, it seemed that no regulatory preemption would be forthcoming in the final days of the Reagan administration. But industry was not to be counted out yet. With the "kinder, gentler," even "environmental" President Bush coming up next, there was a definite sense of urgency. All stops were to be pulled to get the outgoing Reagan administration to preempt. One opponent of preemption noted, "[s]omeone who does not have George Bush's best interests at heart has been trying to set him up. The strategy is to get the Reagan Administration to act at the last minute and leave an enormous controversy for the Bush Administration as it comes in the door."[49]

Despite the findings and apparent course against preemption set by Frank Young's working group as a whole, Don Pearlman, an aggressive pro-preemption assistant to Interior Secretary Hodel, managed to get the assignment to formalize options from the working group for the next meeting of DPC. When Paul Colborn of my staff and I arrived at one of Pearlman's drafting sessions, it was very clear that Pearlman was pushing for the immediate, total preemption option. When I commented that such would be contrary to the President's executive order and the very findings of Young's working group that had asked him to "formalize, not reformulate" its recommendations, Pearlman seemed unfazed. As the discussion continued, I again observed that the total preemption option he was advocating was contrary to President Reagan's legal direction in the executive order. That may be, I was told, but such obstacles won't trouble the next administration's legal counsel. I was beginning to get the picture. In any event, I had to rush off to another meeting back at the Department, so I left Paul Colborn to guard our apparently waning federalism interests.

When Colborn returned to the Department, we were both troubled by the abrupt change in course Pearlman seemed to be engineering, and we decided to briefly restate the legal ground for Nancy Risque, the presidential assistant, who kept working groups on their assigned course. Doing this made me an even larger target for industry lobbyists who were now frantically watching the Reagan clock wind down. Treating the President's executive order as a matter of law, not policy, I stated that preemption was more a "legal than policy matter." Putting it in these terms reflected a definite OLC perspective; namely, that when the President gives direction by executive order, it is not just something to accommodate if possible, it is a direction backed by all the force of the Constitution's blunt instruction to the President to "take care that the laws be faithfully executed." I acknowledged that the FDA had statutory authority to establish a general, nationwide rule, but as a matter of law—the law of the executive order—the FDA had been directed not to exercise the full extent of that federal power.

It was a distinction lost on Don Pearlman, who had Secretary Hodel write a letter to new Attorney General Thornburgh complaining that my legal interpretation was obstructing the policy choice in favor of total preemption. Hodel had been forum shopping, and he stated in his letter that he knew other lawyers in the administration who disagreed with my interpretation. That was hardly surprising. I am sure there were some lawyers who disagreed in good faith, and some who disagreed because they understood executive orders as nothing more than remote, obscure pronouncements by the same fella who chats with us on the radio every Saturday.

I didn't have a clue what Thornburgh's views were on this subject. We hadn't had a morning senior staff meeting virtually since his arrival. Thus, my only real means of keeping him abreast of the large, ever-changing OLC docket, were my weekly written reports of incoming and completed matters. In this Howard Hughes-like environment, I increasingly annotated these reports as at least a poor substitute for direct communication. What Thornburgh did with these, if he even received them, I do not know. I do not recall ever getting a note back about them of any type, whether "nice work" or "stupid moron, where did you go to law school?" In any event, while I would have welcomed hearing from the Attorney General on almost anything, on this particular matter that was not true. As the Attorney General's in-house ethics advisor, I knew he had financial interests in food companies, and therefore, without an ethics waiver from the counsel to the President, he could not participate in public decisions that might affect these companies or their financial well-being.

Hodel's letter did trigger a call from one of Thornburgh's guarding Pennsylvanians, Robin Ross. Ross informed me that he was one of the Administration lawyers who disagreed with my preemption analysis. Apparently, Ross was guided in this by a Covington and Burling legal opinion prepared for the H. J. Heinz Company of Pittsburgh (where else?). Ross sent me Covington's memorandum complete with the Heinz cover letter stating that it refuted Justice's assertion that FDA preemption must be state specific. That was an easy refutation since OLC never made that claim. FDA's Frank Young had administratively set the working group on the course of looking for the specific conflicts between California's Proposition 65 and federal law. OLC was not about to object to Dr. Young's narrow focus, as it was entirely consistent with the President's federalism direction. Nevertheless, to Covington and Burling,

Heinz, and, I assume, Ross as well, the President's executive order, and OLC's legal analysis written in light of it, represented nothing more than a political or philosophical view of federal-state relations. Again, I took the federalism executive order more seriously.

I reminded Ross that the Attorney General, and any one else on the Attorney General's staff with a financial conflict, could not participate in this because of the ethics laws. Shortly thereafter, I received a copy of Deputy Attorney General Harold Christensen's response to Hodel. The Deputy pointed out to Secretary Hodel that the OLC memorandum had aimed its analysis toward finding an actual conflict between Proposition 65 and federal law because this was the explicit charge of the working group. If the working group wished to depart from those instructions to now consider the total preemption of all state laws dealing with warning labels, that was a decision for the Department of Health and Human Services, Christensen wrote, not the Department of Justice.

Again, on the strength of the executive order, I might have quibbled with the Deputy's lateral to HHS, but frankly, I knew one more volley would just be undone by another of Heinz's 57 varieties. OLC's position was clear, and I suspect for that reason, I did not have anything further to do with Proposition 65. A week or so later, Paul Colborn pointed out that the FDA had submitted draft regulations to immediately, without notice and comment or a factual record of conflict, preempt Proposition 65. In addition, the draft regulatory proposal set out for notice and comment a proposed rule to preempt *all* state and local requirements that were "in addition to, or different from, FDA requirements." This is exactly what the industry wanted, and it makes tremendous sense as a policy matter. However, having taken the President's federalism direction seriously—some would say too seriously—I could not faithfully say that the proposed regulatory course was an implementation of the law consistent with the President's constitutional duty as he saw it.

The inauguration came and went. The environmental President was now in office. William Reilly, Bush's EPA chief, examined Proposition 65 and concluded that "[t]he law simply warns people about their exposure to carcinogenic or reproductively toxic chemicals at levels exceeding 'no significant risk.' It is hard to argue with providing information to the public."[50] The FDA's draft regulations were left on the desk of OMB's Jay Plager, one of the few Reagan holdovers who successfully made the transition to the Bush administration. That's where they remained. Plager stated that unless there was a significant change in California's implementation of Proposition 65 that "substantially implicates important federal interests, no federal preemptive action—either by regulation or otherwise—is warranted."[51]

I couldn't have said it better myself.

NOTES

1. Wash. Post, Jan. 21, 1981, at A1 (President Reagan's inaugural address).
2. *The Federalist No.* 39, at 246 (C. Rossiter ed. 1961).
3. *Id.* at 245.
4. Letters of Agrippa, *reprinted in* B. Schwartz, *The Bill of Rights: A Documentary History*, 510–11 (1971).
5. Working Group on Federalism of the Domestic Policy Counsel, *The Status of Federalism in America*, (Nov. 1986) [hereinafter Federalism Report].
6. U.S. Const. art. I, § 8.
7. *McCulloch v. Maryland*, 17 U.S. (4 Wheat.) 316 (1819).
8. G. Gunther, *Constitutional Law* 79 (quoting Jefferson) (12th ed. 1991).
9. *See generally*, Abel, *The Commerce Clause in the Constitutional Convention and in Contemporary Comment*, 25 Minn. L. Rev. 432, 470 (1941).
10. 3 Farrand, *The Records of the Federal Convention of 1787* 478 (letter of February 13, 1829, from James Madison to J. C. Cabell).
11. *See, e.g., U.S. v. E. C. Knight Co.*, 156 U.S. 1 (1895); *Carter v. Carter Coal Co.*, 298 U.S. 238 (1936).
12. *Wickard v. Filburn*, 317 U.S. 111 (1942).
13. 469 U.S. 528 (1985).
14. *Id.* at 588 (O'Connor, J., dissenting).
15. *U.S. v. Butler*, 297 U.S. 1, 65–66 (1936).
16. *Steward Machine Co. v. Davis*, 301 U.S. 548 (1937); *South Dakota v. Dole*, 483 U.S. 203 (1987).
17. U.S. Const. art. VI.
18. *Rice v. Santa Fe Elevator Corp.*, 331 U.S. 218, 230 (1947), quoted with approval in *Hillsborough County, Fla. v. Automated Medical Laboratories, Inc.*, 471 U.S. 707, 713 (1985).
19. Federalism Report, *supra* note 5, at 41.
20. *Id.* at prefatory note.
21. Bureau of National Affairs, *Federal Contracts Report* 1058 (1986).
22. Exec. Order No. 12, 612, Sec. 3(a), 52 Fed. Reg. 41685 (1987).
23. *Id.* at sec. 3(d)(2).
24. Kornhauser, *The Public Interest*, Legal Times, Jan. 11, 1988, at 10 (quoting Shannon Ferguson of "OMB Watch").
25. Moore, *Federalism Renewed, with Reservations*, 20 Nat'l J. 274, Jan. 30, 1988 (quoting Jeffrey H. Schiff, executive director of the National Association of Towns and Townships).
26. McCaslin, *Meese: Give Power Back to the States*, Wash. Times, Jan. 31, 1986, at 2A.
27. Veto Message for the Comprehensive Anti-Apartheid Act of 1986 (Sept. 26, 1986).
28. *House Votes to Override Veto of Sanctions Despite Reagan Offer of New Executive Order*, 3 Int'l Trade Rep. (BNA) 1180 (Oct. 1, 1986).
29. *The Federalist No.* 42, (C. Rossiter ed. 1961).
30. *U.S. v. Curtiss-Wright Corp.*, 299 U.S. 304, 319–320 (1936).
31. U.S. Const., art. I, § 10.

32. 389 U.S. 429 (1968).
33. *Id.* at 437.
34. 331 U.S. 503 (1947).
35. *Hughes v. Alexandria Scrap Corp.*, 426 U.S. 794 (1976).
36. *See Reeves v. Stake*, 447 U.S. 429, 438–39 (1980) (upholding South Dakota's right to restrict the sale of state-produced cement to state residents).
37. 475 U.S. 282 (1986).
38. *Id.* at 290.
39. 50 U.S.C. App. 2401 *et. seq.* (1991).
40. Exec. Order No. 12,532, 50 Fed. Reg. 36861 (1985).
41. *Rice v. Santa Fe Elevator Corp.*, 331 U.S. 218, 230 (1947).
42. *See* 132 *Cong. Rec.* S11817 (Aug. 15, 1986) (remarks of Senator Lugar).
43. *Board of Trustees of the Employees Retirement System of the City of Baltimore v. Mayor and City Council of Baltimore City*, 317 Md. 72, 562 A.2d 720 (1989).
44. 110 S. Ct. 1167 (1989).
45. Exec. Order No. 12,612, sec. 4(a), Fed. Reg. 41685 (1987).
46. *Id.*
47. *Drawing Fine Lines Over Preemption*, 20 Nat'l J. 1790, July 9, 1988 (quoting Mr. Graham of the National Food Processors Association).
48. Exec. Order No. 12,612, sec. 4(c), 52 Fed. Reg. 41685 (1987).
49. Savage and Paddock, *Reagan Aides Consider Move to Preempt State on Toxic Rules*, L.A. Times, Jan. 14, 1989, at 28, col. 1 (quoting David Roe, an attorney with the Environmental Defense Fund and a principal author of Proposition 65).
50. Gatty, *OMB Says Federal Preemption of Proposition 65 is Nixed for Now*, Prepared Foods, Aug. 1989, at 22.
51. *Id.*

7

Peace: The Color-blind Society

If there is a higher law background to our Constitution, as I have argued there surely is, there can be no principled distinction among persons on the basis of skin color. Since all persons of whatever race are endowed by their Creator with unalienable rights, nothing could be clearer. Yet, this straightforward proposition has been the source of continued strife in our nation's history.

At first, the expediency of forming a nation left the slavery question unresolved. It may well be that no single sovereign country would have emerged had the slavery question not been set aside, but the price of hiding the moral issue was the deadliest war in our history. As the Civil War subsided, the thirteenth, fourteenth, and fifteenth amendments sought to explicitly rectify the harm of creating two classes of persons. The thirteenth amendment abolished slavery, the fifteenth secured voting rights, and the fourteenth amendment grandly proclaimed that no state "shall deny to any person within its jurisdiction the equal protection of the laws." No sooner had the words been written, however, than a new issue arose. To what extent could race be used not to harm, but to help, an individual? Disagreement over this notion of benevolent or benign racial classifications, or what is modernly referred to as affirmative action, continues to this day.

THE CIVIL RIGHTS DIVISION

Matters of civil rights are delegated by statute and the Attorney General to the head of the civil rights division, a division staffed by close to two hundred lawyers. In this sense, the Office of Legal Counsel was not formally charged with litigating, or necessarily, even giving advice on civil rights issues. However, many civil rights conflicts would implicate constitutional questions, especially the equal protection guarantee of the fourteenth amendment. Thus, there was a formal overlap between the work of civil rights and OLC.

This formal confluence of interests was more noticeable during the tenure of Attorney General Meese because of the very close personal friendship between the head of the civil rights division, William Bradford Reynolds, and two former civil rights deputies, Charles Cooper and Michael Carvin, who played important roles within OLC during the Meese years. Preceding my tenure as OLC head, Cooper would disappear almost every evening about 5:00 PM to run on the mall with Reynolds before both would return to their respective offices frequently to work well into the night. As the two men briskly made their way by the Smithsonian, the issues and conflicts of the day would get a thorough review. Very often, the two would consult on strategy for advancing administration policy through the arguments being made in litigation not just by the civil rights division, but by the entire department. Reynolds was Meese's chair of the litigation strategy group, and he made effective use of that designation to keep tabs on the general direction of the Department.

William Bradford Reynolds

Brad Reynolds first came to Justice in the 1970s working as an assistant to Solicitor General Erwin Griswold, and then, Robert Bork. Working for the Solicitor General as an assistant means relatively low pay and long hours, but it also means having the privilege of arguing before the U.S. Supreme Court, a rare opportunity available to only a few lawyers during their careers. Reynolds well deserved this honor. A high-ranking graduate of the Vanderbilt Law School, he spent his early years as an attorney at New York's Sullivan and Cromwell, a prestigious law firm not known for coddling its young associate attorneys.

Reynolds left Justice before Nixon's firing of Watergate prosecutor Archibald Cox via Bork, becoming a partner specializing in antitrust and commercial litigation in a Washington, D.C., law firm. In 1977, Reynolds was invited back to Justice by Griffen Bell to possibly head the antitrust division. While admiring Bell, Reynolds was unsure of his "comfort level" with the Carter administration generally, and he declined. The election of Ronald Reagan removed any discomfort, and at the invitation of William French Smith, he became the head of the civil rights division in 1981.

Bob Jones: An Opening Misstep

Early on, Reynolds became ensnared by a controversy that looks greatly different from public and legal perspectives. Bob Jones University is a fundamentalist Christian school in Greenville, South Carolina. In 1970, the IRS revoked the school's tax-exempt status, the university paid taxes, and then sued for a refund. Bob Jones did not discriminate on the basis of race in admissions, but based on its interpretation of the Bible, forbade interracial dating and marriage. Arguing that the IRS' action was both unauthorized by statute and a transgression of its free exercise of religion, the university initially won in federal district court, but the decision was reversed on appeal. The Supreme Court then granted review.

Operating from a narrowly focused, legal perspective, Reynolds thought the IRS action needed to be checked to prevent federal bureaucracies from making decisions not authorized by statute. Section 501(c)(3) of the tax code plainly provided for tax-exempt status to a university organized on a nonprofit basis and uninvolved in lobbying activities or political campaigns. Bob Jones met these criteria. Nevertheless, because of the school's limitations on interracial marriage and dating—whether or not religiously inspired—the IRS decided that Bob Jones was not operating consistently with the common law definition of a charity. Simply stated, the university's actions were termed contrary to "public policy." Yet, this IRS position had not been statutorily sanctioned by Congress. Indeed, in the midst of the controversy, then Congressman (now Senator) Grassley observed that "[n]obody argues that racial discrimination should receive preferred tax status in the United States. However, the IRS should not be making these decisions on the agency's own discretion. Congress should make these decisions."[1]

It is undoubtedly important to keep any federal agency, perhaps especially the IRS, within statutory bounds, but *Bob Jones* was the wrong case in which to make the point. As it turned out, the subtleties of executive and legislative supervision of administrative agencies were entirely, and properly, swamped by the more profound abhorrence for racial decisions. Even the religious genesis of Bob Jones' race-based policy could not change the "atmospherics" of the case. After all, Bob Jones, and similarly situated institutions,[2] were not being *prohibited* from exercising their religious beliefs, the express concern of the first amendment, they were only being denied the economic benefit of a tax-exemption for them. Reynolds lost *Bob Jones* badly before the Court.[3] The arguments he advanced were not wrong in isolation, but in context, they clouded his sounder inclinations in support of a color-blind Constitution. Perhaps, most regrettably, *Bob Jones* disfigured the public's perception of Reynolds' genuine and sincere commitment to eliminating society's immoral reliance upon race in schooling, employment, and housing in the years to come.

Race and Original Intent

Some 30 years after the passage of the equal protection guarantee in the fourteenth amendment, the Supreme Court decided *Plessy v. Ferguson*,[4] upholding a state law requiring "separate but equal" railway accommodations on the basis of race. In a vigorous dissent, the senior Justice Harlan wrote: "But in the view of the Constitution, in the eye of the law, there is in this country no superior, dominant, ruling class of citizens. There is no caste here. Our Constitution is color-blind, and neither knows nor tolerates classes among citizens." Eighty years later, Thurgood Marshall, the Court's first black Justice in its history, would dispute Harlan's claim to support a race-conscious admissions policy at a public university. Marshall wrote: "[Had] the Court been willing in 1896, in [*Plessy*], to hold that [equal protection] forbids differences in treatment based on race, we would not be faced with this dilemma in 1978. We must remember, however, that the principle that the 'Constitution is color-blind' appeared only in the opinion of the lone dissenter."[5]

The Harlan-Marshall quotations frame the historical debate of the original intent of the fourteenth amendment. What did the amendment mean by "equality"? Were white persons, as well as black, thought to be within the scope of the equal protection guarantee, and if so, did the drafters and ratifiers of the amendment ever contemplate that long-term programs of special treatment in favor of one race would be constitutional?

In terms of equality, the drafters of the amendment understood that the law could create conditions of equality of opportunity, but not result. For example, Congressman Butler, the chairman of the House Judiciary Committee, a few years after the amendment's ratification, explained the meaning of equality in reference to the similar principle in the Declaration of Independence. Butler stated:

> I believe that "equal" in the Declaration of Independence is a political word, used in a political sense, and means equality of political rights. All men are not equal. Some are born with good constitutions, good health, strength, high mental power; others are not. Now, we cannot by legislation make them equal. God has not made them equal, with equal endowments. But this is our doctrine: Equality . . . —and I will embody it in a single phrase, as the true touchstone of civil liberty—is not that all men are equal, but that every man has the right to be the equal of every other if he can.[6]

Butler's perspective is clearly that of someone intending to provide individual opportunity, not the redistribution of benefits to a racial group. In this, it is much different from that of Justice Marshall, who asserts that

> [i]t is unnecessary in 20th century America to have individual Negroes demonstrate that they have been victims of racial discrimination; the racism of our society has been [ ] pervasive... [and] we now must permit the institutions of this society to give consideration to race in making decisions about who will hold positions of influence, affluence and prestige....[7]

Also in direct contrast to the recently retired Thurgood Marshall is the Constitution's history. The guarantee of equal protection in the fourteenth amendment was to apply to citizens of all races. Senator Howard at the time reflected that it is Congress' intent to "abolish all class legislation and do away with the injustice of subjecting one caste of persons to a code not applicable to another."[8] Similarly, Senator Stevens commented that "no distinction would be tolerated in this purified republic but what arose from merit or conduct."[9] Finally, Senator Wilson pointedly stated: "we have advocated the rights of the black man because the black man was the most oppressed; but we mean that the poorest man, be he black or white, ... is as much entitled to the protection of the law as the richest and the proudest man in the land."[10]

Wilson's comment is revealing because it helps explain some arguably race-conscious behavior on the part of the 39th Congress that drafted and passed the fourteenth amendment. During the Civil War, a proposal was considered to establish a Bureau of Freedmen's Affairs to assist freed slaves in leasing property, entering into employment contracts, and other related matters. The bill did not pass because of strong opposition to the race-based benefits it provided, and, as unfamiliar as it may sound to present ears, because members of Congress strongly felt that social welfare schemes were the sole province of the states. One House report stated flatly:

> A proposition to establish a bureau of Irishmen's affairs, a bureau of Dutchmen's affairs, or one for the affairs of those of Caucasian descent generally, who are incapable of properly managing or taking care of their own interests by reason of a neglected or deficient education, would ... be looked upon as the vagary of a diseased brain.... Why the freedmen of African descent should become these marked objects of special legislation, to the detriment of the unfortunate whites, your committee fails to comprehend....[11]

In response, the proponents of a Freedmen's Bureau subtly changed their arguments. The bill, it was argued, was merely a temporary expedient to rectify the past mistreatment of the slaves. The Bureau was needed "not because these people are negroes, but because they are men who have been for generations despoiled of their rights."[12] Thus, the Bureau was not a permanent recognition of race, but an effort to help former slaves become self-sufficient.

It was a reasonable "special case" argument, but even it was contested. For example, the proponents of short-term assistance to the recently freed slaves attempted to analogize the Bureau legislation to that giving special benefit to Indian tribes. Few thought the analogy apt, however, insofar as tribes were effectively separate sovereign units, and the special federal efforts in their behalf reflected that fact as well as their prior possessory claim on the territory of the United States.[13] Modernly, the Supreme Court still recognizes Indian tribes to be the subject of special solicitude, even against equal protection challenge.[14] This differential treatment applies to tribes, not individual Indians, and OLC has made this clear several times in recent years.

When the next Congress took the Bureau legislation up again, it passed and was signed into law by President Lincoln in March 1865.[15] But this time there was a crucial difference. The 1865 legislation specifically provided that the relief was intended for the freed slaves as well as for white refugees from the rebel states. This diluted the racial nature of the original proposal and focused the new law on those injured. The assistance to the generation of freed slaves could be justified in 1865 as reparation for recent, government-fostered deprivation. So too, the extension of assistance to refugees *from the rebel states* tended to confirm that the Congress viewed the legislation as needed because of the specific and extraordinary devastation of the Civil War.

Eric Schnapper, a counsel to the NAACP, argues that notwithstanding the inclusion of white refugees in the 1865 act, most of the aid went to the freed slaves.[16] This is hardly surprising, but it does not contradict the race-neutral intent of the statute itself. Again, the freed slaves were specific victims of discrimination, and any benefit allocated to them would be compensatory for the actual injuries they had suffered. Samuel Alito, Jr., a former deputy in OLC and now a U.S. Appellate Judge, made this point very persuasively in the government's brief in *Wygant v. Jackson Bd. of Education*,[17] in which the Court struck down a lay-off scheme giving preference to less senior minority teachers.

When the Freedmen's Bureau was sought to be reauthorized in 1866, renewed objection was made to any "class legislation—legislation for a particular class of the blacks to the exclusion of all whites. . . ."[18] It was strongly argued that any such partiality would be "in opposition to the plain spirit pervading nearly every section of the Constitution that congressional legislation should in its operation affect all alike."[19] Again, the supporters of the legislation pointed out the measure's victim-specific nature and that the measure was temporary. For example, the bill's author argued that "[w]e shall not long have to support any of these blacks out of the public Treasury if we educate and furnish them land upon which they can make a living for themselves."[20]

The bill passed, but Andrew Johnson, concerned about its class implications, the displacement of state authority, and the extent of Congress' constitutional authority, vetoed the measure. While the vote in the Senate was insufficient to override Johnson's veto, even the Senate arguments made in favor of override stressed the legislation's victim specificity and idiosyncratic nature in several ways. This was a measure for four million recently emancipated people, it was said, and "never before" had such necessity for aid arisen. Moreover, that the Congress viewed its special assistance to be for *these* freedmen, and not black Americans more than a century later, was made plain by their explicit reliance upon the abolition of slavery provisions of the thirteenth amendment for constitutional authority.[21] The Freedmen's Bureau, using revenue generated by fees and some later appropriations, continued for another few years providing assistance to former slaves and the poor generally. Consistent with its designedly temporary status, the Bureau was abolished in 1872.

Laurence Tribe has admitted that the history of the Freedmen's Bureau does not support modern affirmative action because its benefits were going to actual victims of slavery.[22] Nevertheless, Tribe would argue for affirmative action on the basis that some of those supporting the fourteenth amendment did not think the guarantee of equal protection meant the end of segregated public schools.[23] Yet, this is surely building on the shakiest of foundations. First, legislative history ought never be used to contradict text. Second, that these members of Congress indulged a notion unpalatable and inconsistent with any common definition, then or now, of "equality" is no reason to perpetuate and compound the error. Third, these fragmentary comments could be seen as largely uninformed since public schooling was relatively new, available to only a few children, white or black. Fourth, and perhaps most importantly, what the school comments suggest is that the nation had yet to understand the social significance of abolishing racial classes. Indeed, it would have been quite remarkable for a Congress that just a few years before had contemplated slaves as property to suddenly and fully comprehend the social implications of their freedom. As explainable as such partial understanding might have been in 1866, it is indefensible in 1991. The segregated public schools of the post–Civil War era do not lead to preferential, or more correctly segregated, schooling, employment, and housing benefits today.

THE ELEMENTS OF MODERN RACIAL PREFERENCE

With the history of the fourteenth amendment in mind, the contemporary push for race preferences can be evaluated. These preferences have been insinuated into the law in a variety of ways, with the intent of blurring the line between the prohibition of racial discrimination and its use. In remarkable Orwellian fashion, the proponents of race preference have defined the absence of racial preference as "discrimination."

Brown v. the Board: Correcting *Plessy*

The official sanctioning of the "separate but equal" doctrine in *Plessy* was fundamentally at odds with the history of the fourteenth amendment, and the reconstruction Congress' rejection of class-based legislation. That it took 60 years for this proposition to be clearly articulated by the Supreme Court in *Brown* is an embarrassment of our history as a nation. Chief Justice Warren's opinion in *Brown v. Board of Education*,[24] striking down the segregation of public schools by law, is sometimes misinterpreted as a sociological essay to the effect that segregated schools retard educational and mental development. In context, Warren does rely on a substantial amount of nonlegal material to demonstrate the ill consequence of segregation on a child's educational development. However, the greater import of *Brown* is its general acknowledgement that the official separation of people on the basis of race "generates a feeling of inferiority."

In this, Warren came very near to embracing Harlan's dissent in *Plessy* that the Constitution is color-blind. Indeed, Warren notes that the strongest proponents of the fourteenth amendment intended it "to remove all legal distinctions among 'all persons born or naturalized in the United States.' "[25] Yet, Warren did not come right out and take this expansive, color-blind view himself. In fact, Warren would later acquiesce in *Brown's* declaration of nondiscrimination becoming a mandate for more discrimination.

The Transformation of Nondiscrimination to School Assignment by Race

When Thurgood Marshall argued the *Brown* case for the NAACP before the Court, he made it very clear that he was not arguing for the public school system that had been poisoned by racial assignment to be further weakened by that practice. At oral argument, Marshall stated:

> [t]he only thing that we ask for is that the State-imposed racial segregation be taken off, and to leave the county school board . . . to work out their own solution of the problem, to assign children on any reasonable basis they want to assign them on. . . .[26]

As Brad Reynolds later observed, it was Marshall's view at the time of *Brown* that "[s]o long as the children were assigned 'without regard to race or color, . . . nobody would have any complaint.' "[27] Yet, Thurgood Marshall and his liberal brethren on the Court would subsequently allow the appropriate commitment to nondiscrimination to be turned inside out as the remedies for school segregation came to be fashioned.

After *Brown*, it was initially the equitable impulses of district court judges, not Supreme Court Justices, that started down the treacherous path of using race to counter racial discrimination. The Supreme Court simply remanded the school cases to the lower federal courts with the instruction to place schools on a nondiscriminatory basis "with all deliberate speed." Predictably, some school districts resisted. One state governor said the ruling didn't apply to his schools.[28] Another school district sought to go slowly to avoid the flight of white parents and children into the suburbs.[29] Another refused to fund the public schools, but provided grants to all-white private academies.[30]

These circumventions of the law rightly could not be tolerated. But the Court's rejection of this resistance ultimately became too unrefined. In *Green v. New Kent County*,[31] the Court invalidated a freedom of choice plan, fashioning a decree that not only mandated nondiscrimination, but an affirmative duty of integration. With this the Court came to subscribe to the illogic that more discrimination was the way to end discrimination. Moreover, educational quality—the primary concern of parents—took second place to racial mix. As Reynolds relates:

> [t]he social issue of racial balance in the classroom—rather than the civil rights issue of racial neutrality in student assignments—became the overriding concern in school desegregation decrees, and the Supreme Court's acknowledgment in *Swann* that race-conscious assignments and mandatory student transportation are legitimate desegregation techniques evolved into nothing short of a judicial obsession with forced busing to achieve racial balance.[32]

Reynolds sought to change this. His method was not to deny the value of an integrated school environment, but to have it result from voluntary choice. In 1984, Reynolds pointed to a consent decree entered into with Bakersfield, California, as his blueprint for the desegregation of the future. The core of the settlement of this school discrimination case relied upon so-called magnet schools, that is, public schools with a variety of special programs in science, computer-assisted instruction, the performing arts, as well as programs for gifted and talented students. This voluntary approach was an anathema to liberal civil rights activists. The voice of liberal editorial opinion, the *New York Times*, sarcastically opined that Reynold's emphasis on voluntariness, rather than mandatory busing, was "certainly a blueprint: for evasion and for continuing the Administration's lax approach to school desegregation."[33]

Beyond busing, Reynolds soundly questioned having school districts perpetually in the hands of federal judges rather than local school officials and parents. This was a natural corollary of his emphasis on voluntariness. The objective of federal involvement in public schools was to ensure free choice without racial bias, not statistical racial balance in particular public schools. Even had the objective been statistical racial balance, it would have been unattainable given the dynamics of population shifts and private choice. When racial imbalance does not result from intentional discrimination, it was not unconstitutional. Reynolds took this position for this first time in an *amicus* brief filed with the Fourth Circuit in late 1984.[34] As might be expected, it was immediately denominated as "outrageous" by those who would deliver local public schools into federal hands indefinitely.[35]

The Supreme Court took Reynolds' side less than a year after he left office. Rejecting the argument that federal supervision of a local school district should only end under extraordinary or unforeseen circumstances, the Court remarked that school desegregation decrees were "not intended to operate in perpetuity. Local control over the education of children allows citizens to participate in decision making, and allows innovation so that school programs can fit local needs."[36] Whether federal court supervision of a school system, including mandatory busing, would end would now depend on whether the school board had "complied in good faith with the desegregation decree since it was entered."[37] This was the standard for which Brad Reynolds had consistently argued. Perhaps it signals a recognition by the Court that it neither can, nor should, remake every facet of society—where people live, work, worship, and recreate—by simplemindedly moving children around on school buses on the basis of race. In its own words, the Court's energies are best concentrated upon ensuring that "*de jure* segregation ha[s] been eliminated as far as practicable, . . ."[38]

Children ought to have never been used as pawns in the Court's social engineering. Indeed, it can be forcefully argued that racial mix and busing are patently insufficient remedies for any child or family who personally experienced discrimination by school officials. To say that a particular child's discrimination injury is rectified by a court-ordered transportation plan affecting large numbers of other students, or even a new magnet school, is the equivalent of telling someone injured by a negligently designed highway that better highways will soon be built. A child discriminated against is in school today, not next year or five years from now, when the magic racial statistics, which no one can really meaningfully define or secure for very long, may come to exist in the school system. Moreover, even to suggest that school system racial balance is the correct remedy is to misperceive the nature of the harm. It is *not* a numerical harm. It is *not* a group harm. It is, as Earl Warren and John Harlan would have likely acknowledged, an individual deprivation of equality. Just as the highway victim will receive money damages for his personal injuries, the remedy for individually suffered school discrimination should have been from the very start the payment of compensation *to the individual student.* As civil rights lawyer Clint Bolick explains:

> The plaintiffs would point to the futility of busing mechanisms in securing equal educational opportunities, they show that well-integrated urban private schools (and/or suburban public schools) were willing and able to provide such opportunities, and they would ask for their *pro rata* share of public educational expenditures in order to avail themselves of those opportunities. Such a strategy would at once vindicate the principles of equal protection—in a manner far more effective, yet far less divisive, than busing remedies—while empowering individuals to choose among educational alternatives, thereby expanding educational opportunities for those who need them most.[39]

TOO INTELLECTUALLY HONEST TO BE PROMOTED

The positions advanced by Brad Reynolds may now have found a receptive ear in the courts; however, in 1985, Senate liberals were anything but receptive to the prospect of approving his promotion to the position of Associate Attorney General. It was rough going from the onset of the Senate confirmation hearings in early June 1985. Reynolds, himself, perceived the problem. "This administration, and I personally," said Reynolds, "have dared to question [the pro-busing/pro-quota] orthodoxy, and the reaction has been a barrage of charges and criticism from the civil rights 'establishment.' "[40] Writing months later, an observer of the Reynolds hearings would write: "McCarthyism was back in style in the nation's capital. Thirty-five years ago, Joe McCarthy perfected the politics of character assassination and guilt by association, but today it is the Democrats who have mastered these techniques to obtain their ends."[41]

In point of fact, it was bipartisan McCarthyism, as two Democrats and two liberal Republicans would disregard the fact that Reynolds brought more overall civil rights prosecutions than had the previous Carter administration, and that the positions advanced by the civil rights division under Reynolds were vindicated in the federal courts over 80 percent of the time.[42] Instead, the focus of the Senate Judiciary Committee became the magnification of a few, slight errors of recollection by Reynolds during the course of intense, often hostile hearings. For example, after prolonged questioning, Reynolds told Senator Joseph Biden that during a Louisiana voting rights case: "I certainly met with Governor Treen. I met with a large number of representatives of the other side from Louisiana. I met with my staff." As it turned out, Reynolds had relied on his staff to meet with the representatives on the other side. In another redistricting case in Mississippi, Reynolds told the committee that he had consulted with the attorneys representing black voters; to be technically precise, he had met with one attorney representing some of the black voters.

These are not high crimes and misdemeanors; they are not even the stuff of stay-after-school-for-detention. But in Brad Reynold's case, it was enough to virtually brand him a liar, and even at times, to suggest that he was a bigot. After Reynolds had testified that he did not believe he had legal grounds to challenge the move of a polling place in Selma, Alabama, from a minority neighborhood to the town hall a few blocks away, Senator Metzenbaum weighed in: "I do not understand. You are intelligent, you appear to be a decent human being and yet you come down in some of these cases on the side of bigots."[43] And on it went. Hearings that were scheduled for early May, dragged on into several sessions through late June. On June 27, the committee voted 10–8 against sending Reynolds' nomination to the floor with a favorable recommendation. With a 9–9 vote, the committee even declined to forward the nomination to the floor without recommendation.

I had not yet joined the Department at the time of Reynolds' hearings. A few months later, while talking with him about my prospective duties in OLC, our conversation turned to his ordeal. It was clear that the experience had not changed his legal philosophy, as it should not have. However, there was a sense of disappointment at the personal vilification that had occurred. "There's a lot that went on there that I'm troubled about," he would say. "It's more in the nature of how the whole process was sort of distorted and twisted. I am obviously not pleased that some individuals decided to engage in an attack on my character when their real aim was to make a statement about the policies."[44]

Reynolds' superb legal training may actually have heightened the frustration he was feeling the day we talked. Lawyers are trained to be advocates, and good lawyers trained to advocate without belittling the human qualities of one's opposition, or, as we say, argue *ad hominum*. So much of the push and pull of politics wholly contradicts this. The Reynolds hearings were mean-spirited events where the object was to win at any cost, even if it meant ruining reputation and standing in the community. Had Reynolds' opponents been in the least honest, they would have attempted to disprove his interpretation of the civil rights laws or the Constitution. Instead, there was a heavy dose of political rhetoric coupled with the serious distortion of his minor failings of memory.

The frightening thing is that events like Reynolds' political execution, and later Bork's, and of course Meese's general ill-treatment, discourage critical thinking throughout the larger legal profession, if not society. How many times do newspapers have to repeat that those against racial quotas are *anti*–civil rights before citizens generally accept this refrain or remain silent in dissent. More than a few colleagues of mine strongly cautioned me against writing this book because it would adversely affect future opportunities. Ironically, these good people who I know had only my welfare at heart, have been granted tenure for the very purpose of enlivening debate, challenging presuppositions, and undertaking the search for objective truth wherever it may lead.

Reynolds, of course, did not give up his quest for the truth in civil rights—that is, the even-handed, color-blind application of the Constitution and civil rights laws. While there was some speculation that he might resign from the civil rights division following his rejection as Associate Attorney General, his personal aside to his deputy, Chuck Cooper, quickly put an end to such thinking. "Let's go," said Reynolds. "We have a division to run."[45] Moreover, Reynolds' rebuff did not diminish his standing with the Attorney General. When it became generally known that Meese would meet with Reynolds and one or two others pretty much every morning at 7:00 AM in advance of the morning senior staff meeting an hour later, the press and certain predictable members of Congress howled that he was effectively exercising the powers of the job the Senate had denied him. The howling got even louder when Meese two years later formally gave him the additional title of Counselor to the Attorney General, signifying his responsibility as, in Reynolds' self-effacing words, the Department's "traffic-cop," because of the counselor's role of determining the flow of people and information to the Attorney General. Contrary to Senator Metzenbaum's assertion that Meese had deliberately given Reynolds the title to show "his contempt for Congress," it can be faithfully reported that the Attorney General was merely rewarding someone he viewed as an exceptional lawyer. Meese did not give an instant's thought to the petty venality ascribed to him by the Senator.

Employment: Discriminatory Intent vs. Effect

A crucial part of the contemporary pressure for racial preference can be found in the effort to define discrimination in terms of the *effect* of race-neutral public or private decisions rather than actual proof of discriminatory intent. As stated earlier, this is Orwellian. Employers are alleged to discriminate when they do nothing more than reasonably require a high school diploma as a condition of employment. If more white applicants than blacks happen to be high school graduates in the local community, an employment discrimination lawsuit is likely. Employers can raise their particular employment goals or the purposes served by the educational qualification, but it is often unavailing. In effect, these employers are presumed to have discriminated if there is a statistical racial imbalance in their workforces. The fact that the statistical disparity could be traced to any one of thousands of factors from geography to work commuting distance to more attractive job choices competing for the same labor pool largely doesn't matter.

This is outright favoritism by racial class, and it might be wondered how Congress could dare justify such fatuous regulation under the Constitution, especially in light of the strong disavowal of class legislation by the fourteenth amendment. This question becomes even more intriguing when it is coupled with the fact that the modern Supreme Court has held unequivocally that to prove a violation of constitutional equal protection, there must be evidence of discriminatory intent.[46] Technically, it might be responded that these cases against employers are usually not premised directly on the Constitution, but Title VII of the Civil Rights Act of 1964.[47] As will be seen below, however, this lawyer obfuscation is nonresponsive.

Had it been fairly interpreted, the statutory language of the 1964 Act creating Title VII required proof of discriminatory intent every bit as much as constitutional equal protection. In a nutshell, the 1964 Act made it unlawful to "discriminate . . . *because of* race."[48] Indeed, when the sponsor of Title VII was pressed to assure the Senate that the legislation would *not* be used to sanction racial quotas and preferences wherever a work force was statistically imbalanced, Senator Hubert Humphrey stated that "[the bill] does not provide that any quota systems may be established to maintain racial balance in employment. In fact, the title . . . prohibit[s] preferential treatment for any particular group, and any person, whether or not a member of any minority group, . . . "[49] To further emphasize the point, it was explicitly provided in Title VII that nothing in the legislation should be interpreted to require preferential treatment because of race.[50]

Until the civil rights law was amended in 1991, the characterization of a reasonable employment qualification like a high school diploma as discrimination could not be attributed to either the Constitution or statute but only the statutory make-believe of the Supreme Court. In *Griggs v. Duke Power Co.*[51] the Court, via the not always precise pen of former Chief Justice Burger, sweepingly opined that Title VII "proscribes not only overt discrimination but also practices that are fair in form, but discriminatory in operation."[52] Thus began a judicial odyssey of statutory disfiguration. Justice Scalia describes the process as a transformation in favor of racial bias, moving toward proportionate representation in the workplace.[53] When the Court slightly moderated the pace of transformation in 1989 in *Wards Cove v. Atonio*,[54] by requiring job applicants to at least specifically identify the employment qualification that they thought discriminatory and to show that it serves no business purpose, the racial preference lobby was outraged by the Court's temerity.

By this time, conditioned by the Court's willingness in *Griggs* to label innocent statistical imbalance as evil discrimination, a liberal Congress passed legislation in 1990 to reverse the small ingredient of sanity evidenced by *Wards Cove*. President Bush vetoed the measure arguing that it effectively was a "quota bill." Of course, the legislation did not explicitly demand quotas, but any employer who did not have the politically correct statistical balance was, quite obviously, highly vulnerable to litigation. In 1991, another attempt at reversing *Wards Cove* was launched, this time with the proponents agreeing to add language that ostensibly excludes quotas. It is not clear that the language as drafted accomplishes its purpose, and anyone with a memory of Senator Humphrey's original statutory reassurance against hiring by race must certainly be skeptical.

In all this skirmishing over whether the language of the original Title VII mandates racial preference, or could be amended to do so, a fundamental point has yet to be satisfactorily answered. No one has explained how Congress or the Court can trump the Constitution. In brief, no one has yet come to grips with the fact that regardless of what Congress says, or what the Court says Congress has said, Congress *lacks* the power to impose practices that amount to hiring by race. The two sources of power that have been suggested from time to time cannot justify such mischief. First, it has been claimed that Congress has the power to define equal protection in the fourteenth amendment differently than the Court. For this proposition, Justice Brennan placed reliance on section 5 of the fourteenth amendment providing that "Congress shall have the power to enforce, by appropriate legislation, the provisions of this article." But a majority of the Court has never acceded to Brennan's view, because it fundamentally displaces the Court's own role to "say what the law is." Alternatively, hiring by race has sometimes been offered up as part of Congress' power to regulate interstate commerce. The commerce power has been given an almost limitless range by the Court. The justification for the original 1964 Civil Rights Act, including Title VII, was premised on Congress' ability to remove impediments to the free flow of goods and persons that result from intentional racial discrimination. As broad as the commerce power is, however, it is hard to see how commerce is advanced by *de facto* racial employment quotas. In actual fact, commerce is very likely burdened, not advanced, by such social engineering.

Nevertheless, the acceptance of Title VII as a remedy for statistical racial imbalance in the work force is, at the moment, commonplace. The *Wards Cove* decision required more specific proof of either statistical imbalance (between the employer's work force and the qualified labor pool and not just the general population) or lack of business justification for the employment qualifications alleged to produce the imbalance, but it was still fundamentally based on racial numbers rather than any evidence of discriminatory intent. *Wards Cove* thus narrowed, but did not close, the unexplained gap between the constitutional command of equal protection and the Court's statutory misinterpretation favoring equality of result. As much shouting and quota hurling as went on between Congress and President Bush, *none* of the President's antiquota alternatives ever directly addressed the anomaly of relying upon discriminatory impact rather than intent. One wonders why President Bush bothered to expend so much political capital on his own proposal which, at its core, was only slightly less quota-ridden than Congress'.

Bush flopped, flipped, and ultimately totally flopped over the Civil Rights Act of 1991.[55] Bush insisted to the very end that he would not sign a quota bill, but despite his almost humorous denials to the contrary,[56] he did just that. Amending Title VII, the 1991 Act for the first time statutorily moves from a discriminatory intent to the bogus discriminatory impact standard. The 1991 Act recites as one of its key purposes the provision of "statutory guidelines for the adjudication of disparate impact suits."[57] Moreover, the 1991 Act proclaims to statutorily repeal the Supreme Court's decision in *Wards Cove*. Now a person complaining of impact discrimination need not even identify the particular source of the impact if that would be too difficult.

Executive Order 11246

Part of the explanation for the President's paradoxical behavior may be traced to the Faustian bargain that the business community has made with proponents of racial preference. Business is naturally interested in economic stability and as few impediments (including litigation) to profitability as possible. Thus, it would seem that the immorality—and unconstitutionality—of hiring people on the basis of skin color is less of a concern than just having one clearly stated set of rules. If the government says the firm must have X percent of workers of a given race or gender, that's just a cost of doing business like any other economic regulation pertaining to the environment or worker safety. For businesses with government contracts and the even larger number of firms that are subcontractors of those businesses, Executive Order 11246 has come to represent a pragmatic accommodation with those arguing for race-conscious employment decisions.

As first issued by President Johnson, the order was not intended to call "the merit system into question, [but] attempted only to eliminate the institutional and informational barriers that stand in the way of the minority individual's ability to compete *equally* with others for jobs and promotions."[58] Thus, the order as drafted was color-blind. It specifically provided that "[t]he contractor will not discriminate against any employee or applicant for employment because of race, color, religion, sex or national origin."[59] The order further mandated that each contractor "take affirmative action to ensure that applicants are employed without regard to their race, color, religion, sex, or national origin."[60]

While the term *affirmative action* has since been coopted by the racial quota crowd, this was not its original meaning as incorporated into the executive order. As Duke law professor William Van Alstyne has written, affirmative action under the order is "action of a positive character, discriminating against none, dispreferring no one, involving neither quotas nor queues nor targets nor presumptions of what is the 'right' mix or 'proper' share of each according to race."[61] What is meant, quite simply, was that employers had an outreach obligation to identify and recruit employees of all races. The rub, of course, came in the implementation.

By delegation, the executive order has been implemented by the Secretary of Labor and the Secretary's Office of Federal Contract Compliance Programs (OFCCP). By regulation, OFCCP has required employers to first analyze their work force to determine whether minorities and women are "underutilized," and then, upon a finding of underutilization, to establish a goal of proportionate work force representation and timetables for achieving the goal.[62] Sounds like quotas, doesn't it? While lots of "ah-hemming" goes on to deny that goals are quotas, the characterization is close enough. More importantly, most business managers reason, if devising these quota-goals satisfies the government, so be it. Indeed, from a business perspective, compliance with the order might, in some cases, be used as a defense to a claim brought under Title VII. Since the Court's misinterpretations of Title VII are something of a moving target, the goals and timetables provide a meager security blanket for business against civil rights liability.

Security blanket or not, the executive order is being misused to serve the interests of those who want jobs allocated by race. A close legal analysis would again suggest that such racial practices are inconsistent with the constitutional guarantee of equal protection. The Supreme Court has not decided the issue, however.[63] In part, this is because the Court has yet to agree even on the underlying principles that govern race-conscious affirmative action generally. Nevertheless, as the Court's opinions require greater evidence of past discrimination or "narrow tailoring" for plans using race as a factor, the OFCCP's regulations interpreting the order are drawn into greater question. For now, several lower courts have accepted the validity of the executive order based on a variety of theories including congressional acquiescence—the legally weak proposition that legislative silence means consent.

It is sometimes argued that the order as implemented by the OFCCP merely *requires* what private employers may *voluntarily* do under the Court's interpretation of Title VII. This would be plausible, but for one problem: the allowance of voluntary, private racial discrimination, is itself a prime example of statutory misinterpretation borne of judicial activism. Specifically, in *United Steelworkers v. Weber*,[64] Justice Brennan denied the discrimination claim of a white steelworker who had been refused a place in a training program that, under the union's voluntary affirmative action plan, was half-reserved for blacks. Brennan acknowledged that a "literal interpretation of . . . [Title VII]" makes it unlawful to discriminate on the basis of race, but nevertheless allowed it anyway. This kind of sleight of hand is beginning to wear thin on the Court. As Justice Scalia in dissent in *Johnson v. Santa Clara County*[65] observed, *Weber* ought to be overruled because the statutory language in Title VII against such racial discrimination was enacted "with a clarity which, had it not proven so unavailing, one might well recommend as a model of statutory draftsmanship. . . ."[66]

Harvard Law Professor Charles Fried, who served as Solicitor General during my service at the Department, disagrees with Scalia and supports the Court's "jurisprudentially disingenuous" result in *Weber*,[67] as Fried calls it. In Fried's mind, private employers ought to be allowed to use race in beneficent ways. The problem, of course, is that one man's beneficence is another's arbitrary burden. Even if one can overlook the hardships imposed on the randomly burdened employees, special preference is seldom the asset it seems to be. Race-conscious hiring may be especially odious to those within the preferred race who obtained their positions on merit, since their achievement is then dimmed by the shadowy stigma of preference given to others. As the late Alexander Bickel warned: "[t]he history of the racial quota is a history of subjugation, not beneficence. . . . A quota is a divider of society, a creator of castes, and it is all the worse for its racial base, especially in a society desperately striving for an equality that will make race irrelevant."[68] In all events, Fried's endorsement of *Weber*, the product of blatant statutory misinterpretation, is hardly in keeping with a rule of law.

Even Fried admits, however, that the Court's mistaken invitation to private employers to voluntarily discriminate on the basis of race is no justification for the federal government to *require* racial preferences. Yet, this is exactly what the executive order, as interpreted by OFCCP, does. Brad Reynolds struggled for more than a year to try to revise the executive order to make it compatible with the Constitution. The draft submitted by Reynolds would have amended the order to state that it could not be:

> interpreted to require or to provide a legal basis for a government contractor or subcontractor to utilize any numerical quota, goal, or ratio, or otherwise to discriminate against, or grant any preference to, any individual or group on the

basis of race, color, religion, sex, or national origin with respect to any aspect of employment, . . .[69]

The message was clear, and the reaction was predictably swift. Liberal activists called the draft a declaration of "outright war on equal employment opportunity."[70] Once again, Reynolds' attempt to remove race from the landscape of public decision making yielded the perverse, twisted characterization that his actions were themselves racist. Once again, the personal attacks began, as Reynolds' efforts to return federal contracting to merits-based hiring were assailed as being of "great comfort to bigots everywhere."[71] Nevertheless, Reynolds had the unflinching support of the Attorney General and both carried Reynolds' draft to White House Chief of Staff Don Regan, ultimately, it was hoped, for consideration by the President.

Presidential consideration was long delayed, and it is not entirely clear that it ever formally occurred. While the President was certainly made aware of the draft, it was standard operating procedure at the White House to not ask the President for a decision until all affected cabinet agencies had an opportunity to fully discuss the issue and then agree on a range of options for the President's decision. In addition to this usual practice, there was special reason for Regan to "go slow" on this proposal. As the former chairman of Merrill, Lynch, Regan was no stranger to the business community, and he well knew that his former colleagues opposed tampering with an executive order that was thought to reduce their liability risk under Title VII. For example, a spokeswoman for the National Association of Manufacturers stated that she "hated to see the Administration move on this" and she didn't want the administration to move prematurely from "one extreme to another."[72] Meanwhile, Ralph Neas and the racial preference fraternity were continuing their verbal assaults calling the draft "a pernicious proposal," and turning the rhetorical knife with the quip that "the Bob Jones strategy team [was] at it again."[73]

In the fall of 1985, however, the pace picked up a bit with Labor Secretary Brock indicating that he was "near agreement" with Meese and Reynolds on a draft revision of the order. The rough outline of this revised draft would have encouraged private firms to use goals and timetables, but coupled that encouragement with a blanket prohibition against all racial discrimination, whether or not it was intended to be "benevolent." This may have sounded good politically, but this type of doublespeak was exactly what the business folks wanted to avoid. In essence, the private discrimination permitted under *Weber* was seemingly being both prohibited and encouraged. Ralph Neas exploited this ambiguity to further divide business from the color-blind efforts of Reynolds and Meese stating that "employers would be facing 'double jeopardy' because they might . . . face Civil Rights Act Title VII suits on the one hand and reverse discrimination suits joined by the Department of Justice on the other, if they decided to voluntarily set goals and timetables."[74] Business got the message, and following visits by lobbyists, so did close to 200 members of Congress who wrote President Reagan a letter urging him to reject the proposed revision of the executive order.

In addition to his role as Attorney General, Ed Meese served as the chairman of the White House Domestic Policy Council (DPC). This body, which coordinated the formulation of administration domestic policy among directly affected cabinet agencies, took up the draft next. Three options for presentation to the President were agreed upon: (1) revise the order along the lines suggested by Reynolds but also as amende (and confused) by Labor's insistence on voluntary goals and timetables; (2) leave the order unchanged, but somewhat revise OFCCP regulations; and (3) make changes in both the order and the regulations that would address abuses. Meese favored the first option, Brock the second. The third was a make-weight. So much for compromise. In effect, the unamended race-neutral version of the draft order was off the table. The version revised to satisfy Brock distressed business interests and now didn't satisfy Brock. In this "heads you win, tails I lose" setting, little positive was likely to emerge.

It didn't. Following the DPC meeting, more members of Congress, on behalf of their business constituents, wrote the President suggesting that amending the order would "open the floodgates to a proliferation of litigation and legislation. Such a result would engender instability in the business community and a serious disruption of the legislative process."[75] Business before principle was the order of the day. Clarence Thomas, who was appointed by President Bush to replace Thurgood Marshall on the Supreme Court, explains:

> It should . . . come as no surprise that large firms, . . . and groups such as the National Association of Manufacturers were falling over each other to applaud . . . affirmative action. [Goals and timetables] will decrease the chances that employers will be forced to hire those persons actually discriminated against (who would be entitled to back pay) and will increase the probability that employers will escape fully addressing discrimination by merely hiring a certain number of blacks or women (who are not entitled to back pay). Moreover, the approval of goals and timetables allows yet-undetected discriminators to create a numerical smokescreen for their past or present violations.[76]

The discussions for revising the order dragged on into 1986. Don Regan opined that the President should be given a single option agreed to by the cabinet, instead of three. As Regan surely knew, this would likely end any effort to revise the order because the cabinet was not of one mind. It did.

The Twists and Turns of Racial Preference: The Supreme Court's Affirmative Action Decisions

While revisions to the executive order were being debated, the Supreme Court had considered a host of affirmative action cases, allowing both sides to claim that case law was evolving to support their respective positions, and thus, thoroughly muddying the waters. Brad Reynolds argued that the Court's decision in *Wygant v. Jackson Board of Education* demonstrated that the existing executive order was at odds with the Constitution.[77] Absent prior discrimination, *Wygant* invalidated the extension of preferential protection against layoffs to minority teachers as violating the fourteenth amendment. Pointing out the fact that the executive order as implemented by OFCCP requires hiring goals without a finding, or even an allegation, of prior illegal discrimination, Reynolds argued that the requirement was inconsistent with the Court's insistence in *Wygant* upon, in the words of the Court's plurality, "some showing of prior discrimination by the governmental unit involved."[78] Moreover, Reynolds stated, *Wygant* required that any remedy adopted must be "narrowly tailored" or constitute the least intrusion upon the rights of innocent third parties. Hiring goals, said Reynolds, did not meet this standard either.

The Labor Department immediately disputed Reynolds' interpretation of the case. Since the Court was not writing with clarity and several members of the Court wrote separate opinions, it was relatively easy to give emphasis to one part of the Court's work over another. A spokeswoman for Labor thus asserted that *Wygant* "provides a basis for cautious optimism by proponents of reasonable and flexible goals and timetables, . . ."[79] Indeed, the Court seemed to emphasize that hiring goals were more likely to be found acceptable because they "impose a diffuse burden," unlike the preferential layoffs at issue in the case. A few months later, the Court stirred the waters again approving race-conscious remedies for nonvictims, even though this was seemingly contrary to the language of Title VII and equal protection, and its own prior opinion in *Wygant*.[80]

The equivocation on the Court completely short-circuited further efforts to eliminate the racism inherent in OFCCP's implementation of the executive order. While the focus on the executive order receded, the Department continued to press in litigation for greater acceptance of the view that race-conscious preferences should be undertaken only under the most extraordinary or compelling of circumstances. *Richmond v. Croson*[81] was the the next case of significance. The city had adopted an explicitly racial policy of requiring contractors with the city to subcontract at least 30 percent of the dollar volume of each contract to so-called minority business enterprises. Minority was defined to include, among other persons, Aleuts and Eskimos, even though there was no evidence any lived, worked, or regularly visited Richmond.

By the time *Croson* was argued in October 1988, Dick Thornburgh had replaced Ed Meese and moved Reynolds out of the position of Counselor to the Attorney General. While Reynolds and the civil rights division continued to have their internal say on civil rights matters, including *Croson*, it was apparent to all that the aggressive pursuit of a principled, color-blind Constitution had been pragmatically slowed. This suited Charles Fried, the gentlemanly, if somewhat academically showy, Solicitor General. Fried reports that *Croson* was his "particular project,"[82] and he tried to navigate an indeterminate course. In my judgment, he gave up the sounder view that race is almost never appropriately considered[83]—indeed, not even in the case of remedy because there the remedy is for a party injured by discrimination, not an injured party of a particular race. Nevertheless, Fried had convinced himself that racial preferences could be awarded to nonvictims and even to counter the prior discrimination of entities other than the one awarding the preference.

Despite Fried's equivocation, *Croson* invalidated the Richmond set-asides, and briefly supplied greater clarity to this troubled area. The Court rejected the highly unspecific predicate of the Richmond plan that had not been based on any findings related to the particular field (contracting) nor the particular problems of the Richmond area. Thus, the Court seemingly rejected societal discrimination as a basis for racial preferences. The Court also found the plan not to be "narrowly tailored," since the rigid 30 percent set-aside rested on the unrealistic assumption that minorities would choose to enter into construction in "lockstep" proportion to their representation in the local population. In addition, while the Court previously had accepted racial preferences that were not victim specific, it expressed dismay in *Croson* that no effort was made to inquire "whether or not the particular [minority business enterprise] seeking a racial preference has suffered from the effects of past discrimination by the city or prime contractors."[84]

Regrettably, the *Croson* Court accepted Fried's proposition that an entity, in this case the city, could adopt racial preferences even when it was not seeking to rectify the effects of its own past discrimination. This was directly contrary to the plurality opinion in *Wygant*. Later, Fried would claim that, had the Court not agreed with him, a city "could not pass an antidiscrimination ordinance applicable to anyone other than itself."[85] Nonsense. Nothing precludes a local government from mandating nondiscrimination on the basis of race. Indeed, that is the whole point of objecting to Richmond's set-asides or any local government's use of race in the award of its contracts. What a local community could not do, had the Court disagreed with Fried, is mandate racial preference.

Croson's most significant contribution was its forthright rejection of generalized societal discrimination as a sufficient justification for racial preferences. In the parlance of the Court, a compelling state interest is required for *any* racial preference, regardless of the color of the beneficiary. However, in striking down Richmond's racial set-asides, the Court had to find some way to distinguish a virtually identical program the Court had earlier sanctioned by the federal government in *Fullilove v. Klutznick*.[86] The distinction the Court fixed upon was Congress' separate enforcement power under section 5 of the fourteenth amendment. Thus, the Court writes: "[t]hat Congress may identify and redress the effects of society-wide discrimination does not mean that, *a fortiori*, the States and their political subdivisions are free to decide that such remedies are appropriate."[87] There is some historic logic to this distinction since the fourteenth amendment was drafted as a constraint against the states, or in the Court's words, "from a distrust of state legislative enactments based on race. . . ."[88] However, insofar as the Court had previously held that the Congress is constrained in its actions by the same standard of equal protection as the states,[89] the distinction is more anomalous than real.

The anomaly of the federal-state distinction drawn in *Croson* came back with a vengeance in a subsequent case, to limit and obscure *Croson*'s clearest message that racial classifications always require strict scrutiny and compelling justification. In *Metro Broadcasting v. FCC*,[90] the Court upheld two race-conscious programs mandated by Congress. Under one program, minorities were given preferences for broadcast licenses and under the other only minorities were eligible to purchase such licenses. Writing for a five-Justice majority, Justice Brennan opined that these particular racial preferences need not be justified by a compelling interest, but need only to be related to the achievement of an "important" governmental interest. This was no standard at all. The "important" governmental interest in *Metro Broadcasting* was supposedly broadcast diversity, but there was no necessary relationship demonstrated between minority ownership and the content of radio and television programs. Indeed, there is every reason to believe that market demand shapes program content far more than does the skin color of the station's operator. To think otherwise is to engage in the grossest of stereotypes.

Beyond the flimsy governmental interest, *Metro Broadcasting* greatly distorted Congress' section 5 enforcement authority. The unique remedial power said to be possessed by the federal government in *Croson* was a power to constrain the states. *Fullilove* had required the states in the presence of demonstrated past discrimination to set aside federal construction money on the basis of race; it did not authorize Congress to adopt racial preferences whenever it felt like it. In *Metro Broadcasting*, the preferences neither applied against the states nor were they premised on a showing of past discrimination. In effect, the federal government was being given a license by Justice Brennan to discriminate at will so long as it thought its discrimination was "benign." As Justice O'Connor wrote for the dissent:

> [h]istory should teach greater humility. Untethered to narrowly confined remedial notions, "benign" carries with it no independent meaning, but reflects only acceptance of the current generation's conclusion that a politically acceptable burden, imposed on particular citizens on the basis of race, is reasonable. The Court provides no basis for determining when a racial classification fails to be "benevolent."[91]

Unthinkingly, the judicial activism of Justice Brennan and the Court's contortions to allow *some* racial preferences *some* times, have led us away from the color-blind path embodied in the fourteenth amendment, and articulated by Justice Harlan in his *Plessy* dissent rejecting the doctrine of "separate but equal." It is good to remember that "separate but equal" at its core was built on the very same specious notion that some racial preferences are benign. The *Plessy* majority, like the Brennan Court in *Metro Broadcasting*, rejected the assumption that racial division—separateness—yields inferiority or discrimination. "If this be so," insisted the *Plessy* Court, "it is not by reason of anything found in the act, but solely because the colored race chooses to put that construction upon it."[92] As Justice Kennedy wrote in his separate dissent in *Metro Broadcasting*,

> [t]he history of governmental reliance on race demonstrates that racial policies defended as benign often are not seen that way by the individuals affected by them. [Racial preferences] . . . impose "stigma on its supposed beneficiaries," and "foster intolerance and antagonism against the entire membership of the favored classes."[93]

The Court has still not found its way in matters of civil rights. It is not for lack of sound guidance from William Bradford Reynolds. Against tremendous odds and at great personal cost, Brad Reynolds, like Harlan before him, championed the principle that "[o]ur Constitution is color-blind, and neither knows nor tolerates classes among citizens."

NOTES

1. 125 Cong. Rec. 18444 (1979).
2. The plight of Bob Jones was argued together with the Goldsboro Christian schools. The Goldsboro policies were even more racially exclusionary insofar as the schools maintained a racially discriminatory admissions policy based upon biblical interpretation.
3. 461 U.S. 574 (1983).
4. 163 U.S. 537 (1896).

5. *Regents of University of California v. Bakke*, 438 U.S. 265 (1978).
6. *Cong. Globe*, 43rd Cong., 1st Sess., 1874, H. at 413.
7. 438 U.S. 265, at 400 (Marshall, J., concurring).
8. *Cong. Globe*, 39th Cong., 1st Sess., 1866, S. at 2765.
9. *Id.* at 65.
10. *Cong. Globe*, 39th Cong., 1st Sess., 1866 at 343.
11. H. R. Rep. No. 2, 38th Cong., 1st Sess. 2–4 (1864).
12. Senator Sumner quoting Secretary of War Stanton, *Cong. Globe*, 38th Cong., 1st Sess. app. at 2800 (1864).
13. *See Cong. Globe*, 38th Cong., 1st Sess. 3346 (1864) (statement of Senator Hendricks).
14. *Morton v. Mancari*, 417 U.S. 535, 551–55 (1974).
15. Act of March 3, 1865, ch. 90, 13 Stat. 507, 508.
16. Schnapper, *Affirmative Action and the Legislative History of the Fourteenth Amendment*, 71 Va. L. Rev. 753, 761 (1985).
17. Brief of the United States as *amicus curiae* supporting petitioners at 14–15 *Wygant v. Jackson Bd. of Education*, 476 U.S. 267 (1986) (No. 84–1340).
18. *Cong. Globe*, 39th Cong., 1st Sess. app. 544 (1866) (Congressman Taylor).
19. *Id.*
20. *Cong. Globe*, 39th Cong., 1st Sess. 322 (1866) (statement of Senator Trumbull).
21. *Cong. Globe*, 39th Cong., 1st Sess. 941 (1866).
22. Tribe, *In What Vision of the Constitution Must the Law Be Color-Blind*, 20 J. Marshall L. Rev. 201 (1986).
23. *Id.* at 204 (citing Bickel, *The Original Understanding and the Segregation Decision*, 69 Harv. L. Rev. 1 [1955]).
24. 347 U.S. 483 (1954).
25. *Id.* at 489.
26. *Argument: The Oral Argument Before the Supreme Court in Brown v. Board of Education of Topeka 1952–55*, 47 (L. Friedman ed. 1969).
27. Reynolds, *Individualism v. Group Rights: The Legacy of Brown*, 93 Yale L. J. 983, 998, (quoting Marshall's oral argument) (1984).
28. *Cooper v. Aaron*, 358 U.S. 1 (1958).
29. *United States v. Scotland Neck City Bd. of Educ.*, 407 U.S. 484 (1972).
30. *Griffin v. County School Board of Prince Edward County*, 377 U.S. 216 (1964).
31. 391 U.S. 430 (1968).
32. Reynolds, *supra* note 27, at 1002.
33. *A 'Blueprint' All Right—for Segregation*, N.Y. Times, Feb. 1, 1984, at A26, col. 1.
34. Werner, *U.S. Says Cities Can Put an End to Busing Plans*, N.Y. Times, December 7, 1984, at 18A, col. 6. *See also*, E. Witt, *A Different Justice* 142–43 (1986).
35. Werner, *U.S. Says Cities Can Put an End to Busing Plans*, N.Y. Times, Dec. 7, 1984, at A18, col. 6 (quoting Napolean B. Williams, Jr. of the NAACP Legal Defense Fund).
36. *Board of Educ. of Oklahoma City v. Dowell*, 111 S. Ct. 630, 637 (1991).
37. *Id.* at 638.
38. *Id.* at 638.

39. C. Bolick, *Unfinished Business* 124 (1990).
40. Kurtz, *Reynolds to Lay Error To "Faulty Recollection"; Justice Nominee to Testify Again Today*, Wash. Post, June 18, 1985, at A3 (quoting Reynolds).
41. Wolfson, *The New McCarthyism; William Bradford Reynolds and the Politics of Character Assassination*, Policy Review 60 (Winter 1986).
42. *Id.*
43. Lewis, *Hostile Questions Greet Nominee for Justice Dept. Post at Hearing*, N.Y. Times, June 5, 1985, at B, col. 1.
44. Shenon, *Reynolds: Not Gone and Not Forgotten*, N.Y. Times, Oct. 3, 1985, at B8, col. 3.
45. Wolfson, *supra* note 41, at 64.
46. *Village of Arlington Hgts. v. MDHC*, 434 U.S. 1025 (1978); *Washington v. Davis*, 426 U.S. 229 (1976).
47. 42 U.S.C. 2000(d) *et seq.* (1991).
48. Pub. L. No. 88–352, § 701, 78 Stat. 240, 253 (1964) (codified as 42 U.S.C. § 1983 (1988).
49. 110 Cong. Rec. 11,848 (1964).
50. Section 703(j), 42 U.S.C. sec. 2000e–2(j).
51. 401 U.S. 424 (1971).
52. *Id.* at 431.
53. *Johnson v. Trans. Agency, Santa Clara County*, 480 U.S. 616 (1987) (dissenting opinion).
54. *Wards Cove Packing Co. v. Atonio*, 490 U.S. 642 (1989).
55. Pub. L. 102–166, 102nd Cong, S. 1745 (November 21, 1991).
56. Quoting himself, Bush told an audience of Republican faithful:

> "Look, I want a civil rights bill. I do not want a quota bill." And we stayed with it. They thought they were going to ram the political decision down against me with the American people. I vetoed a bad bill. And now we have a civil rights bill that is good, . . . And that's what you have to do. You've got to beat down bad legislation before you can get good legislation.

Remarks at a Bush-Quayle Fundraising Luncheon in New York City, 27 Weekly Comp. Pres. Doc. 1634 (November 12, 1991).
57. Disingenuously, the 1991 Act suggests that it is "confirming" the statutory authority for discriminatory impact law suits, when in fact, as discussed in the text, the impact theory of discrimination was a judicial creation.
58. Abrams, *Affirmative Action: Fair Shakers and Social Engineers*, 99 Harv. L. Rev. 1312, 1318 (1986).
59. 3 C.F.R. 339 (1964–65), *reprinted in* 42 U.S.C. sec. 2000(e) app. (1988).
60. *Id.* at sec. 202(1).
61. U.S. Comm'n on Civil Rights, 1 *Selected Affirmative Action Topics in Employment and Business Set-Asides* 180, 182 (1985) (testimony of William W. Van Alstyn on March 6, 1985).
62. 41 C.F.R. pt. 60–61 *et. seq.* (1986).
63. In *Chrysler Corp. v. Brown*, the Court stated "[f]or purposes of this case, it is not necessary to decide whether Executive Order 11246 as amended is authorized by [various civil rights statutes and procurement statutes] or some more general notion that the Executive can impose reasonable contractual require-

ments in the exercise of its procurement authority." 441 U.S. 281, 304–305 (1979).

64. 443 U.S. 193 (1979).
65. 480 U.S. 616 (1987).
66. *Id.* at 657.
67. C. Fried, *Order and Law* 130 (1991).
68. A. Bickel, *The Morality of Consent* 133 (1975).
69. *White House Considering New Executive Order Without Job Goals*, Daily Rep. for Exec. (BNA), at A–2 (Aug. 16, 1985).
70. *Id.* (quoting Nancy Kreiter, research director of Women Employed).
71. *Id.*
72. *White House Calls Draft Order an "Analysis" of Position on Goals*, Daily Rep. for Exec. (BNA) at A–3 (Aug. 19, 1985) (quoting Sharon Spigelmyer, director of human resources at NAM).
73. *Id.* (quoting Neas, executive director of the Leadership Conference on Civil Rights).
74. *House Panel Chairman Critical of New Version of Affirmative Action Executive Order*, Daily Rep. for Exec. (BNA) (Oct. 16, 1985).
75. *No White House Action Imminent on Affirmative Action Executive Order*, Daily Rep. for Exec. (BNA) (Oct. 31, 1985).
76. Thomas, *Affirmative Action Goals and Timetables: Too Tough? Not Tough Enough!* 5 Yale L. and Pol'y. Rev. 402, 406 (1987).
77. 476 U.S. 267 (1986).
78. *Id.* at 280.
79. Pear, *Justice Dept. Says Opinion Narrows Job Equality Rule*, N.Y. Times, May 23, 1986, at A1, col. 4.
80. *Local 28 Sheet Metal Workers v. EEOC*, 478 U.S. 421 (1986) (where a majority of the Court rejected a suggestion in the earlier opinion in *Firefighters Local Union No. 1784 v. Stotts*, 467 U.S. 561 (1984), that race-conscious relief under Title VII could only be awarded to identifiable victims of discrimination). On its face, section 706(g) of Title VII seemingly precludes relief to nonvictims.
81. 488 U.S. 469 (1987).
82. C. Fried, *supra* note 67, at 127.
83. Justice Scalia suggests that "a social emergency rising to the level of imminent danger to life and limb—for example, a prison race riot requiring temporary segregation of inmates, . . . can justify an exception" to the color-blind principle of the fourteenth amendment. *City of Richmond v. J. A. Croson Co.*, *supra* note 77, at 578 (Scalia, J., concurring in the judgment).
84. *Id.* at 509.
85. C. Fried, *supra* note 67, at 128.
86. 448 U.S. 448 (1980).
87. *Id.* at 490.
88. *Id.* at 491.
89. *Bolling v. Sharpe*, 347 U.S. 497 (1954).
90. 110 S.Ct. 2997 (1990).
91. *Id.* at 3033.
92. 163 U.S. at 551.
93. 110 S.Ct. at 3046 (Kennedy, J., joined by Scalia, J., dissenting) (citations omitted).

8

Freedom: Iran-Contra and the Criminalization of the Separation of Powers

So much has been written about Iran-Contra, it is hard to justify even a single word more. Ronald Reagan viewed the support of the contras, whom he called the Nicaraguan Freedom Fighters, as important to the nation's security in this hemisphere. It is fair to say that many Americans viewed neither the contras, nor their Soviet and Cuban-backed antagonists, the Sandinistas, as a matter for serious concern. At heart, Americans are isolationist, not imperial. We expect others around the world to treat us in the same "hands off" manner. Live and let live.

This "live and let live" credo was challenged, however, in an odd confluence of ways in the 1980s. First, American hostages were taken in Iran in late 1979 in the last year of the Carter presidency. After a prolonged period, these hostages were released, but more were taken in seven separate incidents in 1984 and 1985. One of those taken, and later killed, was William Buckley, CIA station chief in Beirut. Americans respond when provoked, but this type of terrorist provocation was difficult to grapple with. No national soil or interest could be identified and reclaimed. The whereabouts of the hostages was unknown, and even the aggressors were shadowy, distant figures. While it was generally thought that the Americans were being held by a Shiite terrorist group, the Hezbollah, no one really fully knew what they wanted. Like random violence on the streets of Washington, D.C., few foreign policy experts, let alone the average American, could understand the deep instability in Iran. For the previous quarter century, until the death of the Shah, Iran had been the steadfast ally of the United States.

Because of its geographic position in the Middle East, American military analysts stressed the strategic importance of Iran. Suspicious that the Soviets had more than a little to do with the nascent instability in the region, some method, it was thought, had to be found to reopen relations with Iran. Since Iran was in the midst of a conflict with Iraq, it desperately wanted American munitions. That was impossible—U.S. policy against dealing with terrorist nations and an arms embargo dating from the 1979 hostage taking stood in the way. To hurdle the problem of direct U.S. support, various members of the National Security Council (NSC) staff and some of our friends in Israel suggested that a small amount of arms could be transferred by Israel to Iran, if the United States would agree to replenish the Israeli inventory. The President apparently agreed with this approach, although at what time the President consented and whether it was to the extent of the arms shipments that later occurred remains obscured.

This, of course, became known as "arms for hostages." Some hostages, but not all, were released. The President denied this was his principal motivation, but given the pleas of the hostage families, it was humanly impossible for this not to be weighing heavily on his mind. The President's insistence that the arms transfer was a diplomatic endeavor to establish friendlier relations with Iran met either cynicism or reproach. The success or failure of this venture was quickly eclipsed, however, by the Attorney General's discovery that the Iranians had been overcharged for the U.S. weaponry supplied by Israel, and part of this "residual" or "surplus," through the rogue ingenuity of certain NSC staff members, ended up in the hands of the contras, at a time when U.S. military assistance was prohibited.

Oliver North and John Poindexter, the principal NSC characters in this drama, are either heroes or goats depending on your perspective. One thing is certain, they took advantage of weak links in the National Security decision-making process to design and implement a course of action that may well have not been taken, or been taken differently, had that process kept all of the principals—the President, the Secretary of State, the Secretary of Defense, and the Attorney General—fully informed. North and Poindexter were relieved of duty, and subjected to presidential (the Tower Board)[1] and congressional inquiry.[2]

North and Poindexter have also been prosecuted by Independent Counsel Lawrence Walsh in a court of law. However, they were not prosecuted for the diversion plan itself. The two main charges against them—conspiracy to defraud the United States and theft of government property as it related to the residuals—were dropped by the independent counsel when, pursuant to the Classified Information Procedures Act,[3] Dick Thornburgh prevented the use of certain classified information Judge Gesell ruled necessary for trial. I have every reason to believe that Thornburgh reached his decision in the honest, informed belief that public disclosure of the classified material would damage the national security. Nevertheless, the decision meant that North and company would be tried for largely minor offenses. Ultimately, North was convicted on three federal charges: altering federal documents, misleading Congress, and improperly accepting a gift of a security fence. Even these convictions have been overturned,[4] either because of an incorrect jury instruction or the possibility that witnesses, jurors, or prosecutors were improperly influenced by immunized testimony that North was compelled to give to Congress.

Many people are wondering what the point of Mr. Walsh's continuing prosecution is. Having expended well over $35 million, there is precious little to show for it. Mr. Walsh has recently breathed new life into his costly effort by arranging for a plea bargain by Alan Fiers, the former head of the CIA's Central American Task Force. Under the plea bargain, Mr. Fiers pleaded guilty to the misdemeanor of refusing to testify before Congress. However, in the words of the *Wall Street Journal*:

> [t]his plea bargain is bizarre because everyone agrees that Mr. Fiers did appear before Congress when he was called to testify. Nor has anyone cited any pertinent question he has "refused" to answer.... What apparently happened was that when Mr. Fiers refused to admit to perjury or any other felony, Mr. Walsh was only too happy to accept a misdemeanor plea to an act Mr. Fiers did not commit. Mr. Fiers can hardly be faulted for copping a false plea. Most career government officials (indeed, most American citizens) don't have millions of dollars set aside to defend themselves in a federal trial.[5]

Whether understandable or not, Mr. Fiers' plea agreement ordinarily wouldn't amount to much, except that it occurred at the very time when Robert Gates, another career CIA employee, was scheduled to have confirmation hearings for the CIA directorship. Gates himself hasn't been accused of anything, save of being at the CIA during the time period when North and Poindexter across the river at the NSC were accused of hatching and implementing their Contra diversion scheme. In true "damned if you do, damned if you don't" Washington tradition, the congressional rumor mill speculates either that Gates knew a lot about Iran-Contra and isn't talking, or that he knew nothing, in which event, he's not alert enough to direct the CIA.

The Gates' dilemma is reminiscent of Ed Meese's troubles with the Independent Counsel. It matters less what is actually proven in court than what is alleged in the newspapers. This is troubling generally, but it is especially problematic in the area of foreign affairs. Here the allocation of constitutional power between the President and the Congress is imprecise, and subject to historical dispute. To criminalize this aspect of the separation of powers is likely to paralyze executive action in ways that will yield far greater threats to our national security than anything afoot in Iran-Contra.

VIOLATING THE BOLAND AMENDMENT

But didn't Oliver North violate the Boland Amendment? The Boland Amendment was actually not one amendment, but five. The 1985 version, provided that:

> During fiscal year 1985, no funds available to the Central Intelligence Agency, the Department of Defense, or any other agency or entity of the United States involved in intelligence activities may be obligated or expanded for the purpose or which would have the effect of supporting, directly or indirectly, military or paramilitary operations in Nicaragua by any nation, group, organization, movement or individual."[6]

Whether this was transgressed by Oliver North was highly contested within Congress itself.[7] There is much to suggest that Boland had no applicability to the National Security Council, to which North was assigned. In this regard, the phrase "agency or entity involved in intelligence activities" are words of art that had been used by Congress and the President throughout the 1970s and 80s to mean a designated list of agencies that *produced* intelligence, like the CIA, not the NSC, which *consumed* intelligence. The NSC served a foreign policy coordinating function within the White House; it was not an intelligence agency. In addition, the Boland prohibition covered only certain appropriated funds, contained as it was in a Defense appropriation which did not include the NSC. Given its nonintelligence functions, the NSC was separately funded together with the White House. If Congress had wanted to extend a broader prohibition it knew how to do it. For example, at other times and in other laws, Congress has employed language like "notwithstanding any other provision of law, no assistance of any kind may be provided."

Doubt over the applicability of Boland to the NSC apparently even divided the staff of the Independent Counsel. Jeffrey Toobin, a former member of that staff, records that "[a] criminal charge based on the Boland amendment divided us not by political inclination but by professional background. By and large, the professional civil litigators and full-time defense lawyers... wanted to bring the Boland case. The experienced prosecutors did not."[8] The professional prosecutors wanted real crimes—like lying, stealing, and cheating. Like many members of Congress, the experienced prosecutors on Walsh's team were not prepared to say that North violated the Boland amendment. Boland did not clearly apply to the NSC, and it wasn't clear what "funds" North had illegally expended. When it was suggested that they could "say that North spent his own salary to aid the contras,"[9] the chief FBI agent assigned to Walsh sniffed "don't forget the price of the paper clips."[10]

Besides being penny-ante, the thought of basing the violation of Boland on North's salary raised a further problem. The Constitution does not allow Congress to "prevent the President or his designated agents from communicating with the Nicaraguan resistance or from encouraging other countries and private citizens to support the resistance."[11] This does not mean that Congress cannot place limitations on appropriated funds. It can. But "Congress may not use its control over appropriations, including salaries, to prevent the executive or judiciary from fulfilling Constitutionally mandated obligations."[12] It was partially this concern that prompted Abe Sofaer, the legal advisor to the State Department, to urge Attorney General Thornburgh at the end of October 1988 to examine the filings of the independent counsel with special care for positions "inconsistent with established policies of the Department of Justice and Executive Branch."[13] This task fell to OLC.

Abe Sofaer

Before I was nominated for the OLC post by the President, I knew Abraham Sofaer only by his erudite treatise on foreign affairs.[14] Small in physical stature, Sofaer had dominated legal thinking in foreign matters since he resigned a federal judgeship to become the State Department's legal advisor in 1985. Sofaer extended his great ability by attracting others of equal merit, such as Nicholas Rostow, a former aide to Sofaer and presently general counsel to the National Security Counsel. One of Sofaer's first assignments was to reexamine the 1972 Antiballistic Missile (ABM) Treaty to determine if it precluded testing the President's Strategic Defense Initiative (SDI). After a painstaking analysis, Sofaer concluded that the treaty's terms were unclear and did not place strict limits on spaced-based antimissile systems. When Robert McFarlane, then the President's NSC advisor, somewhat prematurely revealed Sofaer's interpretation on national television, a storm of controversy erupted. Apparently, Nixon's advisors had mischaracterized this aspect of the ABM treaty when it was before the Senate for ratification, and now some members of the Senate insisted on relying upon these misinterpretations rather than the treaty's actual provisions. Sofaer stuck to his position.

Given the importance the President assigned to SDI, the press attempted unfairly to portray Abe as a "yes-man." In fact, he was anything but. When an initial draft of prepared testimony for William Casey in 1986 was misleading in its description of one of the first shipments of arms to Iran, Sofaer insisted that it be removed. This was a gutsy thing for a subcabinet official to do with regard to any member of the cabinet; it was downright courageous given Casey's long-standing personal relationship with the President.

I don't know if Thornburgh responded to Sofaer's October letter urging review of the independent counsel's filings in the *North* case. However, Sofaer and I had talked directly, and I kept Robin Ross, Thornburgh's surrogate, as closely informed as possible. Shortly thereafter, I included Ross in a meeting in my office with Sofaer, Bill Landers, the associate counsel to the President monitoring Iran-Contra matters, Ed Dennis, the head of the criminal division, Russ Bruemmer, general counsel of the CIA, and a number of others. While Ross didn't stay, he was there long enough to understand that the State Department was asking OLC to file an *amicus* brief in the *North* case opposing some of the positions taken by Walsh in order to protect the interests of the President and the executive branch. As best as I could glean from his nods and silence, Ross concurred with our involvement, and I assumed that meant Thornburgh would as well.

Sofaer was trenchant in his criticism of Walsh's filing, even though it was obvious that Sofaer was pained to have to address the matter *after* Walsh had publicly filed his memorandum in opposition to North's motion to dismiss the principal count in the indictment. Sofaer had asked Walsh to let the executive branch see what he intended to file in court before the fact, but received only the back of Walsh's hand and the invitation to separately file our views. We didn't need Walsh's personal invitation, as the independent counsel statute expressly authorizes the same.[15] Nevertheless, the fact that the President has to speak through an *amicus* brief to execute the law and protect the nation's foreign policy interests surely illustrates—again—the lunacy of the independent counsel statute. Here was Walsh, held by the Supreme Court to be an inferior officer to the President and the Attorney General,[16] effectively saying that it would be impertinent of the President to review in advance law enforcement pleadings in order to protect constitutional and national security interests. The President was not about to interfere in Walsh's narrow and specific duties. He had publicly stated numerous times that he wanted justice to run its course in the North case. By the same token, the President could not let positions be taken in this isolated case that would have constitutional and foreign policy ramifications that Walsh could neither know nor contemplate. Had Walsh thought about it, it was even in his narrow interests to let the executive comment in advance merely to avoid the inevitable press speculation that a public filing was an attempt to derail his prosecution of North.

Sofaer underscored in our meeting that we needed to make it very clear in our brief that we were not commenting on the merits of Walsh's prosecution. We did this right up front. On page 2, I included the following: "our purpose in filing this brief is not to address the underlying facts of the case, but rather to correct legal misstatements."[17] Thus, while the brief was captioned *U.S. v. North,* in actual fact, because of

Walsh's obtuse behavior, it was really *U.S. v. U.S.* Sofaer pointed out that the most troubling misstatements were those that were "potentially damaging to the President's capacity to conduct foreign policy, particularly intelligence and secret diplomacy."[18] Ticking off a lengthy list of concerns, the meeting participants generally agreed that Walsh's pleading improperly sought to use a criminal conspiracy statute to prosecute a political disagreement. Walsh tried to make the political disagreement look sinister by highlighting that activities were conducted in secret. However, secrecy itself is not against the law; in fact, it is an indispensable aspect of a covert operation within the President's constitutional or statutory authority. This much has been recognized by the Supreme Court:

> The President, after all, is the "Commander in Chief of the Army and Navy of the United States." . . . His authority to . . . control access to information bearing on national security . . . flows primarily from this constitutional investment of power in the President and exists quite apart from any explicit congressional grant. . . . The authority to protect such information falls on the President as head of the Executive Branch and as Commander in Chief.[19]

OLC and the criminal division set about the task of drafting the brief. As we worked through the weekend, we commented that it was about the same time in late November two years earlier that the first diversion memorandum had been discovered in North's files by Brad Reynolds and brought to the attention of Attorney General Meese. We laughed lightheartedly that we would have to find some more pleasant exercise to celebrate the Thanksgiving season in the future. For now, however, it was all business.

It will be recalled that Walsh's staff had been divided over whether to charge North with a violation of the Boland amendment. The career criminal prosecutors thought this fairly ridiculous. Walsh's filing, however, made things even more sublime by arguing that North could be guilty "even [if he] technically compl[ied] with all relevant statues and regulations."[20] I tried to bring this point home at a press briefing on the afternoon of our filing, by observing that "[w]hen you tell a citizen that they can be charged [with a crime] even if they have not violated any law, that's a pretty novel theory." The theory had several noticeable constitutional problems, including that ours is a government of law, not unenacted policy.

We admitted that a criminal conspiracy could be filed where a crime had been committed, or even more broadly, where there had been a conspiracy to "defraud the United States," in the sense that some civil law or regulation had been violated. But there had *never* been a reported case in which executive branch officials had been imprisoned for violating the "unenacted 'policy' or similarly diffuse 'intent' of Congress."[21]

This meant that Walsh had to prove that the NSC was within the scope of the Boland amendment, and that what North did was prohibited by that noncriminal appropriations limit. Yet, Walsh resisted doing this, arguing instead that:

> [E]ven if it were the case that the activities of North and his co-conspirators had fallen within some sort of loophole in the Boland Amendment, or were found not to violate specific provisions of the structure of legal control over covert action, the broader problem with their deceitful activities would remain: the defendants . . . chose to hide their activities from Congress to ensure that Congress would not have the opportunity to consider whether to close any such loophole.[22]

This was indeed a strange view of the separation of powers. While the framers envisioned that the divided powers would lead each branch by its own initiative to resist the usurpations of the others, Walsh envisioned a congressional supremacy where it was the duty of the other branches to refrain from exercising constitutional authority until it could meekly ask Congress for further direction. In the end, while we were willing to stomach what the professional prosecutors on North's staff resisted—the transformation of an alleged civil law (Boland) violation into a crime pursuant to the general criminal conspiracy statute[23]—we could not tolerate the mutation of a legal act into a crime.

When Walsh's pleading wasn't spinning unconventional criminal theories, it was misstating, actually vastly understating, the President's foreign affairs authority. While Jefferson recited that "[t]he transaction of business with foreign nations is Executive altogether,"[24] Walsh argued that the framers intended for Congress to have "plenary" or "ultimate" or "primary" authority over foreign matters. Actually, as we noted in our brief, Walsh's pleading was schizophrenic, as other parts of his work suggested that his constitutional conscience was getting the better of him. For example, after demeaning the President's assigned responsibility, he would say "[t]here is no need to insist upon such an extreme position."[25] Walsh's equivocation gave us the greatest difficulty in the implication that somehow Congress, pursuant to its appropriation power, could revoke the President's constitutional authority. We stated:

> Congress' appropriation power is quite broad, and includes as a general matter the authority to attach conditions to appropriations, [but] it is not limitless. . . . That Congress appropriates money for the Army, however, does not mean that it can constitutionally require, as a condition on appropriations, that the armed forces conduct a specific tactical operation.[26]

We made a similar point about the President's absolute and exclusive authority to recognize foreign governments. To this, Walsh's original pleading lamely stated that "Congress *may* lack the power to control the exercise of that prerogative by the appropriations power."[27]

Responding to Sofaer's concerns about protecting the authority for legitimate covert action, we observed that Walsh's view that "secrecy by itself is a species of deceit that criminalizes actions . . . cannot be squared with the nature of foreign relations, and the President's constitutional role in the conduct of foreign affairs."[28] Indeed, we illustrated how secret diplomatic and intelligence missions are at the core of the President's foreign affairs authority. We reminded the court of the words of the late Justice Stewart that it was "elementary that the successful conduct of international diplomacy and the maintenance of an effective national defense require both confidentiality and secrecy."[29]

Finally, we sought to disabuse Mr. Walsh of the view that presidential efforts to gain assistance for the contras from foreign nations or private American citizens could be constitutionally restricted by Congress. Urging foreign governments to supply funding for the contras could not be meaningfully distinguished from other presidential acts of diplomacy. In this sense, the President has a "monopoly on communications," as Professor Henkin, a distinguished foreign affairs author has remarked.[30] For similar reasons, no law could constitutionally prevent the President, or his aides, from urging private citizens to contribute funds for foreign policy purposes. The Boland amendment, remember, precluded the use of some *federal* money. Constitutionally, it could do no more.

As expected, the press portrayed our filing as a brief in support of Oliver North.[31] To the extent that North was operating with the President's knowledge and approval within the parameters of his constitutional authority, I suppose that could loosely—very loosely—be said to be accurate. But as we blared across our brief, we were not "address[ing] the underlying facts."[32] It was up to Walsh to prove his case, and North to raise a "reasonable doubt." Our concern was directed at insuring that neither Walsh nor North won their case under a dangerously mistaken understanding of either criminal law or the President's role in foreign affairs.

Walsh responded to our brief by conceding much of it or declaring that the Court should overlook as irrelevant his comments about the respective foreign affairs authority of the President and Congress. Walsh denied that he was trying to prosecute North on the basis of unenacted policy. Instead, he more clearly premised his prosecution on "a series of congressional enactments and rules promulgated by the executive branch."[33] He further stated that he was not denying the need for secrecy in diplomacy, but rather that his concern was with "the effort to defeat operation of the law through 'deceit, craft, or trickery, or at least means that are dishonest.' "[34] This was fine by us. We had no brief for fraud, properly understood and defined.

As to the President's foreign affairs authority, Walsh stated that he had "no quarrel with most of the general propositions asserted. . . . [And that he] expressly recognizes the existence of significant—and, indeed, exclusive—Executive authority in various areas relating to foreign affairs."[35] More specifically, Walsh conceded that "the Boland Amendment does not, and constitutionally could not, prohibit the President from urging foreign governments or private citizens to contribute to the support of the Contras."[36] Walsh had thus sufficiently refined his pleading to satisfy the President's interests, and the point of our *amicus* was well accomplished.

This was not an "academic dispute within the Department of Justice," as Judge Gesell characterized it, it was the sum and substance of what was wrong with the principal counts in the North prosecution. What Walsh called "obstruction," the U.S. Court of Appeals noted in reversing North's convictions, may often be nothing more than "legitimate political jousting between the executive and legislative branches."[37] While the appellate court based its reversal on the possible improper use of immunized testimony, the reality was that in large part North was being tried for political crimes. That exercise is reserved to the political branches. That was what the Tower inquiry was about; that was the entirely proper thrust of the congressional hearings on Iran-Contra. It was what fundamentally distinguished Iran-Contra from Watergate. As Watergate prosecutor Henry Ruth observed: "I think Walsh made a mistake in charging a conspiracy to violate the world. Trying to prove a crime in foreign policy is very difficult and maybe it shouldn't be undertaken. . . . In Watergate, we had true perjury, . . . "[38]

Nevertheless, Walsh persisted. His political count "violating the world," as Ruth put it, did not last long. A month and a half later, Gesell would dismiss what Walsh had earlier described as the "heart of the case"[39] for reasons pertaining to the inaccessibility of classified information. The truly noncriminal counts in the indictment should have never been brought in the first place. They were political questions, and if the Constitution is to mean what it says, those can never be crimes.

NOTES

1. *The Tower Commission Report* (N.Y. Times ed. 1987).
2. Report of the Congressional Committees Investigating the Iran-Contra Affair, H.Rep. No. 100–433, S.Rep. No. 100–216, 100th Cong, 1st Sess. (1987) [hereinafter "Congressional Iran-Contra Report"].
3. Pub.L. 96–456, 94 Stat. 2025, 18 U.S.C. App. (Supp. 1983).
4. *U.S. v. North*, 910 F.2d 843 (D.C. Cir. 1990).
5. *"Terminator 3,"* Wall St. Journal, July 18, 1991, at p. A12, col. 1.
6. Continuing Resolution, Department of Defense Appropriations Act, Sec. 8066(a), Pub. L. No. 98–473; 98 Stat. 1837 (Act approved Oct. 12, 1984).

7. Congressional Iran-Contra Report, *supra* note 1, *compare* majority report at 395 *with* the minority report at 489 (1987).

8. J. Toobin, *Opening Arguments A Young Lawyer's First Case: United States v. Oliver North* 35 (1991).

9. *Id.* at 36.

10. *Id.*

11. Congressional Iran-Contra Report, *supra* note 1, at 489 (minority report).

12. *Id.* at 476.

13. Letter to Attorney General Thornburgh from Abraham D. Sofaer (Oct. 31, 1988).

14. A. Sofaer, *War, Foreign Affairs, and Constitutional Powers* (1976).

15. 28 U.S.C. 597(b).

16. *Morrison v. Olson*, 487 U.S. 654 (1988).

17. *Amicus* brief of the United States filed by the Department of Justice, at 2 n.1, (Case No. 88–0080–02) [hereinafter "OLC North Brief"].

18. Memorandum to Douglas W. Kmiec from Abraham D. Sofaer 2 (Nov. 16, 1988).

19. *Department of the Navy v. Egan*, 484 U.S. 518, 527 (1988).

20. OLC North Brief at 5 (quoting Walsh's memorandum).

21. *Id.* at 9.

22. *Id.* at 17–18 (quoting Walsh's memorandum).

23. 18 U.S.C. 371.

24. 16 *The Papers of Thomas Jefferson* 378, 379 (J. Boyd ed. 1961) (Jefferson's Opinion on the Powers of the Senate Respecting Diplomatic Appointments April 24, 1790). The only exception, noted Jefferson, were those matters specifically submitted to the Senate. And "*[e]xceptions* are to be construed strictly." *Id.* (emphasis in the original).

25. OLC North Brief, *supra* note 17, at 19, quoting Walsh's memorandum at 31.

26. *Id.* at 24.

27. *Id.* at 25, quoting Walsh's memorandum at 81.

28. *Id.* at 11 n.6.

29. *New York Times Co. v. United States*, 403 U.S. 713, 727–30 (1971) (Stewart, J., concurring).

30. L. Henkin, *Foreign Affairs and the Constitution* 301 (1972).

31. Bell, *Justice Department Files Brief in Support of Oliver North*, Newsday, Nov. 19, 1988, at 9.

32. OLC North Brief, *supra* note 17.

33. Independent Counsel's Memorandum of Points and Authorities in Response to the Memorandum of Law Filed By the Department of Justice as Amicus Curiae with Respect to the Independent Counsel's Opposition to the Defendant's Motions to Dismiss or Limit Count One (Case No. 88–0080–02) at 4.

34. *Id.* at 5 (citing cases).

35. *Id.* at 9.

36. *Id.* at 11.

37. *U.S. v. North*, 910 F.2d 843, 882 (D.C. Cir. 1990), and mod., *reh. den.*, in part, en banc, 920 F.2d 940 (D.C. Cir. 1990), *cert. den.*, 114L.Ed.2d 477 (1991), rejecting a legal presumption that any obstruction of a congressional probe would

fulfill the requirement that one "corruptly" obstruct an inquiry by either House of Congress. 18 U.S.C. 1505. The court stated:

> No one can seriously question that people constantly attempt, in innumerable ways, to obstruct or impede congressional committees. An executive branch official, for example, might call the chairman of a congressional committee convened to investigate some wrongdoing and say, "We both know this investigation is really designed to embarrass the President (or a Senator), not to investigate wrongdoing. Why don't you call it off?" The official surely intends to obstruct or impede the inquiry, but it does not necessarily follow that he does so corruptly.

Id. at 882.

38. Sciaroni, *Time to Pull the Plug on Lawrence Walsh*, 60 Human Events 1 (June 8, 1991) (quoting Henry Ruth).

39. Lardner, *Major Counts Against North Are Dismissed; Justice Asks Shield for Bush, Reagan*, Wash. Post, Jan. 14, 1989, at A1 (quoting Walsh).

PART III

The Finale

"I have refused to bend to the constant drumbeat of political and media pressure because I have a responsibility to uphold an important principle, not only for myself and this Administration but for future government officials who are subjected to untrue allegations."

Attorney General Meese
July 6, 1988

Good-bye Thornburgh. In his office, "Thornburgh, with some relish, said, 'We hope you'll tell us if there is any way we can improve our management operations here.' I hesitated, not knowing if he was serious, or seriously disingenuous" (p. 219). (Photo courtesy of the U.S. Department of Justice)

9

Ethics, Give Us More Ethics

There are few things more important than integrity in public office. This is especially true for those who exercise law enforcement authority. Nothing shakes a citizen's faith in government faster than a corrupt police officer or vengeful prosecutor. Despite some very one-sided press reporting, the Reagan administration held the importance of ethical conduct in high regard. The first White House memorandum I received as a presidential nominee dealt with ethics. The memorandum stated:

> A conflict of interest may exist whenever a government official has a personal interest (financial or otherwise) in a matter which is related to his or her official duties . . . or the activities of the official's department or agency. . . . [F]or purposes of conflicts of interest, not only must you consider interests held in your own name but also those of your spouse, minor children and other members of your immediate household. [W]hen considering whether an interest creates a conflict it is just as important to avoid even the *appearance* of a conflict as an actual conflict; . . .[1]

The memorandum went on to highlight specific provisions of Title 18 of the U.S. Code. As might be expected, these criminal provisions forbid bribery or making any decision, even of a general policy nature, that might affect private investments. The prohibitions also greatly limit the continued receipt of financial benefits from a previous employer. Other regulations require highly detailed financial disclosures. Finally, there are postemployment restrictions, which preclude contact for designated periods of time ranging from one year to life with one's prior agency after leaving government service.

All of these provisions are important. Many of them were enacted or greatly strengthened in the late 1970s in the wake of Watergate, making the Reagan team the first administration to be subject to their full regulatory enforcement. But as important as these ethics statutes and regulations are, they do not insure character or integrity. No statute or regulation could. The qualities of being an unbiased and caring decision maker are not to be found in the numbers on a financial disclosure form. An appreciation for an objective right and wrong is instilled in a person long before any serious acquaintance with the U.S. Code.

This quality of personal integrity, in my judgment, ran deeply in Edwin Meese. Guileless, and a man of his word, he expected others around him to be similarly inclined. In this, he was sometimes mistaken. His unwillingness to see the dark side of former associates invited the attribution of their financial conflicts to him. In this, the Attorney General was seriously libeled. The Attorney General's trusting nature also, ironically enough, was sometimes the very trait leading him astray of the more formal, statutory, or regulatory ethics standards. Those who do business with a handshake seldom see the need for contracts—or, for that matter, detailed disclosure forms.

THE RETURN OF THE INDEPENDENT COUNSEL

Wedtech

In May 1987, Edwin Meese was once again brought within the scrutiny of an independent counsel. As before, the impetus for the probe originated with his political opposition in Congress:[2] Senator Joseph Biden and Congressman Peter Rodino urged the independent counsel to investigate whether Meese—while serving in the White House in the early 1980s—had improperly received anything of value for asking that the Army fairly consider a contract application of Wedtech, a South Bronx military contractor. Over a year later, independent counsel James McKay would conclude that no "evidence [was] discovered that Mr. Meese, at any time, knowingly received any money or thing of value from anyone in return for or on account of any official act he performed which benefitted the company."[3] In the interim, Meese would be constantly harangued and defamed with questions about the "Wedtech scandal." For the Attorney General, the so-called scandal amounted to no more than asking his White House deputy to ensure that Wedtech was getting a fair hearing in the government contracting process. Such "constituent referrals" are the constant diet of much of government. Congressmen incessantly contact government agencies about everything from housing projects to why Aunt Mabel didn't receive last month's social security check. No one blinks an eye, but then, Congress has never applied stringent ethics rules to itself. That is not to say there was no one making the Attorney General look bad. E. Robert Wallach, a former Meese law school classmate, received substantial monetary and stock benefits from Wedtech. The independent counsel record alleges that Wallach, unbeknownst to Meese, was asking Wedtech for compensation largely for his access to Meese. Mother always said, be careful what friends you keep. Mom would not like E. Robert Wallach.

Have I Got an Investment for You!

In assuming the post of Attorney General, Edwin Meese agreed to divest himself of stock ownership in a number of firms that might be particularly affected by legal decisions then pending within the Department. This was a common thing for a new Attorney General to do, and in Meese's case, it did not greatly intrude on his family financial planning, since the number of shares involved were usually small. Selling stock, of course, leaves one with cash on hand that then rationally requires reinvestment somewhere.

Reenter E. Robert Wallach. It seems Wallach had a landlord, Dr. Rusty Kent London, who had a friend, Franklyn Chinn, who was in the investment business. Chinn bought new issues and quickly traded them, making a pretty good return. Meese turned over the money from his ethics-related stock sales to Chinn who opened up a new account for the Meeses. Because the Attorney General wanted the account to be a blind investment vehicle (again, for ethics reasons), trades were to be made by Chinn without Meese's knowledge.

Meanwhile, Wallach was afoot. He got Chinn hired by Wedtech as a consultant, and later, a director. There was no reason for Ed Meese to know this, and he didn't. When he found out, Meese promptly terminated his account with Chinn. But it was too late; the newspapers were already filled with speculation that Chinn was investing Meese's money in Wedtech. None of the money was so invested, but there were reams of news stories written implying the contrary.

Meese didn't hide his investment with Chinn. He had no reason to. On his public financial disclosure form, he listed the name of Chinn's investment company, Financial Management International. But he would come under criticism even for this. The Office of Government Ethics (OGE) claimed that such listing was inadequate.[4] Meese, it was said, had to list every stock trade undertaken by Chinn. Of course, that would completely undermine Meese's ethical desire for a blind investment vehicle. That's true, said OGE, but that's Meese's fault, too, since he used the wrong form to establish his blind account.[5] Rules are rules. But to "handshake" Edwin Meese, life was getting as complicated as a Franz Kafka play. While his personal ethical drama was excruciatingly long, at the final curtain, the independent counsel cleared Meese of any wrongdoing. Chinn had treated Meese like any other investment client and Meese had received no "unlawful gratuity."

Hang Up the Phone, Ed

The independent counsel did, however, keep casting his net wider. Almost every time, E. Robert Wallach was the only person ensnared.[6] When he wasn't, some other quirk of financial ill fate seemingly defeated the Attorney General's every good intention. For example, the Department of Justice helped break up the A.T.&T. monopoly into seven regional telephone companies, so-called baby bells. By the terms of the antitrust consent decree resulting in the breakup, certain restrictions on baby bell service areas were devised that were subject to periodic review by the Department and the court. As mentioned earlier, the Attorney General had committed to sell stock in companies that were the subject of such departmental activity. In May 1985, Meese sold all of his A.T.&T. stock, but he couldn't find, and thus couldn't immediately sell, 17 shares in each of the baby bells. To keep his ethics promise, Meese had a lawyer prepare a "transfer of property" document in 1985 for the missing baby bell stock, the total market value of which at the time was approximately $8,900.

Part of Meese's obligation under the transfer of property document was to either find the lost baby bell shares or seek replacements. They were not to be found, so the Attorney General wrote for replacements. The transfer agent sent the Meeses forms which they filled out, had notarized, and returned. You'll never guess. Upon receipt, the transfer agent discovered he had sent the Meeses the wrong forms. In September 1986, the Meeses resubmitted the correct forms, but this time, the Meeses forgot to complete a few lines on the back of one of the forms. The transfer agent—you guessed right again—returned all the forms to the Meeses, and replacement certificates were not issued until June 1987.

While all this back and forthing was going on with the transfer agent, another baby bell issue came before the Department. Knowing that the Attorney General had still not obtained the replacements for the lost stock certificates, John Richardson, Meese's chief of staff, came to see me in December 1986, to see if Meese could nevertheless participate in the baby bell discussions. It was Richardson's view that by the transfer of property document, Meese had transferred beneficial ownership in the baby bell stock and had committed to turn over legal title as soon as the replacement certificates were issued. That might be true, I told him, but since the Attorney General still had *some* interest in a stock he had committed to sell, he should obtain a formal ethics waiver from the counsel to the President before participating in any baby bell discussions. Richardson asked me to draft a waiver request, and I agreed to do so if he would provide me with a copy of the transfer of property document. Richardson looked in his files, but was unable to immediately locate it. It was just as well. When the document resurfaced some months later, it did not accomplish a sufficient transfer of ownership to be the basis for a waiver. The sounder course was thus to ask for a waiver premised not on the attempted transfer but on the relatively small value of the shares. The Attorney General obtained a waiver on this basis from the counsel to the President in January 1987.

But there was a problem. Richardson did not tell me, and may not have known himself, that the Attorney General had participated in previous baby bell discussions within the Department.[7] Had the transfer of property document been sufficient to transfer ownership, Meese could have participated, but if it was ineffective, he had a financial conflict at the time of his participation. Of course, since he was assuming the document's validity, Meese didn't know he had a financial conflict, and logically, the law only punishes *knowingly* acting in a matter where one is financially interested. If the Attorney General didn't think he owned anything, his decisions could not possibly have been biased.

When Meese put this tortured telephone tale before the independent counsel, McKay rightly concluded "that a criminal prosecution of Mr. Meese . . . [was] not warranted under the particular facts of this case."[8] Unfortunately, the independent counsel went on to suggest that "a trier of fact would probably conclude beyond a reasonable doubt that [Mr. Meese's participation given his financial interest was] in violation of 18 U.S.C. 208." In effect, the independent counsel was saying that, despite Meese's heroic efforts to get rid of the baby bell stock, he technically still violated the law because he was unsuccessful in doing so, and it was only McKay's kindness that forestalled prosecution.

This is very bad prosecutorial form. You either have the evidence or you don't. Prosecutors ought not to be about the business of opining that someone "probably" violated the law. Carter Attorney General Benjamin Civiletti observed: "[a] regular prosecutor has one function: put up or shut up. They investigate and they charge, or they do not charge . . . [;] they don't go about damaging a person's reputation without giving him a forum to clear his name."[9] The Watergate prosecution report also reflected this well-established prosecutorial policy: "It would be irresponsible and unethical for a prosecutor to issue a report suggesting criminal conduct on the part of any individual who has no effective means of challenging the allegations against him or of requiring the prosecutor to establish such charges beyond a reasonable doubt."[10] Nevertheless, in the telephone matter and one in which Meese, relying on his accountant's poor advice, mistakenly filed an inaccurate income tax form, McKay adopted this "probable violation not worth my time" posture.

On close examination the mud generally slung in the Attorney General's direction was not worth either McKay's or Meese's time, let alone the taxpayers' money. The banner headlines pounding in the fact of the Attorney General's investigation day after day probably did more to impede the work of the Department and undermine citizen confidence in the rule of law than Meese's lost baby bell stocks or his late tax payment. This faith was further eroded by the expedient judgment and feeble loyalty of Arnold Burns and William Weld who, knowing the weaknesses of the allegations against the Attorney General, nonetheless tried to force his early resignation. When that effort was rebuffed by White House Chief of Staff Howard Baker, Burns and Weld resigned in March 1988 with great fanfare to the plaudits of the press.[11] President Reagan brushed aside such obvious posturing and reiterated his full confidence in the Attorney General, quipping "We have people resigning all the time, especially late in the Administration."[12]

Edwin Meese was subject to intense personal scrutiny. In my judgment, much of it was politically motivated. Independent counsel McKay did his job. I do not doubt his competence or integrity in carrying out the mandate he was given. The question that better needs an answer is whether his mandate was warranted. Some sense of proportion, of judgment, is needed. There are definite costs to specious investigations beyond the very high million dollar price tags of the independent counsels themselves, including misleading the public and discouraging rational people from devoting time to public service. We can ill-afford to have independent counsels appointed merely to cast aspersions upon our highest officials in lengthy reports. In these reports, it is often difficult to find any wrongdoing, let alone to separate significant public misbehavior from the trivial. In point of fact, there is little agreement on what even constitutes wrongdoing. As the head of a nationally recognized ethics institute recently reported:

> [d]espite the proliferation of government ethics codes and standards of conduct . . . , a recent survey reveals a level of disagreement as to what is proper and what is not that is both startling and disturbing. It paints a landscape of practical politics so seeded with land mines that even the most conscientious politician has reason to be confused and frustrated . . . [T]he problem is not simply one of shifting standards over time; there is strong evidence to suggest that whether or not an act will be criticized as unethical will depend in large part on what particular reporter or editor is making the decision.[13]

In rereading the independent counsel's report, one finds the following:

> [a] full investigation of financial transactions of Mr. and Mrs. Meese since 1980 was conducted by Internal Revenue Service agents assigned to the staff of the

independent counsel. A complete set of records of the financial affairs of the Meeses was assembled and thoroughly examined by the independent counsel. The financial records of Mr. and Mrs. Meese did not evidence any unexplained income or expenditure, unusual asset, concealed transaction or any other unexplained improvement in their financial condition since 1980.[14]

How many members of Congress could withstand the same level of examination and have the same said about them?

The Final Hour: Meese Gives Congress a Dose of Its Own Medicine

When McKay filed his voluminous report with the court finding no basis for criminal proceedings in early July, the Attorney General announced that he would resign from office the following month. He held his head high, stating: "I have refused to bend to the constant drumbeat of political and media pressure because I have a responsibility to uphold an important principle, not only for myself and this Administration but for future government officials who are subjected to untrue allegations."[15] Congressional Democrats like Senator Carl Levin immediately rejoiced, calling his resignation "long overdue" in light of what they disingenuously called serious "ethical shortfalls."[16]

But the worm was about to turn. When Congress drafted the independent counsel law, it exempted itself. There was no need for an independent counsel for Congress, the argument went, because the members can ethically regulate themselves. We now know how poorly this works from the Keating 5 savings and loan scandal. Congress' self-regulation is a sham. Even the former vice-chairman of the Senate Ethics committee states: "[y]ou can't divorce yourself from knowing you have to live with these people. Next time you turn around, you'll need that person's vote."[17]

Congressmen also resisted subjecting themselves to independent counsel investigations, with the argument that the Department of Justice could always investigate. True, it could and did. It is not surprising that Congress would prefer the quiet, responsible prosecutorial discretion of the Department to the blaring, media-feeding independent counsel process. But fair is fair. If there were perceived conflicts of interest between an everyday prosecutor investigating a high level executive official, similar pressures and conflicts could exist between Congress and the executive. Given Congress' vast control over budgetary and personnel resources, it is not farfetched to imagine scenarios in which high political prices might have to be paid for the prosecution of ranking members.

That this type of executive-legislative conflict is possible may have been obliquely recognized by the independent counsel statute itself. The law provides that the Attorney General can ask for an independent counsel to be appointed where investigation by the "Attorney General or other officer of the Department of Justice may result in a personal, financial, or political conflict of interest."[18] A day or two before he was scheduled to leave the Department, Attorney General Meese asked that I stop by his office to discuss this very provision. Point blank, the Attorney General wanted to know if this meant the law covered Congress. Even though a few members of Congress had opined to the contrary, on the face of the statute, I agreed that the words might admit of Meese's interpretation. But I wanted to look into the legislative history. I reminded the Attorney General that up to then, this phraseology had only been applied to widen the scope of executive branch officials covered by the law. For example, it was this provision that allowed the independent counsel law to be applied to the otherwise uncovered Oliver North. Meese knew this very well, but he was disturbed by the apparent inequality of having high-level officials in government treated differently merely because they performed executive rather than legislative duties.

As I left the Attorney General's office via the small rotunda that separates his offices from OLC, I must have looked troubled because as I passed Mark Levin of the Attorney General staff, he asked if I was all right. "Fine," I said, "just lost in thought." After the ordeal of the past 18 months, I was reluctant to exhaust the Attorney General's final hours defending what I was sure would be promptly attacked on Capitol Hill. Couldn't Meese express his "equal treatment" concerns to Thornburgh, and let the new guy bear the burden of this law reform. And what, in fact, did Thornburgh think of this? In a couple of days, he would be sitting in Meese's chair. Thornburgh was in the midst of his confirmation hearings, and over the past several weeks, I had been counseling both Meese and Thornburgh.

Back in my office, I reviewed the legislative history of the independent counsel law. There, the quoted language was explained largely in relation to a situation in which a Department official might have a "conflict" investigating someone close to the president from his campaign, or with Billy Carter in mind, a brother or relative of the president. There was little solid evidence that the drafters of the Act were thinking that they were covering themselves. It did occur to me, however, that there was nothing precluding the Attorney General from crafting his own internal independent counsel mechanism. Under the broadly worded statutes conferring authority on the Attorney General to run the Department, he can pretty much assign particular duties to whomever he wishes. That being so, he could denominate a "special government employee" or a particular U.S. Attorney as an independent prosecutor for the purpose of conducting an investigation into a member of Congress. Leon Jaworski had this arrangement in the Watergate investigation.

I reported my findings to the Attorney General. He liked the idea of relying on his departmental authority because it freed us from some of the more unfair aspects of the independent counsel Act. In particular, having just been found not to have violated any laws but nevertheless openly pilloried by an independent counsel report, Meese emphasized that his independent counsel order for Congress should avoid this breach of prosecutorial ethics. I told him I could have the order for his signature by the day's end, if he was certain that he wanted to proceed. Meese could sense my discomfort, and, while he was under no obligation to do so, he assured me that he had discussed the idea with the President and Thornburgh. That allayed my concern, although I confess that in speaking with him later in the afternoon on the telephone, I was still trying to dissuade him. "The press will dismiss your concerns about 'evenhandedness' and see the order as a 'parting shot.' " I said. He understood. But by now, if I knew anything about Ed Meese, it was that press criticism would not forestall his pursuit of a course he had determined to be right.

My last recollection of Edwin Meese as Attorney General is as he signed the order creating an independent counsel for members of Congress. I thanked him one final time for the privilege of serving with him. Meese smiled and, as he shook my hand, the phone rang. It was the White House budget director checking on some of the details of the President's legislative package before Congress. Here, amid the half-packed boxes and temporarily barren walls, the hectic pace was continuing, even as it was fast approaching 8:00 PM. Taking the signed order in hand to file with the Federal Register, I left, looking back briefly as I turned from his outer office to see him still at work. I like to remember him that way.

HELLO THORNBURGH

Dick Thornburgh always struck me as being right out of central casting. Indeed, as I briefed him on the work of OLC in those early weeks, I couldn't help likening his countenance to Henry Fonda. I had seen Fonda some years earlier play Clarence Darrow in Los Angeles, and Thornburgh seemed to have every bit of the intensity and studied look of the great actor.

In the first days of his tenure, when the guarding Pennsylvanians had not yet arrived, Thornburgh seemed relaxed, open and anxious to get on with the business of the Department. We all did our best to demonstrate that we wanted him to succeed. In response, we got some tough talk. He said unequivocally that he wanted "no surprises," and Thornburgh made it clear that he was not fond of any of us talking with the press in ways that undermined the work of the Department. This made tremendous sense, and I was pleased to see him act in this "take charge" or "no nonsense" fashion. There was only an occasional uneasiness.

While Thornburgh assiduously avoided talking about Meese, his actions seemed subtly calculated to show Meese up. My imagination, I thought. Nevertheless, there was a "fair-haired boy" aura about Thornburgh that at times seemed more planned than natural.

With the arrival of the Pennsylvanians, Thornburgh became distant. Thornburgh's three principal aides were Robin Ross, a savvy former counsel from Thornburgh's governorship, Murray Dickman, his non-lawyer personnel guru, and David Runkel, a press aide. At first, the troika sealed Thornburgh off from direct contact with the work of the divisions. Shortly thereafter, they sealed him off from the division heads as well.

Thornburgh did invite the heads of each office and their deputies to lunch with his Pennsylvania friends soon after their arrival. The lunch in the fall of 1988 may have been our last collegial meeting. One hint of the guardedness of Thornburgh and his people stands out to this day. Somewhere in the chicken salad, I jokingly observed that there was now an abundance of "low-numbered" Pennsylvania license plates in the Department garage and that perhaps the spaces should be reassigned sequentially. My deputies laughed, but Thornburgh and company froze over this innocuous banter. Thornburgh looked at Dickman and said: "See, what did I tell you." The next day, I noticed Dickman backed his car into his parking space so that you couldn't see his plate.

One of my deputies at the Thornburgh lunch, Carol Ann Williams, was really an "acting deputy," having accepted my invitation to step into a deputy slot when I was nominated to head the office. Carol had been with the Department for over ten years as a career lawyer. A graduate of the Harvard Law School, she has an excellent legal mind and an open, cordial personality that was respected throughout the Department and the government. It had long been my belief that OLC needed a "career deputy" to maintain objectivity and continuity from one political administration to the next. I had even contemplated such a post for myself before my nomination by the President. Thornburgh's emphasis on professionalism seemed like the opportune time to press this idea. I asked Kathleen O'Day Murphy, my personnel assistant, to put the necessary documentation together to ensure Carol's permanent promotion to a career deputy position. My second hint, after the license plate *faux pas*, that maybe I didn't have "a friend in Pennsylvania" was Dickman's refusal to forward the paperwork for Carol's promotion to the Attorney General. Since it could not possibly have had anything to do with Carol's unquestioned merit, I called Dickman and Ross on it. Dickman was evasive and Ross eerily said, "none of us know where we will be after the election." "Maybe so," I argued, "but here was an excellent opportunity for Thornburgh to tangibly demonstrate his recently articulated commitment to high, professional standards."

The promotion was never made, and to this day, OLC is without a career deputy. Carol took matters in stride. Her work continued to be exceptional. Part of it was helping me draft numerous orders, first modifying, then rescinding, then suspending, then modifying again, Attorney General Meese's order extending an independent counsel structure to members of Congress. By this time, I was no longer granted frequent audiences with Thornburgh, but his Pennsylvania friends conveyed the impression that at least—collectively—they couldn't make up his mind. When the subject did come up in his presence, Thornburgh would look at me with a steely squint and muse out loud, "I sure would like to know how or why that order got drafted."

It wasn't much of a mystery. As the Attorney General's lawyer, I followed my duty to carry out his lawful instructions. It was that simple. I had questioned Meese about the wisdom and timing of the order as far as it was appropriate. Beyond this, the order as drafted fully reflected Attorney General Meese's concerns about "remov[ing] any real or apparent concern that a particular investigation may be politically motivated."[19] As Meese further explained, the independent counsel order for members of Congress will "demonstrate to the public that neither political hostility nor political favoritism played a part in the final decision."[20]

As drafted, Meese's order was a vast improvement over the independent counsel Act. First, independent counsels under the order—unlike the more equivocal statements in the law—were obligated to follow departmental policies. Second, an independent counsel under Meese's order was to utilize departmental personnel, not hire wholly new staffs, to investigate and prosecute. Third, none of the arbitrary limitations in the independent counsel law that preclude the Attorney General's consideration of the absence of criminal state of mind applied under the order. Fourth, as already mentioned, independent counsels under the order were admonished to prosecute or remain silent, and not to issue gratuitous "what ifs" as was the case with the McKay report on Ed Meese.

This is not to suggest that there was not a respectable, opposing view on the order. To the extent that the order further entrenched the notion that the Department was unable to investigate crime wherever it found it, it could be argued as bad for the long-term interests of the Department. But good or bad, somebody had to make up the "keystone" mind.

Thornburgh meanwhile continued to vacillate. First, he publicly stated that "having all high officials covered by the same general procedures makes good sense."[21] Shortly thereafter, Thornburgh was hinting that he might not keep the order, stating that he "hadn't had the opportunity to review with others what the basis for the order was."[22] Thornburgh then considered revising the order to limit the eligible independent counsels to U.S. Attorneys. Then the thought was to revoke. Finally, in

April 1989, citing President Bush's introduction of an ethics reform package, Thornburgh suspended the order.[23] The only problem with that rationale was that Bush's ethics reform package was described by C. Boyden Gray, Bush's White House Counsel, as going in the opposite direction. Gray stated that "there is a comparable argument that could be made that Department of Justice investigations of powerful individuals in the legislature can be extremely awkward."[24]

The awkwardness of raising ethical issues with "powerful individuals" was soon to be brought home to me.

Ethics in Transition

Frank Q. Nebeker became the head of the Office of Government Ethics (OGE) in early 1988. A former appellate judge in the District of Columbia, Nebeker gave every impression of being a strict adherent and implementer of ethical standards. After the McKay independent counsel report was issued, Nebeker, on his own, decided to issue a 17-page memorandum publicly chastising Meese for ethical lapses, notwithstanding the McKay report finding that there was no basis for criminal proceedings. Saying that he could not remain silent in the face of Meese's claim of vindication, Nebeker's memorandum contained no new information, only new invective.

Nebeker argued that Meese had breached his promise to divest himself of the baby bell stock and otherwise to institute a recusal policy whenever that divestment did not occur. It will be recalled that Meese attempted, and in good faith believed, that his transfer of property document accomplished this divestment, and that therefore, there was no need for recusal from telecommunications matters. Yes, the lawyer who drafted the document could have done a better job of it. Yes, Ed and Ursula misplaced the stock certificates, and perhaps Ed and Ursula should have spent even more time searching the garage and family room for the lost certificates, but all of this could not justify Nebeker's gratuitous effort to publicly shame Edwin Meese.

What then was the point of this ethical "piling on"? Giving Mr. Nebeker the benefit of the doubt, it might have been to accomplish two purposes: one derived peculiarly from the Meese situation and one for the future. As to the first, Edwin Meese's tolerance of E. Robert Wallach arguably deserved special mention. The evidence unequivocally demonstrated that Meese never sought personal gain from his public position, but the independent counsel report does suggest that Meese may have too generously allowed Wallach the benefit of Meese's influence. Nebeker stated: "[t]he most troublesome aspect of the information in the independent counsel's report is the extent to which Mr. Meese or Mr. Meese's official position was used for the benefit of Mr. Wallach. The standard against using public office for private gain includes the private gain of others, not simply the personal gain of the employee. . . ."[25] This was an observation well worth making. Almost every government official faces the problem of the good friend in need of government assistance. It is an awkward position. While some uncompensated assistance can be given, it must remain within tolerable limits, as Nebeker stressed, if "for no other reason than to avoid the appearance that the employee is, in fact, misusing his position or that he is making government decisions outside official channels. . . ."[26]

Nebeker's second contribution was more overarching. He stated that his memorandum should be "of particular interest to those about to form a new administration of federal executive affairs."[27] A good point. This was an election year, and whether Meese's treatment was fair or not, the new executive officers—whoever they would turn out to be—needed to fully comprehend the Meese experience for their own sakes. Cynically, it was suggested that Nebeker was merely posturing for public recognition by the prospective Bush administration that had been making high ethical pronouncements on the campaign trail. "Maybe," I observed to a colleague over our brown-bag lunch. But whatever his personal motivation, the memorandum was a helpful warning flag to new government officials who may be unfamiliar with what Nebeker himself said may seem like "strange and overly restrictive" rules.[28]

In November, I became a bit more cynical. A week after the election, Nebeker called me about an ethics question dealing with the Bush transition team. Apparently, he had been asked whether someone who was a member of the transition team had to observe the ethics rules limiting contact with government agencies with which they were formerly associated. These rules are stringent criminal statutes, and on their face, admit of no exception.[29] Basically, they provide that certain high level officials may not contact their former agency on behalf of others for one year or longer. With respect to specific matters that the officials decided, contact is barred for life. Nebeker related that, in his opinion, these criminal prohibitions would *not* apply to former high-ranking government officials on Bush's transition team.

I couldn't have disagreed more, and I thought this was a curious leniency from the ethics czar. Presidential transitions are highly sensitive times in government. Existing government employees, for obvious reasons, are often more than anxious to show their loyalty to the new man or his representatives. Moreover, transition representatives, who are generally highly compensated lawyers and business executives, can have more than a little interest in the internal decision making of government departments for their existing clients and firms. If the ethics laws were concerned about a former high level official contacting his former colleagues at his former agency in normal times, that concern would be heightened, not lessened, in the midst of a transition. That this apprehension was well founded on my part was confirmed by a *Legal Times* story shortly thereafter where it was reported that many private lawyers, some of them quite prominent former officials, were "already busy pushing policies and personnel, in some cases on behalf of their clients, to the Bush team."[30]

Nebeker was somewhat flustered when I told him I wanted to think about it. "You don't have much time," he said, giving me the definite impression that the transition people would be unhappy by the delay. Nebeker had tried to persuade me that these criminal statutes had an implied exception for a presidential transition in light of the unique governmental purpose that they serve. In this, Nebeker referenced the Presidential Transition Act.[31] Carol Williams and I pulled the Act and its legislative history to see if Nebeker's claim could be sustained. It could not. True, the Transition Act acknowledged that presidential transitions served an important public function, but it hardly followed that criminal prohibitions against illicit contacts with government agencies were thereby lifted. A former high official serving in the transition who is now a highly compensated private sector employee clearly may not make decisions on behalf of the United States and his loyalties are certainly not undivided. An obvious hypothetical, it seemed to me, might be a former Department of Defense officer now working for a military contractor contacting the Pentagon on behalf of the transition. Given that Justice was in the midst of a major Pentagon fraud investigation, this did not seem in the least farfetched.

The Transition Act did suggest that the postemployment restrictions might not apply in two limited circumstances: either where the transition worker held no outside employment and was compensated by government funds under the Transition Act or where the transition worker held no outside employment since leaving government other than with the campaign of the now president-elect. While the Act was not entirely clear on even these exceptions, a fair-minded effort to construe the criminal conflict laws together with the Transition Act could lead to this conclusion. Moreover, we were persuaded to admit these exceptions on the strength of the criminal division's concurrence with our analysis. Nevertheless, those aiding the transition who did not fit neatly into one of these two narrow exceptions were fully covered by the postemployment limitations on contacting their former agencies.

In light of the time limitations, I related my opinion to Nebeker by telephone. Nebeker apparently conveyed it to the transition team, as he called back an hour or so later asking that I put the opinion in writing. I was given to understand that the transition people, whoever these anonymous souls were, were less than pleased. "Sorry," I said, "I cannot change the law to suit their happiness." Nebeker agreed, though I suspected he still disputed my interpretation. After I hung up the telephone with Nebeker, I wondered whether President-elect Bush, having been elected in part on a "government of integrity" theme, knew that he was being ill-served by his transition representatives.

Following the transition ethics opinion, the transition team did everything possible to avoid another written legal opinion from OLC. The Presidential Transition Act had appropriated $3.5 million to the General Service Administration (GSA) for transition purposes, and the GSA frequently called me for advice on the proper legal standards governing the allocation of those funds. The questions from GSA and the White House became more numerous, and I asked A. B. Culvahouse, the counsel to the President, if he would like a written summary of the governing principles in particular areas. "Yes," he said, but he doubted whether the transition people would want me to put it in writing unless they could see it first. Culvahouse knew, without asking, that OLC would never permit the prescreening of its draft opinions. We didn't.

Rumors, Rumors, Rumors

In late November 1989, John McGinnis and I were working later than usual one night and our thoughts turned to what lay ahead. We assumed that Bush would automatically keep Thornburgh. Both were politically moderate. Except for an overreliance on his Pennsylvania buddies, Thornburgh had served his interim function of steadying the ship and keeping Justice out of the news during the campaign. It was surprising, therefore, to read press rumors immediately following the election that Bush was contemplating Jim Thompson, a recent former governor of Illinois, as his Attorney General. The word on the fifth floor a few doors down from Thornburgh's office was that Dick was mighty surprised as well. "What lies ahead for OLC?" John wondered aloud. I posited that we had been doing excellent work, had hired superior new attorneys, and had done a thorough job of answering a high volume of complex legal questions in a difficult time. Raising an eyebrow over his Oxford-trained eye, McGinnis just looked at me and said dryly, "these jobs are seldom determined strictly on merit." Smiling, I knew he was right.

In late November, I filled out a form that had come my way from Chase Untermeyer, who was handling personnel for the President-elect. It asked if I was interested in staying on in the new administration and in what capacity. While I ultimately hoped to return to Notre Dame, I viewed my continued government service positively, and I was reasonably certain the university did as well. Thus, the form was simple to complete: "I enjoy my work as head of the Office of Legal Counsel," I wrote. "It would be a privilege to continue." There was no official response, but the newspapers were filled with the comments of Bush transition officials "threatening to sweep out more than 90 percent of the 5,700 Reagan political appointees, ..."[32] If that bit of general inhospitality didn't sink in, the *Wall Street Journal*'s "Washington Wire" column reported the day before Christmas Eve that I had "improved my standing with conservatives because of my brief in the Iran-Contra case," but that I was "not likely" to be kept on by Bush.[33] The column was curious for two reasons: first, I didn't know my standing with conservatives needed improvement, and second, I didn't have a clue what that had to do with George Bush.

After the holidays, the rumor with the greatest currency was that Bush told Thornburgh he could stay, but only on condition that the heads of all, or most all, the divisions be replaced. This rumor may well have been the truth. We all eventually were. A week or so later, as I walked down the corridor to my weekly general staff meeting, McGinnis pulled me aside and asked if I had seen this week's *Legal Times*. "No," I said. Saying that I might want to look at it before the meeting, we stepped into his office. John handed me the paper in which the new Bush team for Justice was either named or rumored. It was reported that William P. Barr, Bush's campaign counsel and former legislative aide at the CIA, would be the new head of OLC. "Looks like a good choice," I said, "I hope I get to meet him." The following day I got my wish. My assistant, Lawan Robinson, buzzed my phone, and with a tinge of loyal disgust in her voice (which I very humanly appreciated), said, "Bill Barr is on the line for you." "Welcome to the Department," I exclaimed with all the diplomatic enthusiasm I could muster. "Why don't you come over to the office, and we will get you started." Bill replied that, as a matter of fact, he was calling from Robin Ross' office down the hall.

Before Barr arrived, Ross appeared at my door. "We just learned," declared Ross, "that Bill Barr has been selected for OLC." Thornburgh was unavailable, Ross said, but he knew Dick would like me to hear the news personally before it became public. Even though the sentiment was about three weeks behind the Washington press, to relieve the pressure of an awkward moment, I took the comment at face value. "I will regret not getting to know you and the Attorney General better," I told Ross. Obviously, I would also miss sharing in the work of the Department. Ross intimated that some would still be coming my way until Barr was confirmed—a process, as it would turn out, that would take another four or so months. The director of a scholarly research project on presidential appointments has since reported that the Bush transition was probably the "slowest ever."[34]

Over my last months in OLC, the work did not slacken. Legal issues surrounding the Eastern Airline strike, the *Valdez* oil spill off the coast of Alaska, and the savings and loan bailout all took considerable time. As mentioned earlier, the constitutional defects in Congress' whistleblower protection measure also had to be negotiated and repaired. In addition to these novel factual occurrences, novel legal claims were also pressed. A group of "inspectors general," or internal government auditors, had mistakenly gotten it into their heads that their job was not to maintain the integrity of the government regulatory process but to directly displace appointed government regulators. In an age of ethical sensitivity, any legal opinion suggesting that watchdogs were wandering beyond their assigned territory was certain to stir controversy, and it did.[35]

One of the most demanding assignments given to the old OLC by the new President was the expeditious drafting of his ethics reform package. There was not inconsiderable irony in this, stemming in part from the fact that there was mounting evidence that it was "the impact of the [ethics laws] and subsequent efforts to tighten even further the regulation of the actions and personal finances of executive branch officials," that was backlogging the presidential appointment process,[36] and thus, lengthening my stay. It was also humorous to think that the person entrusted with the new President's first major initiative in fulfillment of his ethics campaign promise was the very person who apparently irritated the President-elect's transition team by insisting that existing ethics laws be enforced.

Ethics, Give Us Some Ethics

In his first full working day in office, George Bush told his newly assembled staff: "[i]t's a question of knowing right from wrong, avoiding conflicts of interest, bending over backward to see that there's not even a perception of conflict of interest."[37] It made good news copy, and Bush presumably was sincere, even though in a backhanded way it unfairly suggested that what had gone on in the Reagan era was the opposite. But what exactly did it mean? To find out, this old Reagan hand, at the request of the new Bush White House, was drafting an executive order that would create the President's Commission on Federal Ethics Reform Law.[38] The order directed the Commission to report back with its recommendations by March 9, a relatively short time frame. Chaired by Malcolm Wilkey, a genial former head of OLC and federal judge, the Commission set up shop upstairs from OLC in the Justice building, and started the arduous task of making sense of existing ethics laws, and in all likelihood, recommending a few new ones to fill out the "details" in Bush's declaration. It would not be an easy task.

Meanwhile, the Bush team was apparently having some difficulty complying with the old ethics rules. It was widely reported that Boyden Gray, Bush's close friend and White House Counsel, was receiving, and had received throughout his years as counsel to the then-vice-president, substantial compensation from a large communications firm.[39] After the disclosure, he promptly resigned from the company's board, somewhat sheepishly acknowledging that he had not fully understood the outside income and deferred compensation rules. Now that he was getting the hang of the ethics rules, however, Gray, as the White House ethics advisor, started to apply them to others besides himself. For example, Gray required Secretary of State James Baker to grudgingly divest himself of corporate stock that he had inherited from his grandfather. By February, Bush was starting to understand that "ethics" is not a self-defined term, commenting that "I hope I haven't created something that just carries things too far. I want to have high ethical standards, but I don't want to have it so it goes so far, bends so far backward that a person that knows something about a subject matter is disqualified from serving, or a person that has some means is disqualified from serving."[40] In less than a month, Bush had prescribed "bending over backward" twice—but in two different directions. Ethics reform was turning out to be a more difficult contortionist routine than first thought.

On time, the Commission devised 27 recommendations. I was pleased to be of service to the Commission throughout its deliberations, although, given my run-in with the transition team over ethics, the Commission staff was a bit leery of acknowledging this publicly. Whenever staff members would drop into my office in OLC, it was as if they were leaving with drive-thru advice in a discrete brown bag. Amy Schwartz, the associate White House counsel and executive director of the Commission, told me that there was some thought of openly thanking OLC for its assistance, "but well, you know. . . . " Some weeks after the Commission's report was released, I did receive a much valued cordial, personal note of appreciation from Malcolm Wilkey in the mail, which I shared with my fellow OLC lawyers.

In saying this, I don't mean to suggest that either I or anyone in OLC expected personal credit for the Commission's work. There is no copyright in government work, and there should not be. The work product is collegial, and the objective of every public servant within the executive branch must be the advancement of the President's objectives within the law. My recollections here are more designed to convey the awkwardness of being an active principal legal advisor, but nevertheless politically deceased. In the movie "Broadcast News," an astute, but physically clumsy news producer conveying information to the handsome, on-camera anchorman through an earpiece observes, "I say it here, and it comes out there." I felt much the same advising the Commission and the Bush White House generally.

Many of the Commission's recommendations were aimed at extending at least some of the existing ethics rules that were already applicable to the executive to either Congress, the judiciary, or both. For example, with more sweet irony, the Commission proposed extending to the legislative and judicial branches the executive one-year, no-contact rule that the transition team had tried to avoid.[41] This Commission recommendation to prevent former members of Congress and their senior staffs from immediately returning to lobby their former colleagues upon leaving office, closely paralleled the reasoning in the transition team opinion we supplied Nebeker. With respect to the dubious practice of awarding honoraria for speeches and the like concerning public duties, the Commission "took special note of the extreme lack of uniformity across the three branches of government in the rules governing honoraria and other outside income."[42] Executive officials could receive none, while legislative officials could accept any and all offered up to 30 to 40 percent of the individual's salary. The Commission recommended prohibiting all honoraria and subjecting outside income generally to a 15-percent cap based on a senior employee's salary. In making this recommendation, the Commission was swimming upstream politically, as few members of Congress wanted to lose these lucrative sources of outside income. Federal judges, too, had become accustomed to book royalties and salary supplements from law teaching. Saying that it did not want to "discourage these activities," the Commission nevertheless "believe[d] that paid outside work [was] more likely [than unpaid volunteer work] to engross the federal employee to the extent of creating an interference with the individual's basic duties."[43] One other notable Commission recommendation proposed making the financial reporting requirements uniform across the three branches of government.[44]

Not all executive ethics rules could be easily applied to the other branches. For example, extending the financial conflict-of-interest rules to congressmen on any rigorous basis might preclude their ability to represent a fair cross-section of their constituency. The Commission observed:

> If [the financial conflict of interest laws] were applied to Members of Congress, it would effectively require them to divest themselves of all private financial interests upon assuming office, or, alternatively, recuse themselves on a frequent basis, thereby leaving their constituents without representation as to those matters. The legislative process requires such representation of interests and concomitant interest-balancing among Members of Congress. On the whole, we thus concluded that extension of the conflict of interest recusal or divestment requirements to Members would not be appropriate.[45]

But the Commission did find it appropriate to recommend the extension of the independent counsel law to members of Congress. Without referencing the fact that Ed Meese had already accomplished this administratively (that is, at least, until Thornburgh suspended Meese's order on the basis of the Commission's report), the Commission posited that if there was to be an independent counsel at all,[46] it should apply to Congress as well as the executive. Echoing Meese's final announcement as Attorney General, the Commission wrote:

> Executive branch investigations of [powerful members of Congress] are inherently awkward, and there is at least the prospect that intensive investigations may be discouraged by the risk of offending the target of the investigation.... [In addition,] [e]xtending the Independent Counsel mechanism to Congress could heighten the motivation of the Congress to police itself diligently and could strengthen public confidence in the integrity of the legislative branch.[47]

A few days after the Commission's report was made public, Boyden Gray, Bush's White House counsel, called and asked OLC to chair the working group to draft the President's ethics reform legislation. It felt good to hear from him directly. As a political corpse, I had been receiving most of my messages from the Bush White House through covert couriers. Usually one of Thornburgh's Pennsylvania staffers would suddenly appear to say that they heard that so-and-so in the White House needed legal advice on one thing or another. We would then prepare the advice, as best we could without talking directly with the client, and forward it on—sometimes back through covert courier, and sometimes through the mail. In either event, the feedback from the client was much the same: none.

Not being able to talk directly with my principal clients occasionally resulted in decisions that would cause me to cringe. For example, at about the same time as the ethics review was underway, Secretary of State Baker had negotiated a "side agreement" that allowed Bush to continue to send humanitarian aid to the contras, but only if he received letters of approval from four congressional committees. Had this side agreement been written into the appropriation itself, it would have constituted a classic legislative veto of the type invalidated by the Supreme Court in *INS v. Chadha*.[48] The Reagan administration had fought long to reaffirm this separation-of-power principle. The legislature can speak only as constitutionally prescribed—that is, through the bicameral passage of legislation presented to the President. The isolated approvals or vetoes of committees or individual members concerning the enforcement of a law previously passed by Congress had to be left, as it was constitutionally assigned, to the executive branch. In a *New York Times* story,[49] Boyden Gray criticized the encroachment on presidential power engineered by Baker as "much more than a gentleman's agreement [because] it's in writing and becomes a precedent, ..."[50] He was exactly right, and he expressed "irritation" at not being consulted beforehand. In the same story, I too pointed out that OLC had not been " 'asked for its view as to the propriety or appropriateness' of the agreement negotiated by Mr.

Baker."[51] As one of the politically departed, I had less reason to be irritated, however. My concern was only that a hard-won constitutional principle not be tossed aside for a minor amount of funding in an expedient moment.

In any event, Gray's invitation to write the President's ethics legislation was a momentary political resuscitation. "What did Bush want in it?" I asked. "Ethics" was the response. "When?" Next Week. Using the Commission's recommendations as a base, Carol Williams and I sent out an urgent memorandum to the heads of the relevant Justice Department divisions and Frank Nebeker of the Office of Government Ethics, who would shortly be nominated by Bush to be Chief Judge of a new Veterans Court. We summarized the Commission's report and asked that each division supply us with draft legislative language on particular sections. It was an immense job, and thanks to Carol Williams' patience and coordination ability, got done—although it seemed the laser printer was still churning out the last few pages as Bush and company were reading the preamble. In addition to implementing the Commission recommendations aimed at establishing greater ethical rule uniformity among the branches of government, the legislation contained a few ideas of our own. For example, we included a provision that would eliminate the personal use of campaign funds donated to members of Congress. Some powerful senior congressmen who faced little political opposition in their home districts had become virtual millionaires because of unspent campaign funds, often contributed by political action committees. If outside income and honoraria were to be limited, as the Commission recommended, this little bit of accounting chicanery had to stop as well.

We also dutifully followed the Commission in proposing that the independent counsel law be extended to Congress. However, based on the Meese experience, we tried to build into the legislative proposal a greater amount of procedural fairness. Thus, we prescribed that the Attorney General should be given more time to decide whether an independent counsel investigation is warranted and, in doing so, should be free to consider whether criminal state of mind was present. Any independent counsel appointed should follow departmental policies and rely on Justice personnel for staff. We further provided that independent counsels be selected from a list of past or present U.S. Attorneys or other experienced career prosecutors.

The legislative package got rave public reviews, except of course for the independent counsel extension to Congress, which was described in the press as "wander[ing] from the only rationale for appointing these prosecutors in the first place, which is that above a certain level the executive branch cannot credibly investigate . . . itself."[52] Only later, after the savings and loan scandal and the Keating 5 ordeal, was it more widely understood that Congress could not investigate itself. Bush did skirt a major issue: placing limits on honoraria and outside income for members of Congress. The thinking that emerged from the White House was that since the President was also going to be asking Congress to significantly increase executive and judicial salaries, it was "prudent" to leave Congress' outside income problem for another day.

As it turned out, uniformity of treatment did carry the day—although not exactly in the manner anticipated by the public. All three branches got a substantial pay boost. While some of Bush's ethics reforms have been enacted into law,[53] it remains to be seen whether such reform results in more than the entrapment of the uninitiated and a mild challenge to the ingenuity of influence peddlers.

NOTES

1. Memorandum to Douglas W. Kmiec from Arthur B. Culvahouse, Jr., Counsel to the President 1 (undated).

2. Ostrow, *Unit Looks into Meese Wedtech Ties; Justice Department Weighs Appointment of Special Counsel*, L.A. Times, May 6, 1987, at 4, col. 1 (quoting former Senator Harrison Schmitt of New Mexico, who served as vice-chairman of the Senate ethics committee from 1977–79).

3. Report of Independent Counsel *In re Edwin Meese III* 20 (July 5, 1988) [hereinafter "In Re Meese Report"].

4. *Meese Denies Impropriety on Disclosure of Trust Details*, Wash. Post, July 10, 1987, at A1.

5. *Id.*

6. This was true again with regard to a proposed pipeline from Iraq to Aqaba, Jordan. Wallach was hired to help arrange an insurance fund against the possibility of an Israeli attack on the pipeline. One of the plans involved part of the revenue from the pipeline being paid to Israel. Meese's only role was to introduce Wallach and the idea to Robert McFarlane, the National Security Advisor. However, in one memorandum to Meese, Wallach intimated that part of the Israeli funds would be paid to the Labor Party, an action that arguably constituted a violation of the Foreign Corrupt Practices Act. Wallach was an unstoppable memo writer, and the recipients, Meese and others, often left his memos unread. For a variety of reasons, the pipeline was never built, and because there was no evidence other than Wallach's gratuitous memo that an improper payment was contemplated to be paid to the Labor Party, and more importantly, no evidence that Meese actually knew of this proposal, "[t]he independent counsel... determined that the available admissible evidence [was] insufficient to conclude that Mr. Meese's activities in furtherance of the pipeline project violated the Foreign Corrupt Practices Act." In re Meese Report, *supra* note 3, at 49.

Mr. Wallach was tried and convicted of various federal crimes flowing out of his relationship with Wedtech; however, these convictions were reversed and a new trial ordered because of the perjury of a principal government witness. The perjury was substantively unrelated to the facts as they pertain to Wallach but did go to the veracity of the witness. *See* U.S. v. Wallach, 935 F. 2d 445 (2d Cir. 1991).

7. Nor did I know that some years earlier, when Meese was still at the White House and still held all of his telephone company stock, including that of A.T.&T., that Meese had received an ethics waiver from Fred Fielding, then the counsel to the President. Finding that even this greater stock ownership by Meese was not so substantial as to likely influence his decision making, Fielding granted Meese a waiver to participate "either in meetings to discuss the Administration's policy and strategy for legislatively restructuring the telecommunications industry or in decisions necessary to implement these policy and strategy recommendations." In Re Meese Report, *supra* note 3, at 369 (quoting Fielding). While this old ethics waiver would likely not have been sufficient to cover the new baby bell discussions, because Meese was now Attorney General and the particular matter was a slightly different one, it had some precedential value. Had Richardson mentioned it, we would have based the new waiver request immediately on the *de minimus* value of the stock rather than the so-called transfer of property document.

8. In Re Meese Report, *supra* note 3.

9. Greenhouse, *Washington Talk: Independent Prosecutors; Law Offices Are Abuzz over Report on Meese*, N.Y. Times, July 28, 1988, at A22, col. 1 (quoting Civiletti, who suggested that perhaps McKay should have just relied upon a "well-designed summary").

10. *Id.* (quoting the Watergate Report).

11. Ostrow, *Top Meese Aides Abruptly Resign*, L.A. Times, Mar. 30, 1988, at 1, col. 5. Burns was said to be fearful that "he would be tarnished by criticism of Meese's conduct." It was further reported that Weld "[was] interested in pursuing Republican politics in Massachusetts, [and] was described by friends as becoming convinced that failing to step away from Meese would prove a nearly insurmountable burden in that liberal state." Weld has since been elected Governor of Massachusetts. They deserve each other.

12. Shenon, *High Justice Aides Quit Amid Concern over Meese's Role*, N.Y. Times, Mar. 30, 1988, at 1, col. 6 (quoting the President).

13. Josephson, *Politics and the appearance of impropriety*, Chicago Tribune, Aug. 12, 1991, at 13, col. 2. Josephson's commentary summarizes a survey of over 350 legislative leaders, senior aides and journalists. He found large disagreement on the propriety of fundraising, outside income, representing others before government bodies, junkets, and constituent services.

14. In Re Meese Report, *supra* note 3, at 34.

15. Ostrow and Ingram, *Meese to Quit; Claims Probe Vindicates Him; Says Report Lifts "Burden" of Allegations*, L.A. Times, July 6, 1988, at 1, col. 6.

16. *Id.*

17. Phillips, *Ethics committee: Senate's hot seats*, USA Today, Aug. 12, 1991, at 5A, col. 2.

18. 28 U.S.C. 591(c).

19. Office of the Attorney General, Order No. 1297–88, 28 CFR Part O, 53 Federal Register 31322 (1988).

20. *Id.*

21. Shenon, *Meese Takes a Parting Slap at His Foes*, N.Y. Times, Aug. 13, 1988, at 6, col. 1 (quoting Thornburgh).

22. Ostrow and Jackson, *Reviewing Meese Move for Special Counsels in Such*

Inquiries; Thornburgh Unsure on Congress Probes, L.A. Times, Aug. 24, 1988, at 19, col. 1.

23. Marcus, *Thornburgh Lifts Order On Counsel*, Wash. Post, April 13, 1989, at A28.

24. Lauter and Ostrow, *Bush Proposal Would Curb Special Prosecutor Powers*, L.A. Times, April 13, 1989, at 1, col. 5.

25. Memorandum of the Office of Government Ethics regarding Edwin Meese (September 12, 1988), *reprinted in Meese's Conduct: Ethics Office's View*, American Lawyer, Sept. 19, 1988, at 21.

26. *Id.*

27. *Id.*

28. *Id.*

29. 18 U.S.C. 207.

30. Kornhauser and Ladd, *Unofficial Transition*, Legal Times, Dec. 5, 1988, at 1.

31. 3 U.S.C. 102 note (as amended by Pub. L. No. 100–398, 102 Stat. 985 [1988].

32. Houston, *Bush's Broom Stirs Up Cloud of Job Seekers*, L.A. Times, Nov. 25, 1988, at 1, col. 5.

33. Wall St. Journal, Dec. 23, 1988, at A1, col. 5.

34. Mackenzie, *Appointing Mr. (or Ms.) Right—The Bush Administration's transition has been the slowest in at least 30 years*, National Journal 11 (April 1990). Professor Mackenzie is professor of government at Colby College and director of the presidential appointee project of the National Academy of Public Administration. "[T]he Bush Administration took an average of 8.1 months to get its appointees confirmed, as compared to 5.3 months for Reagan and 2.4 for Kennedy." *Id.*

35. *Congress Set to Review Dispute over Jurisdiction at Labor Department*, Daily Labor Report (BNA) No. 147, at C–1 (Aug. 2, 1989).

36. *Id.*

37. Schorr, *The Battered Bush Principles*, 72 New Leader 3, (Mar. 6, 1989) (quoting President Bush).

38. Exec. Order 12,668, 25 *Weekly Comp. Pres. Doc.* 114 (Jan. 25, 1989).

39. *Id.*

40. *Id.*

41. The President's Commission on Federal Ethics Law Reform, *To Serve With Honor*, 53 (March 1989) [hereinafter "Ethics Report"].

42. *Id.* at 35.

43. *Id.* at 37.

44. *Id.* at 83.

45. *Id.* at 15.

46. At my suggestion, the Commission expressed doubt about the need for any independent counsel law at all. The Commission noted that "[e]ven within the executive branch, . . . the theoretical conflict[s of interest are] easily overstated." *Id.* at 112 n.12. Nevertheless, the Commission ducked the ultimate issue and declined to formally recommend that the independent counsel law be repealed.

47. *Id.* at 112.

48. 462 U.S. 919 (1983).
49. Pear, *Unease Is Voiced on Contra Accord,* N.Y. Times, March 26, 1989, at 1, col. 5.
50. *Id.*
51. *Id.*
52. Editorial, *The President's Ethics Proposals,* Wash. Post, April 14, 1989, at A26.
53. Ethics Reform Act of 1989, P.L. 101–194, 103 Stat. 1716. (1989).

Epilogue

Toward the end of April 1989, my tenure as the head of OLC would draw to a close. I relinquished the front office to William Barr upon his confirmation and wrapped up incomplete matters over the next several weeks. I watched the work of this largely unseen, but tremendously important, constitutional law firm continue unimpeded under the direction of an able successor.

Robin Ross called one afternoon and said Dick Thornburgh would like an opportunity to chat before I left. How unusual, I thought. "Of course," I said. On that final day, my family was with me, saying goodbye to colleagues I will always hold dear. My wife, Carol, took charge of our older children and Kolleen and Kloe, our twin daughters, then six months old, as I entered the Attorney General's office. In the company of one of the Pennsylvanians, Thornburgh greeted me warmly, although it was the type of polished warmth extended by a public figure. Innocuous banter about baseball ensued, until Thornburgh, with some relish, said, "We hope you'll tell us if there is any way we can improve our management operations here." I hesitated, not knowing if he was serious, or seriously disingenuous—that is turning the knife a bit on my departure. "You have my every wish for success," I said. We stepped outside his office, took the obligatory photograph, and parted.

As I write this in my Notre Dame office, Dick Thornburgh is spending his last day in the Department, having announced his candidacy for a U.S. Senate seat from Pennsylvania. I don't know how history will assess his stewardship at Justice. He has had some rocky times. At one point, William Safire wrote of Thornburgh, "[n]obody in the Cabinet has fallen farther faster."[1] In my judgment, he had the capacity to be an excellent

Attorney General. If that is not precisely the way it turned out, much of the blame can be attributed to being too highly dependent on a few political aides from his home state, and not sufficiently reliant upon a Department that wanted Thornburgh, and all who are given short-term licenses to guide the rule of law, to succeed.

But, as I say, others must assess Thornburgh's efforts. My task as the Attorney General's lawyer has been to write what the *Wall Street Journal* has recently called the "Meese footnote."[2] This book does indeed stand as a proud "footnote" rebuttal to every off-hand reference to Attorney General Meese's tenure as " 'stormy or worse.' "[3] As the editorialist sagely discerns: "The strategy behind reflexively imputing flaws of character to Ed Meese as Attorney General is that if the public buys it, the public may also devalue Mr. Meese's policy achievements."[4]

As reflected here, the Attorney General's legal and policy achievements were numerous and significant.

NOTES

1. Moore, *Bush's Most Improved Player*, 23 National Journal 103 (Jan. 12, 1991) (quoting Safire, but suggesting that Thornburgh was making a comeback). *See also, Thornburgh's Political Reputation Deteriorates After Less Than Two Years as Attorney General*, Wall St. Journal, March 21, 1990, at A16, col. 1.
2. Editorial, *Meese Footnote*, Wall St. Journal, June 7, 1991, at A10.
3. *Id.*
4. *Id.*

Selected Bibliography

BOOKS

Adams, Charles. *The Works of John Adams.* Boston: Little, Brown and Co., 1851.

Andrews, James. *The Works of James Wilson.* Chicago: Callaghan and Co., 1896.

Aquinas, Saint Thomas. *Summa Theologica.* Philadelphia: Westminster Press, 1954.

Barnett, Randy, and John Hagel III. *Rights Retained by the People.* Cambridge, Mass.: Ballinger Pub. Co., 1989.

Berger, Raoul. *Executive Privilege: A Constitutional Myth.* Cambridge, Mass.: Harvard University Press, 1974.

———. *Fourteenth Amendment and the Bill of Rights.* Norman: University of Oklahoma Press, 1989.

Bickel, Alexander. *The Morality of Consent.* New Haven: Yale University Press, 1975.

Bolick, Clint. *Unfinished Business.* San Francisco: Pacific Research Institute for Public Policy, 1990.

Bork, Robert. *The Tempting of America.* New York: Free Press, 1990.

Boyd, Julian. *The Papers of Thomas Jefferson.* Princeton: Princeton University Press, 1961.

Caplan, Lincoln. *The Tenth Justice.* New York: Knopf, 1987.

Crosskey, William. *Politics and the Constitution in the History of the United States.* Chicago: University of Chicago Press, 1953.

Dumbauld, Edward. *The Bill of Rights and What It Means Today.* 1st ed. Norman: University of Oklahoma Press, 1957.

Elliot, Jonathan. *The Debates on the Federal Constitution.* Philadelphia: J. B. Lippincott, 1836.

Ely, John. *Democracy and Distrust.* Cambridge, Mass.: Harvard University Press, 1980.

Farrand, Max. *The Records of the Federal Convention of 1787*. New Haven: Yale University Press, 1966.

Fish, Stanley. *Is There a Text in This Class?: The Authority to Interpretive Communities*. Cambridge, Mass.: Harvard University Press, 1980.

Fisher, Louis. *Constitutional Conflicts between Congress and the President*. Princeton: Princeton University Press, 1985.

Fried, Charles. *Order and Law*. New York: Simon and Schuster, 1991.

Gunther, Gerald. *Constitutional Law*. 12th ed. Mineola, N.Y.: Foundation Press, 1991.

Henkin, Louis. *Foreign Affairs and the Constitution*. Mineola, N.Y.: Foundation Press, 1972.

Hunt, Gaillard. *The Writings of James Madison*. New York: Putnam's Sons, 1910.

Hutchison, William et al. *The Papers of James Madison*. Charlottesville: University Press of Virginia, 1977.

Inaugural Addresses of the Presidents of the United States from George Washington, 1789 to George Bush, 1989. Bicentennial ed. Washington, D.C.: Gov. Printing Office, 1989.

Jensen, Merrill. *The Documentary History of the Ratification of the Constitution*. Madison: State Historical Society of Wisconsin, 1976.

Kelsen, Hans. *The Pure Theory of Law*. 2d ed. Berkeley: University of California Press, 1967.

Kennedy, John F. *Public Papers of the Presidents: John F. Kennedy*. Washington, D.C.: Federal Register Division, National Archives and Records Service, 1963.

Kurland, Philip, and Ralph Lerner. *The Founders' Constitution*. Chicago: University of Chicago Press, 1987.

Landis, James. *The Administrative Process*. New Haven: Yale University Press, 1938.

Madison, James. *Letters and Other Writings of James Madison*. Philadelphia: J. B. Lippincott and Co., 1865.

McManus, Michael. *Final Report of the Attorney General's Commission on Pornography*. Nashville, Tenn.: Rutledge Hill Press, 1986.

Morris, Clarence. *The Great Legal Philosophers*. Philadelphia: University of Pennsylvania Press, 1959.

Nedelsky, Jennifer. *Private Property and the Limits of American Constitutionalism*. Chicago: University of Chicago Press, 1990.

Office of Legal Policy. *Wrong Turns on the Road to Judicial Activism: The Ninth Amendment and the Privileges or Immunities Clause*. Washington, D.C.: Department of Justice, 1987.

Patterson, Edwin. *Jurisprudence*. Brooklyn, N.Y.: Foundation Press, 1953.

Peterson, Merrill. *The Papers of James Madison*. New York: Harper and Row, 1974.

Report of the Congressional Committees Investigating the Iran-Contra Affair. Washington, D.C.: Gov. Printing Office, 1987.

Rossiter, Clinton. *The Federalist Papers*. New York: New American Library, 1961.

Scanlan, Alfred. *Natural Law Institute Proceedings*. Notre Dame: College of Law University of Notre Dame, 1947.

Schuckers, Jacob. *The Life and Public Services of Salmon Portland Chase*. New York: D. Appleton and Co., 1874.

Schwartz, Bernard. *The Bill of Rights: A Documentary History*. New York: Chelsea House Publishers, 1971.

———. *The New Right and the Constitution*. Boston: Northeastern University Press, 1990.

Shane, Peter and Harold Bruff. *The Law of Presidential Power*. Durham, N.C.: Carolina Academic Press, 1989.

Siegan, Bernard. *Economic Liberties and the Constitution*. Chicago: University of Chicago Press, 1980.

Sofaer, Abraham. *War, Foreign Affairs, and Constitutional Powers*. Cambridge, Mass.: Ballinger Pub. Co., 1976.

Story, Joseph. *Commentaries on the Constitution of the United States*. Boston: Hilliard, Gray and Co., 1833.

Syrett, Harold. *Papers of Alexander Hamilton*. New York: Columbia University Press, 1965.

Toobin, Jeffrey. *Opening Arguments A Young Lawyer's First Case: United States v. Oliver North*. New York: Viking, 1991.

Tower Commission Report. New York: Bantam Books, 1987. *Trial of Andrew Johnson*. Washington, D.C.: Gov. Printing Office, 1868.

U.S. Attorney General's Commission on Pornography. *Final Report*. Washington, D.C.: Dept. of Justice, 1986.

U.S. Department of Justice. *Major Policy Statements of the Attorney General: Edwin Meese III 1985–1988*. Washington, D.C.: Dept. of Justice, 1989.

Warden, Robert. *An Account of the Private Life and Public Services of Salmon Portland Chase*. Cincinnati: Wilstach, Baldwin, 1874.

ARTICLES

Abrams, Morris. *Affirmative Action: Fair Shakers and Social Engineers*, 99 Harv. L. Rev. 1312 (1986).

Aleinikoff, Alexander. *Constitutional Law in the Age of Balancing*, 96 Yale L. J. 943 (1987).

Antieau, Chester. *Natural Rights and the Founding Fathers—The Virginians*, 17 Wash. and Lee L. Rev. 43 (1960).

Bickel, Alexander. *The Original Understanding and the Segregation Decision*, 69 Harv. L. Rev. 1, 58 (1955).

Brest, Paul. *The Misconceived Quest for the Original Understanding*, 60 B.U.L. Rev. 204 (1980).

Caplan, Russell. *The History and Meaning of the Ninth Amendment*, 69 Va. L. Rev. 223 (1983).

Coleman, James. *The Creation and Destruction of Social Capital: Implications for the Law*, 3 Notre Dame J. L. Ethics and Pub. Pol'y 375 (1988).

Corwin, Edward. *The "Higher Law" Background of American Constitutional Law*, 42 Harv. L. Rev. 149 (1928).

Elman, Philip. *The Solicitor General's Office, Justice Frankfurter, and Civil Rights Litigation, 1946–1960: An Oral History*, 100 Harv. L. Rev. 817 (1987).

Grey, Thomas. *Do We Have an Unwritten Constitution?* 27 Stan. L. Rev. 703 (1975).

Holmes, Oliver. *Natural Law*, 32 Harv. L. Rev. 40 (1918).

Jackson, Robert. *A Presidential Legal Opinion*, 66 Harv. L. Rev. 1353 (1953).

Jaffa, Harry. *What Were the "Original Intentions" of the Framers of the Constitution of the United States*, 10 U. Puget Sound L. Rev. 351 (1987).

Kay, Richard. *Adherence to the Original Intentions in Constitutional Adjudication: Three Objections and Responses*, 82 Nw. U.L. Rev. 226 (1988).

Kmiec, Douglas. *Of Balkanized Empires and Cooperative Allies: A Bicentennial Essay on the Separation of Powers*, 37 Cath. U.L. Rev. 73 (1987).

———, and McGinnis, John. *The Contract Clause: A Return to the Original Understanding*, 14 Hastings L.Q. 525 (1987).

Levinson, Sanford. *Law as Literature*, 60 Tex. L. Rev. 373 (1982).

Lupu, Ira. *Untangling the Strands of the Fourteenth Amendment*, 77 Mich. L. Rev. 981 (1979).

Marzulla, Roger. *The New "Takings" Executive Order and Environmental Regulation—Collision or Cooperation?*, 18 Environmental Law Reporter 10254 (1988).

McGinnis, John O. *Principle versus Politics—The Solicitor General's Office in Constitutional and Bureaucratic Theory*, 44 Stan. L. Rev. 799 (Forthcoming 1992).

Nagel, Robert. *The Formulaic Constitution*, 84 Mich. L. Rev. 165 (1985).

Noonan, John. *The Root and Branch of Roe v. Wade*, 63 Neb. L. Rev. 668 (1984).

Perry, Michael. *Noninterpretive Review in Human Rights Cases: A Functional Justification*, 56 N.Y.U. L. Rev. 278 (1981).

Rehnquist, William. *The Notion of a Living Constitution*, 54 Tex. L. Rev. 693 (1976).

Reynolds, William. *Individualism vs. Group Rights: The Legacy of Brown*, 93 Yale L. J. 983 (1984).

Schauer, Frederick. *Easy Cases*, 58 S. Cal. L. Rev. 399 (1985).

Schnapper, Eric. *Affirmative Action and the Legislative History of the Fourteenth Amendment*, 71 Va. L. Rev. 753 (1985).

Thomas, Clarence. *Affirmative Action Goals and Timetables: Too Tough? Not Tough Enough!*, 5 Yale L. and Pol'y. Rev. 402 (1987).

Tribe, Laurence. *In What Vision of the Constitution Must the Law Be Color-Blind*, 20 J. Marshall L. Rev. 201 (1986).

Tushnet, Mark. *Following the Rules Laid Down: A Critique of Interpretivism and Neutral Principles*, 96 Harv. L. Rev. 781 (1983).

———. *The Newer Property: Suggestions for the Revival of Substantive Due Process*, 1975 Sup. Ct. Rev. 261.

Wechsler, Herbert. *Toward Neutral Principles of Constitutional Law*, 73 Harv. L. Rev. 1 (1959).

Index

About the Author

DOUGLAS W. KMIEC is Professor of Law at the University of Notre Dame. He is the author of several books and many articles on constitutional law and other legal subjects. Kmiec directed the Office of Legal Counsel, U.S. Department of Justice, during the years 1985 to 1989, first as deputy, and then as assistant attorney general. He has been honored as a White House Fellow and a 40th Anniversary Distinguished Fullbright Scholar.

www.ingramcontent.com/pod-product-compliance
Ingram Content Group UK Ltd.
Pitfield, Milton Keynes, MK11 3LW, UK
UKHW020206290926
15470UKWH00001B/31